MEXICO: ECONOMIC, POLITICAL AND SOCIAL ISSUES

Mexico: Economic, Political and Social Issues

Maria L. Castro
and
Irene P. Navarro
Editors

Nova Science Publishers, Inc.
New York

LIBRARY OF CONGRESS CATALOGING-IN-PUBLICATION DATA
Mexico : economic, political, and social issues / [edited by] Maria L. Castro and Irene P. Navarro.
p. cm.
Includes bibliographical references.
ISBN 978-1-60456-847-9 (hardcover)
1. Mexico--Economic conditions--1994- 2. Mexico--Social conditions--21st century. 3. Mexico--Politics and government--2000- I. Castro, Maria L. II. Navarro, Irene P.
HC135.M5268 2009
330.972--dc22 2008036856

Published by Nova Science Publishers, Inc. ✢ New York

CONTENTS

PREFACE

Mexico's economic, political and societal issues have become major points of interest to countries all over the globe.Mexico is the second leading market for U.S. exports after Canada, and is the third most important source of U.S. imports after Canada and China. The United States is Mexico's most important customer by far, receiving about 80% of Mexico's exports, including petroleum, automobiles, auto parts, and winter vegetables, and providing about 50% of Mexico's imports. The United States is the source of over 60% of foreign investment in Mexico, and the primary source of important tourism earnings. Mexico is also the leading country in Latin America in terms of U.S.investment, with the total stock of U.S. investment being about $85 billion in 2006. This new book presents in-depth analyses of such issues such as foreign policy, political reform, and overall economic developments.

Chapter 1 - The North America Free Trade Agreement (NAFTA) took effect in January 1994. From that year to 2000, Mexican exports grew three times faster (15%) than in the previous six years. Contrary to widespread beliefs, the cointegration analysis in this paper finds no connection between the two facts. The evidence about imports is less conclusive. The results also suggest that the opening up of the Mexican Economy during the eighties is more likely to have caused a structural change in the trade flows. The boost from the American economy accounts for 96% of the growth of the equilibrium level of Mexican exports from 1994 to 2000.

Chapter 2 - The U.S. goods trade deficit with Mexico was $64.1 billion in 2006, an increase of $14.3 billion from $49.7 billion in 2005. U.S. goods exports in 2006 were $134.2 billion, up 11.5 percent from the previous year. Corresponding U.S. imports from Mexico were $198.3 billion, up 16.5 percent. Mexico is currently the 2nd largest export market for U.S. goods.

U.S. exports of private commercial services (i.e., excluding military and government) to Mexico were $20.6 billion in 2005 (latest data available), and U.S. imports were $14.7 billion. Sales of services in Mexico by majority U.S.-owned affiliates were $8.9 billion in 2004 (latest data available), while sales of services in the United States by majority Mexico-owned firms were $1.2 billion.

The stock of U.S. foreign direct investment in Mexico in 2005 was $71.4 billion, up from $63.5 billion in 2004. U.S. FDI in Mexico is concentrated largely in the manufacturing, banking and finance sectors.

Chapter 3 - The United States and Mexico have a close and complex bilateral relationship, with extensive economic linkages as neighbors and partners under the North American Free Trade Agreement (NAFTA). Bilateral relations are generally friendly, although the U.S. enactment of border fence legislation in October 2006 caused some tension in the relationship. Drug trafficking issues are prominent in relations since Mexico is the leading transit country for cocaine, a leading supplier of methamphetamine and heroin, and the leading foreign supplier of marijuana to the United States.

In October 2007, the United States and Mexico announced the Mérida Initiative to combat drug trafficking, gangs, and organized crime in Mexico and Central America. The Administration requested $500 million in FY2008 supplemental assistance for Mexico as part of a $1.4 billion, multi-year aid package for the Initiative. In legislative action on H.R. 2642, the second FY2008 supplemental appropriations measure, the House approved $400 million for Mexico on May 15, 2008, while the Senate approved $350 million on May 22; the measure will now go to conference. Both versions have human rights conditions. In other action, a bill that would authorize $1.1 billion for Mexico over three years under the Mérida Initiative, H.R. 6048, was approved by the House Foreign Affairs Committee on May 14, 2008. The Administration has also requested an additional $450 million for Mexico under the Mérida Initiative in its FY2009 budget request.

Shortly after taking office in December 2006, President Felipe Calderón of the conservative National Action Party (PAN) launched operations against drug cartels in nine Mexican states. Since early 2008, he has sent more than 25,000 soldiers and federal police to drug trafficking "hot-spots." Calderón has increased extraditions to the United States, and has demonstrated an unprecedented willingness to reach out for counternarcotics assistance from the United States while also calling for increased U.S. efforts on arms trafficking and a reduction in the U.S. demand for illicit drugs.

Migration, border security, and trade issues also have dominated the bilateral relationship in recent years. Comprehensive immigration reform was debated early in the 110th Congress, but the issue was put aside following a failed cloture motion in the Senate on the Comprehensive Immigration Reform Act of 2007 (S. 1348). In September 2006, Congress approved the Secure Fence Act of 2006 (P.L. 109-367) to authorize the construction of a border fence and other barriers along 700 miles of the U.S.-Mexico border. Since 1994, NAFTA institutions have been functioning, trade between the countries has tripled, and allegations of violations of labor and environmental laws have been considered by the trilateral institutions. The Bush Administration argues that NAFTA has had modest positive impacts on all three member countries, but Mexican farmers have strongly criticized the effects of NAFTA. Notable bilateral trade disputes relate to trucking, tuna, sweeteners and anti-dumping measures. For additional information, see CRS Report RL32934, *U.S.-Mexico Economic Relations: Trends, Issues, and Implications*; CRS Report RS22837, *Merida Initiative: Proposed U.S. Anticrime and Counterdrug Assistance for Mexico and Central America*; and CRS Report RL34215, *Mexico's Drug Cartels*.

Chapter 4 - U.S. immigration policy has largely been viewed as a domestic issue and one where the prerogatives of the Congress prevailed over those of the executive and judicial branches. By the 1970s, however, concerns over growing illegal migration led to the creation of an inter-agency task force to study the phenomenon. During the presidency of Jimmy Carter, the Interagency Task Force on Immigration Policy issued its Staff Report in March 1979, which noted that "In the last twelve years, I.N.S. apprehensions of deportable aliens have increased twenty - fold and the vast majority of those apprehended are Mexican nationals." The work of the Interagency Task Force on Immigration Policy was superseded by the creation of the Select Commission on Immigration and Refugee Policy by Public Law 95 - 412 in 1979. The 16 member Select Commission included four presidential appointees, four cabinet members, four U.S. senators, and four members of the U.S. House. It was led by Father Theodore M. Hesburgh, the President of the University of Notre Dame.

An influx of Haitian entrants and the Cuban government-sanctioned outflow, which included numerous Cubans who had been incarcerated for non-political offenses, hurt Carter's bid for re-election. In Arkansas, a riot by Cubans at a detention center in 1980 was widely seen as costing then Governor Bill Clinton re-election. The stakes of immigration and refugee policies for U.S. presidents were rising. This reflected a broader pattern of politicization and securitization of international migration policies in the transatlantic area.

The Select Commission communicated its report and recommendations to President Ronald Reagan. It recommended a legalization policy, imposition of employer sanctions for unauthorized hiring of aliens, a system of more secure identification for all employees and a slightly modified, "streamlined" H-2 temporary foreign worker program which did "...not exclude a slight expansion of the program." The purpose of the Select Commission was to forge a national consensus concerning reform of immigration policy. However, the vote on the question, "Do you favor employer sanctions with some system of more secure identification?" was eight yes, seven no and one pass. The vote concerning temporary foreign workers was an unambiguous fourteen to two, a major setback to proponents of expanded temporary foreign worker policy. The text voted upon included "The Commission believes that government, employers and unions should cooperate to end the dependence of any industry on a constant supply of H-2 workers."

Bills reflecting the Select Commission's recommendations concerning illegal migration were then submitted to both houses of the U.S. Congress but became mired in a protracted and complex debate. Supporters of expanded temporary foreign worker policy helped prevent passage of legislation until 1986 when Congressman Charles Schumer of New York brokered a deal which would authorize a special legalization program for foreign agricultural workers that ended the legislative logjam. President Reagan signed the Immigration Reform and Control Act (IRCA) into law on November 6, 1986. Meanwhile, all major Democratic Party presidential hopefuls in 1984 had announced their opposition to the imposition of employer sanctions. They viewed employer sanctions as damaging their electoral prospects with Hispanic voters. Polls, however, indicated that Hispanic voters were about evenly split for and against enactment of employer sanctions.

One provision of IRCA authorized the creation of a Commission for the Study of International Migration and Cooperative Economic Development (CSIMCED). This Commission would produce numerous reports and studies which would pave the way to President George H. W. Bush embracing a Mexican proposal to enlarge the free trade agreement signed in 1988 between Canada and the United States to include Mexico. Very significantly, the major research finding of the scores of studies commissioned by the CSIMCED held that trade liberalization would reduce illegal migration from Mexico only in the long run. Over the short to medium term, it would significantly increase it. Philip L. Martin would later refine this insight into his theory of a migration hump.

President George H. W. Bush, signed the Immigration Act of 1990 into law, which increased legal immigration into the United States by 35 percent. The new law reflected a growing conservative celebration of international migration as economically beneficial. Both of the principal contenders for the presidency in 1992 touted a North American Free Trade Agreement (NAFTA) as a way to reduce illegal migration. President George H. W. Bush, referred Mexican President Carlos Salinas' proposal for the creation of NAFTA to the National Security Council which, according to Mexican immigration specialist Jorge Bustamente, determined that international migration had created such interdependency between the United States and Mexico that any adverse development in Mexico would affect the United States. It recommended U.S. support for the Mexican initiative which dovetailed with many of the recommendations made by the CSIMCED. During the 1992 presidential campaign, the Democratic nominee criticized President Bush's policy of forcibly repatriating Haitians only to reverse his stand shortly before his inauguration.

NAFTA came into effect on January 1, 1994. Later that year, a sharply contested referendum to deny public benefits, such as education to illegally resident alien children, passed by a large margin in California. Proposition 187 had been openly opposed by Mexican government officials who helped organize protests against the measure. Although implementation of the measure was determined to be unconstitutional, as it clearly clashed with the 1982 Plyler versus DOE Supreme Court decision which upheld the right of undocumented children to attend public schools in Texas, the referendum sounded a tocsin in Washington, DC.

The subsequent flurry of legislative proposals to curtail legal immigration to the United States was defeated, however. President Clinton signed into law the Illegal Immigration Reform and Responsibility act of 1996 and thereby largely defused immigration as a campaign issue in the 1996 presidential election. The far-ranging legislation reflected a hardening of views in that it mandated a massive increase in Immigration and Naturalization Service personnel as well as support for enhanced border interdiction, removal of criminal aliens and expedited abjudication of asylum cases. Very significantly, however, the 1996 law did not reflect the recommendations of yet another federal commission, the Commission on Immigration Reform, which had recommended implementation of a secure employee identification system and other measures to bolster lagging enforcement of employer sanctions. President Clinton had endorsed the Commission on Immigration Reforms recommendations, which included reduction in legal immigration. President Clinton repeatedly voiced his opposition to guestworker policy and threatened to veto any measure expanding admissions of unskilled foreign workers.

While immigration issues did not centrally affect the outcome of the 1996 presidential election, they nevertheless were accorded much more significance than had been the case in elections in the 1960s or 1970s. Influential newspapers scrutinized the positions of Senator Robert Dole and President Clinton on immigration. Senator Dole supported an amendment which would have denied public education to illegal immigrant children whereas Clinton opposed the amendment. The unsuccessful candidacy of Patrick Buchanan also served to heighten awareness of the principal candidates' stances on immigration. By 2000, George W. Bush would conclude that the anti-immigration overtones of the 1996 GOP candidates had hurt the party's performance in the election.

By the 2000 election, international migration could be viewed in a strategic way. Virtually everyone acknowledged that international migration constituted a key dynamic within globalization which, in turn, was viewed as central to the advancement of U.S. foreign and security interests. (See the article by Oliver in this issue.) Moreover, more ideologically-inclined Republicans took a dim view of governmental regulation in general and found confirmation of the accuracy of their views in the flagging effort of the U.S. government to curtail illegal migration despite the vast increases in resources devoted to that task in the Clinton administrations.

Nevertheless, Republican candidate George W. Bush did not articulate a strategic or architect's vision of international migration policy in overall U.S. foreign and national security policy in the 2000 campaign. It was widely known that he had supported a Southwest Governors' endorsement of expanded admissions of temporary Mexican workers. The Republican candidate was generally not viewed as well-versed in foreign policy matters, save for his knowledge of Mexico. He had some Spanish language facility and kin of Hispanic background. Immigration policy issues, however, did not figure centrally in the 2000 race, although both candidates campaigned for Hispanic votes. Thus, if the Republican contender possessed a strategic vision of international migration in regional or world order, it was kept under wraps. In all probability, any strategic or architect's view of international migration in global and regional order came from Vincente Fox Quesada, elected President of Mexico in July 2000 who, shortly after his election, called for the creation of a North American common market that would allow freer flow of merchandise and workers.

Chapter 5 - The objective in this paper is to bring to the attention of businesswomen's organizations in Latin America the importance of collecting data on the increasing participation of women in the economy as entrepreneurs and managers. Why is collecting this data important? As the authors will discuss in this paper, there are two reasons why having this data matters. First, they anticipate that women's gains in education and the labor market should put them in a good position to benefit from business opportunities opened by free trade. However, free trade also brings challenges to women entrepreneurs. Having the data will allow us to measure the net effect of free trade on women entrepreneurs. And, because governments do not necessarily collect this data, it is important for women's organizations to do so. Second, women's organizations in Canada and the United States have already provided an example of why it is important for them to compile data that the government may not be collecting. These organizations have used data that demonstrate the impact of women in business on the economy to successfully lobby legislators to pass policies that benefit women in business. Women's organizations in Latin America can use data they collect in the same way.

Chapter 6 - Defining "entrepreneurs" as workers who declare their professional status to be that of employers or own-account workers (self-employed without full-time, paid employees), the Organization for Economic Co-operation and Development (OECD, 2000) reports that the share of women entrepreneurs as a percentage of all entrepreneurs increased from 29.7 percent in 1980 to 35.2 percent in 1990 in the United States and from 30.8 percent to 37.1 percent in Canada during the same period. The U.S. Economic Census defines "women-owned businesses" as privately held firms in which women own 51 percent or more of the enterprise. According to the most recent economic census data (1997), the number of women-owned firms increased 16 percent from 1992 to 1997. This is almost triple the rate of growth (6 percent) for all U.S. firms during this period. Estimates from the Center for Women's Business Research (1997) show the increase in women-owned businesses holding at 14 percent between 1997 and 2002.

Furthermore, this growth is consistent across all ethnic groups in the United States. This trend, however, is not necessarily well noted. As Robles (2002) has pointed out, "we are bereft of comprehensive knowledge and information about the U.S. minority enterprise population."

These statistics indicate noteworthy increases in the numbers of U.S. and Canadian women entrepreneurs. What factors have contributed to this growth? And do these factors also translate into success for their colleagues in Latin America? How does the experience of women entrepreneurs in Latin America compare to that of their counterparts to the north? What are the relative advantages and disadvantages of entrepreneurship in the emerging economies of Latin America?

Chapter 7 - In growing competitive markets the large and reputed firms are developing strategies to move into the provision of innovative combinations of products and services as 'high-value integrated solutions' tailored to each customer's needs than simply 'moving downstream' into services. Such firms are developing innovative combinations of service capabilities such as operations, business consultancy and finance required to provide complete solutions to each customer's needs in order to augment the customer value towards the innovative or new products. It has been argued that provision of integrated solutions is attracting firms traditionally based in manufacturing and services to occupy a new base in the value stream centered on 'systems integration' using internal or external sources of product designing, supply and customer focused promotion (Davies,2004). Besides organizational perspectives of enhancing customer value, the functional variables like pricing play a significant role in developing the customer perceptions towards new products.

Consumers plan to spread consumption of their total resources evenly over the remainder of their life span at a given time. Such consumption smoothing occurs though current demand for the products and services and buying power may fluctuate over time. Thus, borrowing allows consumers with lower initial assets but higher expected future income to make utility-maximizing consumption choices within the overall, lifetime budget constraint. On the contrary, consumers may not be very capable of taking lifetime budget constraints into account when making repeated consumption choices that are distributed over time and are influenced by the self reference criterion (see Herrnstein and Prelec, 1992). It has been observed in previous studies that value to expenditure ratios increase consumer sensitivity in volume of buying and driving repeat buying decisions for the regular and high-tech products (Carroll and Dunn 1997). Consumers often have enough insight towards limiting their choices by employing self-rationing strategies. Consumers may show suboptimal behavior while adapting to the self-rationing strategies to limit their choice which may induce asymmetric consumer behavior in the long run (Loewenstein, 1996).

This paper attempts to discuss the interdependence of variability in consumer behavior due to intrinsic and extrinsic retail environment which influence the process of determining the choices on products and services. It is argued in the paper that suboptimal choice of consumers affect the demand of the products and services in the long-run and the cause and effect has been explained through the single non-linear equations. A system of demand equations which explains the process of optimization of consumer choice and behavioral adjustment towards gaining a long-term association with the market has also been discussed in the paper.

Chapter 8 - Over half a million clandestine abortions are believed to occur annually in Mexico, many under unfavorable health conditions that lead to the death of several hundred women. Since it first came under scrutiny in the early 1970s, this situation has proved politically sensitive and difficult for both society and state. An uneasy truce has masked over the subject, broken by periodic controversy. The abortion debate became nationwide following several contrasting legal initiatives and high-profile adolescent rape cases as the country entered systemic change in 2000. This paper assesses accessibility to abortion services, the medical demography of abortion, recent attempts to make abortion safer and rarer, the evolution and social construction of the abortion debate, and the strategies and relative influences of the key actors involved. It further examines the international dimensions to this controversy and the barriers to bringing policy more into line with actual abortion practice. Despite increasing political pluralism, societal and elite awareness of existing problems, for now the issue is not judged sufficiently pressing to merit major action due to a host of reasons discussed. On the other hand, incremental changes in post-abortion care have occurred and the question of abortion can no longer be ignored.

Chapter 9 - Acquired Immunodeficiency Syndrome is a global epidemic. Seventy six percent of the total cases are in the age range of 18-35, which provide suspicions that most of the infections occur during adolescence. Adolescents often engage in sexual risk behaviors because they do not have enough information to make the best decisions concerning their sexual behavior. The adolescents' parents play a very important role in the sexual development and promotion of HIV/AIDS prevention. Parent-adolescent communication about sex is an important medium for adolescents because it provides them with a source of information and values that allow them to make safer sex decisions. Due to the fact that communication is a bi-directional process, it is important to take into account the parent-adolescent interaction. Therefore, the purpose of this paper is to explain an interaction model for HIV/AIDS prevention based in parent-adolescent communication about sex with the Hispanic population using the Self-Efficacy Theory. The model conceives the parent-adolescent dyad for HIV/AIDS prevention. There are two central elements that support this model. The first is the interaction of parent and adolescent to achieve the same goal, which is HIV/AIDS prevention. The second is focused on the general cultural characteristics of Hispanic families, such as: allocentrism, time orientation, gender roles, and fatalism. The principle concepts in this model are parent-adolescent interactions, preventive behaviors, and HIV/AIDS prevention as an outcome. The parent-adolescent interactions include: cultural characteristics, attitudes, beliefs, and knowledge. Together parent's and adolescent's efficacy expectations may result in the activation of preventive behaviors. The preventive behaviors for adolescents are abstinence, condom use, and partner discussion. The preventive behaviors for parents are quality and quantity of communication about sex. The maintenance and perseverance of parent-adolescent behaviors are regulated by outcome expectations such as, prevention of diseases, perceived benefits, partner protection for the adolescent, closeness and sexual risk reduction for parents. Thus, the adolescent's and parent's belief about the positive results of their behavior should result in the repetition of the preventive behavior. This repetition will increase the probability of preventing HIV/AIDS in Hispanic adolescents. This model illustrates the importance of working with efficacy and outcome expectations to improve the parent-adolescent behaviors for HIV/AIDS prevention. Health care providers may use this model to develop effective prevention programs in the community, guide the development of parent and adolescent skills in an educational context, and modify it to fit other STD's.

In: Mexico: Economic, Political and Social Issues
Editors: Maria L. Castro and Irene P. Navarro
ISBN: 978-1-60456-847-9

Chapter 1

IS NAFTA BEHIND THE MEXICAN EXPORT BOOM (1994-2000)?

Daniel Garces-Diaz

ABSTRACT

The North America Free Trade Agreement (NAFTA) took effect in January 1994. From that year to 2000, Mexican exports grew three times faster (15%) than in the previous six years. Contrary to widespread beliefs, the cointegration analysis in this paper finds no connection between the two facts. The evidence about imports is less conclusive. The results also suggest that the opening up of the Mexican Economy during the eighties is more likely to have caused a structural change in the trade flows. The boost from the American economy accounts for 96% of the growth of the equilibrium level of Mexican exports from 1994 to 2000.

1. INTRODUCTION

Free trade agreements among a few countries have become common as substitutes or intermediate steps for wider arrangements. A very important one that generated a great deal of expectations and controversy was signed by Canada, Mexico and the USA. The negotiations preceding the North America Free Trade Agreement (NAFTA) were long and difficult, in part because of the uncertainty about its ramifications. To assess the potential economic effects on the three countries involved, a lot of forward-looking research was carried out by means of computable general equilibrium (CGE) models. These models mostly anticipated large benefits for Mexico and less important ones for Canada and the USA.

In this paper, I concentrate in studying the impact of that accord on the value of trade flows and do not discuss any other aspects, such as changes in the composition of trade, income distribution or employment. I explain what role NAFTA played, if any, in the strong performance of Mexican foreign trade since 1994, the year of the inception of that agreement.[1]

The research about the effects of NAFTA is rather scant. Gould (1998) found that Canada's trade with the US and Mexico did not have perceptible effects, but that trade between Mexico and the US did show changes after NAFTA. He based his estimates on a gravity model of bilateral trade where the change in tariff and nontariff barriers due to NAFTA was approximated by a dummy variable that he found significant for the equations of trade between Mexico and the US; by contrast, I found a similar dummy variable to be nonsignificant in the error correction equations I derived.

Krueger (1999) observed that both Canadian and Mexican foreign trade have become more concentrated towards the US and wondered, also in the context of a gravity model, if that phenomenon was the result of trade creation or trade diversion. She concluded that NAFTA did not induce large effects with respect to other processes already underway, such as previous reduction of tariffs and the modification of the exchange rate regime; on the contrary, the results of this paper imply that the adoption of a new exchange rate system did not have any effects on the trade flows. I do find, however, that changes in Mexican trade policy carried out long before NAFTA had important effects on the behavior of the Mexican foreign trade sector. Finally, Gruben (2001) did not find an effect of NAFTA on employment in assembling plants (maquiladoras) in Mexico. This result is strongly consistent with the ones from this paper.

I examine the Mexican trade flows assuming that they are entirely determined by the demand side; i.e., both the import and export supply functions are perfectly elastic within the observable range or, equivalently, the country is a price taker in world markets. This is a reasonable assumption for Mexico. The analysis is based on the estimation of cointegration relationships. The results are robust enough so as not to depend on the estimation method.

The main results are the following: a structural change occurred during the eighties which makes it difficult to estimate cointegration relationships for the period that begins in 1980 and ends in 2000; therefore, I split the sample and estimated long-run relationships for exports and imports for the period 1990-2000. I obtained coefficients with the correct sign and reasonable magnitude. I also found that the equation for exports, as a function of the US index of industrial production and the real exchange rate, is very stable for that period. The US economy's upswing accounts for 96% of the growth of the equilibrium level of Mexican exports from 1994 to 2000. The net effect of the real exchange rate during that period is small because after the sharp 1995 devaluation it appreciated enough to return to its former level. The import demand (as a function of the Mexican index of industrial production, the level of exports and the real exchange rate) shows instability for the same period although the long-run equation fits the data very well, even without considering seasonality and short-run dynamics.

The analysis was extended to disaggregate data and it was found that only in a few individual categories of exports and imports can one find a cointegration vector valid for the whole twenty one years. For the 1990-2000 period I found a stable cointegration vector in all cases, which explains the result for aggregate exports and imports. I also obtained stable and

[1] From that year to 1999 exports grew on average almost three times faster than during the previous six years: 15.5% against 5.5%, annually. The degree of openness of the economy, (defined as the sum of exports and imports over GDP), for the year 2000 (0.77) is twice as big as that of 1993 (0.36).

constant error-correction models for the same period. These results imply that a structural change in Mexican foreign trade during the nineties was very unlikely and therefore NAFTA could not have caused the boom in Mexican exports. In most cases, a cointegration vector was also found for the 1980-1989 subsample although those vectors do not present the stability shown for the 1990-2000 period. This suggests that a structural change occurred during the time Mexico opened up its economy and joined the General Agreement on Tariffs and Trade (GATT). A likely reason for the lack of evidence in favor of NAFTA as a great catalyzer of trade is that many of the structural reforms that that agreement was supposed to bring about were already there when it started.

The rest of the paper is organized as follows: in section 2, I describe the data and test for the presence of unit roots; in section 3, I analyze the behavior of exports and imports at the most aggregate level; in section 4, I carry out the analysis for different types of exports and imports; in section 5, I derive and analyze the error correction models; section 6 concludes.

2. Description and Statistical Properties of the Data

The data is of monthly frequency. Mexican exports (X) and imports (M) are in constant US dollars.[2] Exports are also disaggregated in maquila ($X^{\{Q\}}$), oil-related ($X^{\{O\}}$) and the rest ($X^{\{-QO\}}$). Imports are disaggregated in consumer goods ($M^{\{cons\}}$), capital goods ($M^{\{cap\}}$) and intermediate goods ($M^{\{int\}}$). I also consider imports of intermediate goods for maquila ($M^{\{intQ\}}$) and the rest ($M^{\{int-Q\}}$). The unilateral real exchange rate peso/dollar (RER) is based on the respective consumer price indexes. The indicators of economic activity are the US index of industrial production (IVUSA) and the Mexican index of industrial production (IVPI). I will use small letters to represent logarithms of the series.

Table 1 presents two tests (with three and six lags) to classify the logarithms of the series as being either trend stationary (TS) or difference stationary (DS). The first one is the GLS-DF test proposed by Elliot *et al.* (1996), which is a more powerful version of the well-known ADF test. The second one is the stationarity KPSS test proposed by Kwiatkowski *et al.* (1992). These tests (or similar ones) are jointly used in confirmatory analysis for the presence of a unit root in a series.[3]

It can be seen that in all cases but two (with three lags) the DF-GLS cannot reject the hypothesis for the presence of a unit root in the levels of the series. The result is confirmed by the KPSS test that rejects the hypothesis of stationarity in all but just one case (with six lags). For the differences of the series (rates of growth) the results are the opposite: the DF-GLS test

[2]Exports and imports data are reported every month in current US dollars. For the calculations in the paper, I divide these numbers by the US CPI. From 1980 to 1990 maquila exports were treated differently from the rest of exports and were reported as a separate item. Since 1991 maquila exports are regarded as part of total exports and are also reported separately but the data were elaborated with a different methodology.

[3]The first test has the presence of a unit root as the null while the KPSS test has stationarity as the null. If GLSDF rejects and KPSS accepts, then the series is classified unambiguously as TS; while if GLSDF accepts and KPSS rejects the series is considered stationary. When both tests accept, then we conclude there is not enough information in the series to classify it. When both reject (an unusual situation), it is probably the case that a linear specification for the series is not a good approximation for its stochastic behavior.

rejects the hypothesis of a unit root in all cases and the KPSS test cannot reject the hypothesis of stationarity. Therefore, I consider all series to be $I(1)$.

Table 1. Unit Root Tests and Stationarity

Variable	DF-GLS Test		KPSS Test	
	Levels			
	3 lags	6 lags	3 lags	6 lags
x	-1.8	-0.9	1.3**	0.8**
$x^{\{-QP\}}$	-1.7	-1.3	0.5**	0.3**
$x^{\{Q\}}$	-2.9**	-2.2	0.2**	0.2**
m	-1.5	-1.8	0.7**	0.4**
$m^{\{cap\}}$	-1.5	-1.5	0.7**	0.4**
$m^{\{cons\}}$	-1.8	-2.0	0.6**	0.3**
$m^{\{int\}}$	-1.7	-1.6	0.7**	0.4**
$m^{\{int_Q\}}$	-3.2**	-2.5	0.2**	0.1
$m^{\{int\_Q\}}$	-1.7	-1.7	0.7**	0.4**
$IPI^{\{USA\}}$	-1.1	-1.4	0.7**	0.4**
$ivpi$	-1.8	-1.7	0.8**	0.5**
tcr	-1.6	-1.9	0.5**	0.3**
	Differences			
x	-8.0***	-3.7***	0.0	0.0
$x^{\{-QP\}}$	-8.1***	-3.7***	0.0	0.0
$x^{\{Q\}}$	-10.6***	-6.2***	0.0	0.0
m	-7.8***	-5.4***	0.1	0.1
$m^{\{cap\}}$	-5.2***	-2.8*	0.0	0.1
$m^{\{cons\}}$	-6.8***	-4.2***	0.1	0.1
$m^{\{int\}}$	-6.0***	-3.7***	0.0	0.0
$m^{\{int_Q\}}$	-10.1***	-6.1***	0.0	0.0
$m^{\{int\_Q\}}$	-5.7***	-3.8***	0.0	0.0
$IPI^{\{USA\}}$	-6.7***	-5.1***	0.1	0.1
$ivpi$	-9.5***	-5.6***	0.0	0.0
tcr	-8.3***	-5.5***	0.1	0.1

*** 1% significance
** 5% significance
* 10% significance

3. Analysis of Aggregate Mexican Foreign Trade

Mexico's geographical situation makes the variables that determine the level of its foreign trade easy to identify. Figure 1 shows, with a solid line in both panels, the Mexican trade balance, measured as $x-m$ instead of $X-M$. The dotted line in the upper panel represents the difference of the logarithm of the indexes of industrial production of Mexico ($ivpi$) and the US ($ivusa$), as a measure of relative income. The dotted line in the lower panel represents the path of the logarithm of the real exchange rate (rer).

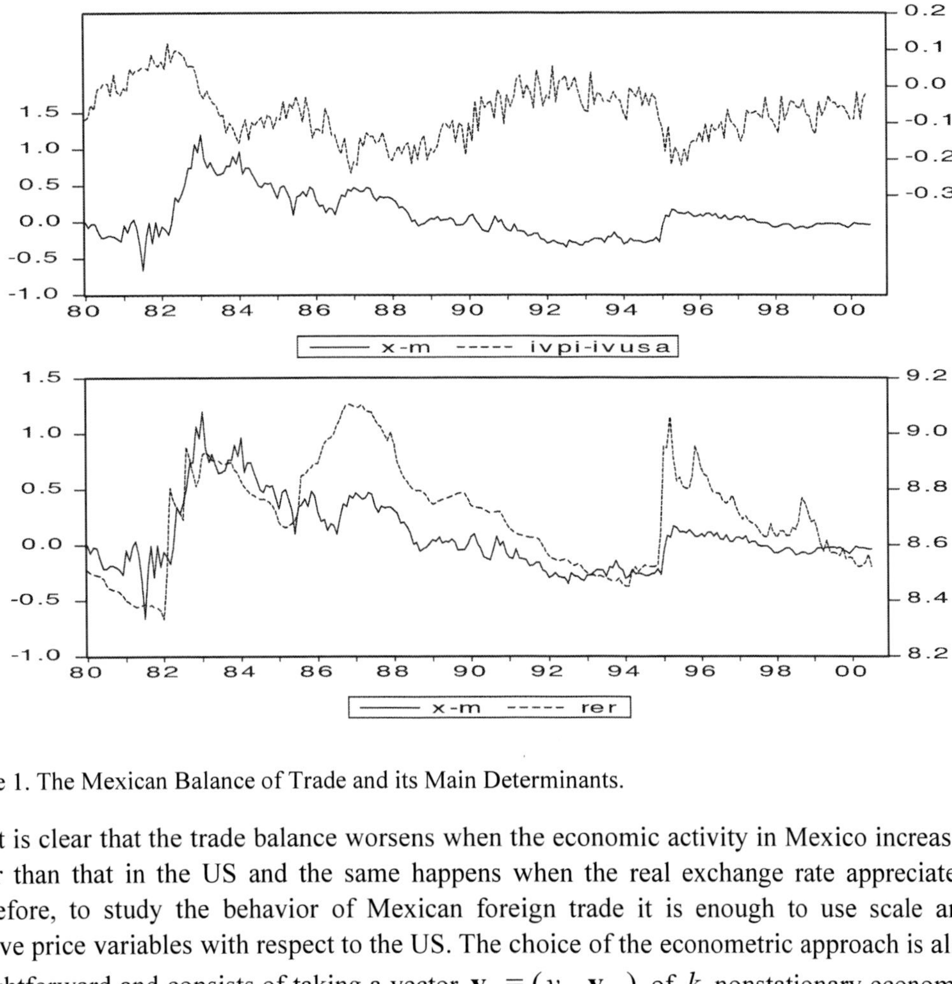

Figure 1. The Mexican Balance of Trade and its Main Determinants.

It is clear that the trade balance worsens when the economic activity in Mexico increases faster than that in the US and the same happens when the real exchange rate appreciates. Therefore, to study the behavior of Mexican foreign trade it is enough to use scale and relative price variables with respect to the US. The choice of the econometric approach is also straightforward and consists of taking a vector $\mathbf{y}_t = (y_{1t}, \mathbf{y}_{2t})$ of k nonstationary economic variables forming a cointegrating system that can be interpreted as a demand y_1 of imports or exports depending on some other $k-1$ variables $\mathbf{y}_2$ in a linear fashion:

$$y_1 = \boldsymbol{\gamma}'\mathbf{y}_2 \tag{1}$$

where γ is the $k-1$ vector of long-run coefficients or elasticities.

In principle, one could try to model the equations for exports and imports simultaneously in the context of a VECM. I tried this approach but, due to the presence of structural changes (to be discussed later), the size of the workable sample was small relative to the number of parameters and, therefore, very sensitive to changes in the number of lags.[4] For this reason I study exports and imports separately.

3.1. Exports

Since 1980 there have been some important changes in the composition, the rate of growth and the destination of Mexican exports, as illustrated by figure 2.

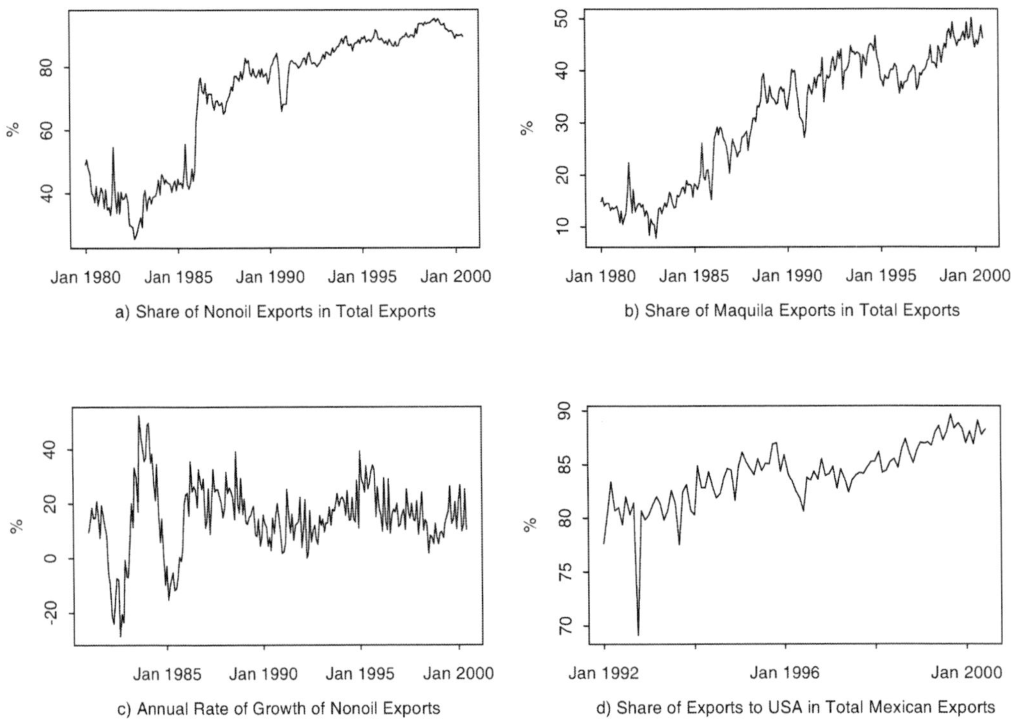

Figure 2. Changes in Mexican Exports.

Panel a) shows how nonoil-related exports have increased their share from about 50% in the early eighties to nearly 90% in 2000. Panel b) suggests a similar behavior of maquila exports, whose portion of total exports has reached nearly 50%, up from some 15% in the early eighties. Panel c) illustrates how the dynamics of exports have changed since the late eighties when Mexico entered into the GATT and gave up trade policy as a tool to correct macroeconomic imbalances. The long swings at the beginning of the sample are due to the implementation of several trade policies. This erratic behavior is reflected in the problem of

[4] The coefficients I obtain in the paper can be approximated by a VECM with nine lags and some restrictions that are rejected by the data.

estimating an export function for the whole sample. The final panel shows that the tendency of Mexican exports to concentrate in a single destination (the US) started before NAFTA.[5]

As a consequence of this complex behavior, it was not possible to obtain an equation for the whole sample period. To try to answer the main question posed by the paper, I modeled the long-run demand for Mexican exports (x) from 1990 to 2000 as a linear function of the US index of industrial production ($ivusa$) and the real exchange rate (rer). The rest of the sample is analyzed in a later section. In this section I apply the Johansen (1988) cointegration procedure to study the system formed by these three variables. The specification includes twelve lags and a constant in the cointegration space. I tried to correct the nonnormaility of the residuals with dummy variables but too many were required so I decided to run the VECM without them.[6] The results are shown in table 2:

Part (i) shows the trace statistics for the sequential hypotheses of zero, at most one and at most two cointegration vectors. Only in the first case is the hypothesis rejected, so I conclude there is only one long-run relationship. This fact reduces the identification efforts to give a unitary coefficient to one of the variables, which I conveniently choose to be exports. This makes the other coefficients interpretable as long-run elasticities.

Part (ii) shows the normalized cointegration coefficients. The coefficients have the correct signs and turn out to be very similar to the ones obtained with other methods. These coefficients imply the long-run export demand function:

$$x = c + 2.80ivusa + 0.32rer \tag{2}$$

Part (iii) shows the exclusion and weak exogeneity tests. The results show that none of the three variables can be excluded from the long-run relationship and that only total exports reject the hypothesis of weak exogeneity. The results shown so far justify the more detailed analysis I carry out in later sections utilizing single-equation methods. Part (iv) shows several specification tests. The problems detected by them might render the conclusions invalid, therefore the results of this section should be interpreted cautiously. I used other estimation methods and the results were not very different. In a later section I will show other estimates and tests.

Finally, a simple test can be applied to decide whether NAFTA, or any other event, caused a structural change in the behavior of Mexican exports during the sample period. The procedure consists in recursively estimating the system, and at each step testing, with a likelihood ratio, the hypothesis of the recursive coefficients being statistically equal to the ones obtained for the whole period. Figure 3 shows the sequence of test statistics. The level of significance is determined by a χ^2 distribution with one degree of freedom.

---

[5] No data of Mexican exports to the US are available for previous years.

[6] This is a serious problem because many of the tests are based on the assumption of normality. All the results shown in this section have to be interpreted with this caveat in mind.

Table 2. Maximum Likelihood Analysis for Exports 1990-2000

(i) Cointegration Analysis				
Eigenvalues	0.215	0.054	-	0.027
Null Hypothesis	$ran. = 0$	$ran. \leq 1$	-	$ran. \leq 2$
λ_{trace}	41.280**	10.520	-	3.460
Critical Values (95%)	29.700	15.400	-	3.800
(ii) Standarized Cointegration Vector and Coefficientes of Adjustment				
Variable	x	$IPI^{\{USA\}}$		rer
Norm. Coint. Vec. γ	1.0000	-2.80	-	-0.318
Coeff. of Adjust. α	-0.399	-0.017	-	0.043
(iii) Significance and Weak Exogeneity Tests for a Given Variable				
Variable	x	$IPI^{\{USA\}}$		rer
Exclusion $\chi^2(1)$	21.247**	19.382**	-	10.656**
Weak Exogeneity $\chi^2(1)$	16.100**	5.168*	-	0.455
(iv) Specification Tests				
Equation	x	$IPI^{\{USA\}}$	rer	Joint Test
AR F(7,102)	4.40[.00]**	0.75[.63]	1.11[.37]	F(63,257)=2.01[.00]**
Normality $\chi^2(2)$	0.99[.61]	5.36[.07]	73.98[.00]**	$\chi^2(6) = 76.44[.00]$**
Heterosk. F(12,96)	1.35[.20]	1.59[.11]	3.08[.00]**	F(72,500)=1.47[.01]*

p-values are between parentheses
* Significant at 10%
** Significant at 5%
*** Significant at 1%
See Hendry (1995) for a detailed description of the tests.

The hypothesis of stable parameters is easily accepted by the data. On the basis of this result, one can claim that there was no structural change in the behavior of Mexican exports during the nineties; however, this result can be a byproduct of the aggregate level in which the estimation is taking place. Therefore, a more disaggregated analysis is necessary. As an example, one can consider the behavior of oil-related exports, which probably do not respond to market factors the way other kinds of exports do. The stability and constancy of the short-run dynamics is demonstrated later. The accuracy of the model is demonstrated graphically in figure 4.

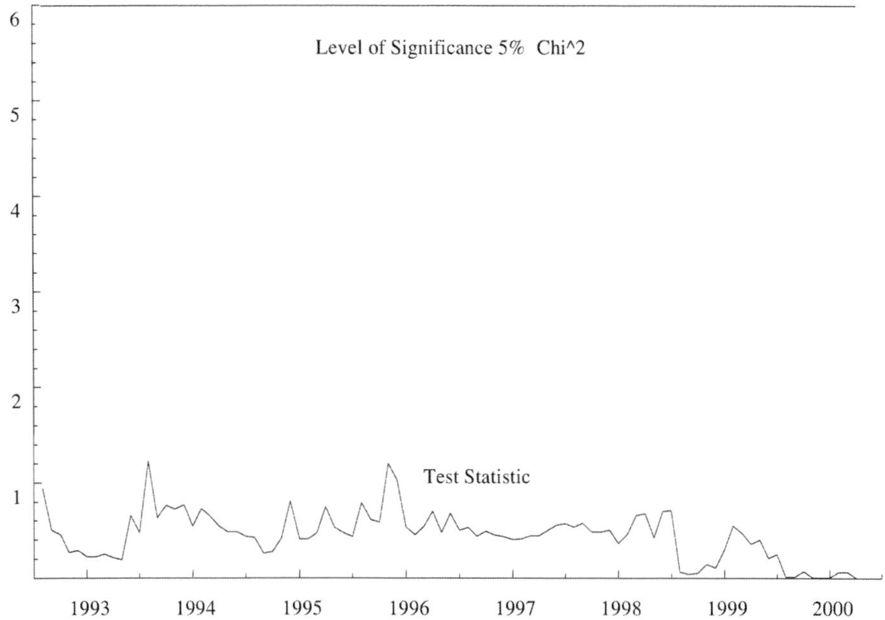

Figure 3. Recursive Test of Stability for Exports.

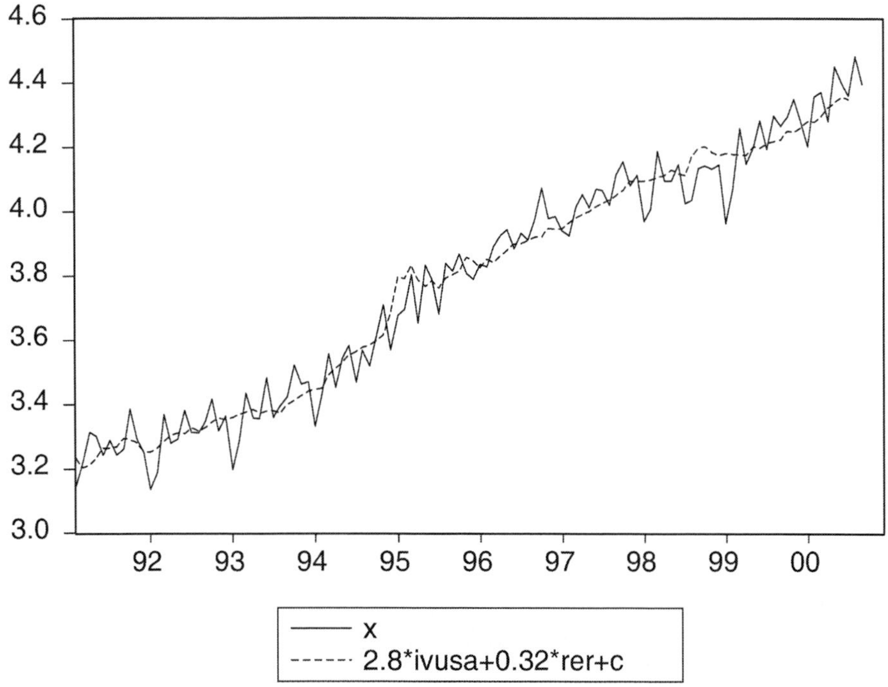

Figure 4. Exports (x) and its Long-Run Level ($2.8ivusa + 0.32rer + c$).

The goodness of fit is acceptable in spite of not including the short-run dynamics or seasonal components. From these results one can make some calculations that explain the fact that the rate of growth of Mexican exports has been much higher since the beginning of NAFTA. For the 1994-1999 period, the growth of the equilibrium level of Mexican exports is due almost completely (97%) to the expansion of the American economy (as measured by its index of industrial production) and only 4% of this growth is related to a modest depreciation of the real exchange rate. From 1990 to 1993 exports grew less because of the American economy's much slower pace and the revaluation of the real exchange rate. For this period, the appreciation of the real exchange rate offset about one third of the positive effect of the scale variable.

3.2. Imports

During the eighties, imports were often subject to a restrictive trade policy and a strategy of recurrent devaluations in order to face balance-of-payments problems. After Mexico entered the GATT in the mid eighties, most nontariff restrictions were removed and tariffs were considerably lowered. The effect of all these changes can seen in figure 5.

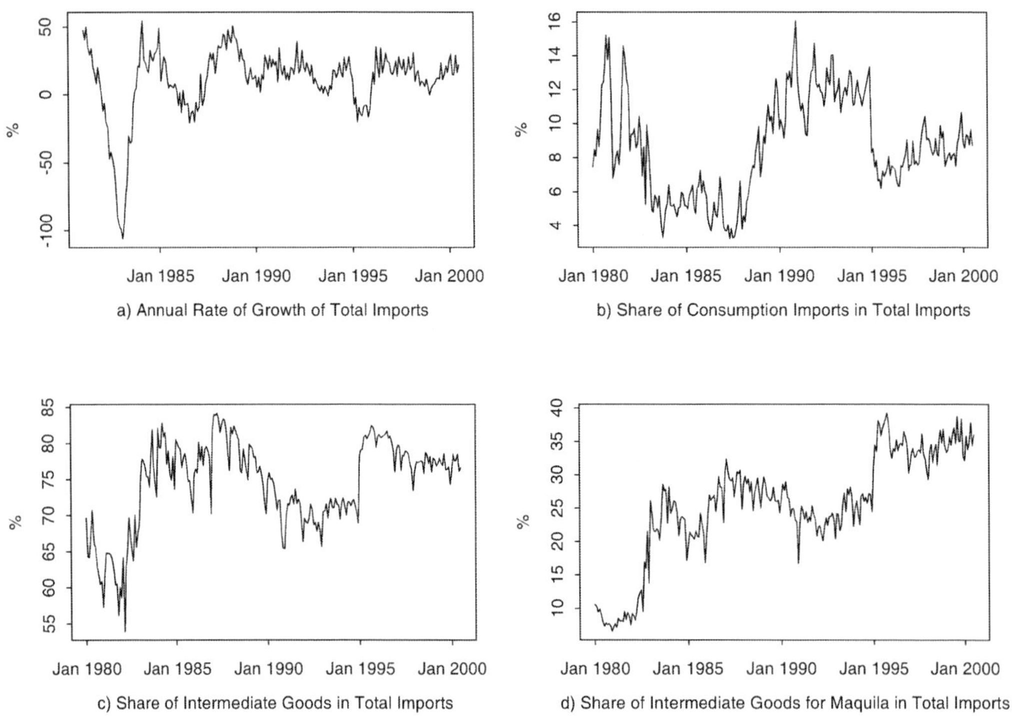

Figure 5. Evolution of Mexican Imports.

Table 3. Maximum Likelihood Analysis for Imports 1991-2000

(i) Cointegration Analysis					
Eigenvalues	0.222	0.136	-	0.29	0.002
Null Hypothesis	$ran.=0$	$ran.\leq 1$	-	$ran.\leq 2$	$ran.\leq 3$
λ_{trace}	48.590**	20.17	-	3.599	0.250
Critical Values (95%)	47.200	29.700	-	15.400	3.800
(ii) Standarized Cointegration Vector and Coefficientes of Adjustment					
Variable	m	$ivpi$		rer	x
Norm. Coint. Vec. γ	1.000	-0.937	-	0.410	-0.530
Coeff. of Adjust. α	-0.713	-0.178	-	0.113	-0.365
(iii) Significance and Weak Exogeneity Tests for a Given Variable					
Variable	m	$ivpi$		rer	x
Exclusion $\chi^2(1)$	27.980**	24.990**	-	17.290**	26.230**
Weak Exogeneity $\chi^2(1)$	16.630**	4.840	-	1.230	4.140
(vi) Specification Tests					
Equation	m	ivpi	rer	x	Joint Test
AR F(7,97)	2.43[.03]*	2.29[.03]*	2.00[.06]	4.97[00]**	F(112,292)=1.83[.00]**
Normality $\chi^2(2)$	0.12[.94]	1.35[.51]	62.46[.00]**	0.61[.74]	$\chi^2(6)=67.74[.00]$**
Heterosk. F(16,87)	1.10[.37]	1.58[.09]*	3.36[.00]**	1.84[.04]*	F(160,685)=1.59[.00]

p-values are between parentheses
* Significant at 10%
** Significant at 5%
*** Significant at 1%
See Hendry (1995) for a detailed description of the tests

Panel a) shows the annual rate of growth of total imports. Major devaluations have always had a strong impact on imports and sometimes they came bundled with severe economic contractions and a discretionary trade policy. The large drop in 1983 corresponds to the beginning of the debt crises that left the country with a low level of foreign currency and a deep economic recession. Panel b) shows the share of consumption imports in the total. This type of imports presents the highest income effect. The economic expansion and the consumption boom from the beginning of the nineties coincides with the largest shares of this type of imports in the total. Panel c) represents the participation of intermediate goods, the most important component of imports. It has been growing since the beginning of the sample and currently makes up nearly 80% of the total. The last panel represents the share of intermediate goods imported by the maquilas. This is by far the most dynamic component of Mexican imports and currently approaches 30% of the total. This fact suggests that Mexican exports must be considered as an explanatory variable for Mexican imports.

I applied the Johansen procedure to a system that includes Mexican total imports (m), the Mexican index of value of industrial production ($ivpi$), the real exchange rate (rer) and the level of total Mexican exports (x). The results are shown in table 3.

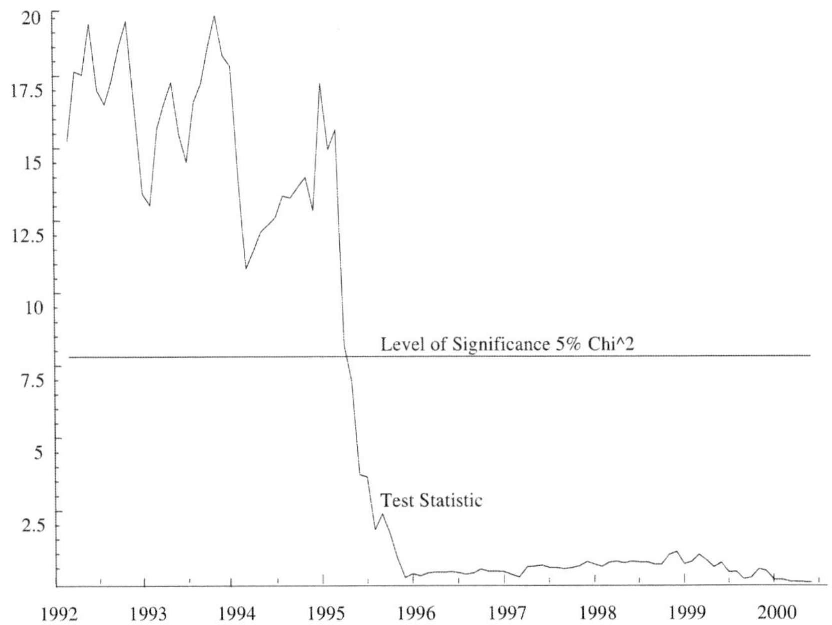

Figure 6. Recursive Test of Stability for Imports.

The results are very similar to the ones obtained in the case of exports: there is only one cointegration vector; the long-run elasticities have the correct sign; none of the variables can be excluded, and only imports reject the hypothesis of weak exogeneity. There are also specification problems as neither autocorrelation nor normality are jointly accepted. The long-run demand for imports turns out to be:

$$m = c + 0.94ivpi - 0.41rer + 0.53x \qquad (3)$$

The outcome of the stability test, however, is different. As figure 6 shows, the sequence of likelihood-ratio statistics crosses the significance line.

This result could be interpreted as indicative of a structural change in Mexican imports during the nineties, but a more detailed analysis is necessary. In spite of the apparent instability shown above, the long-run equation fits the data very well, as figure 7 shows. The fit is quite good even without short-run dynamics or seasonal components.

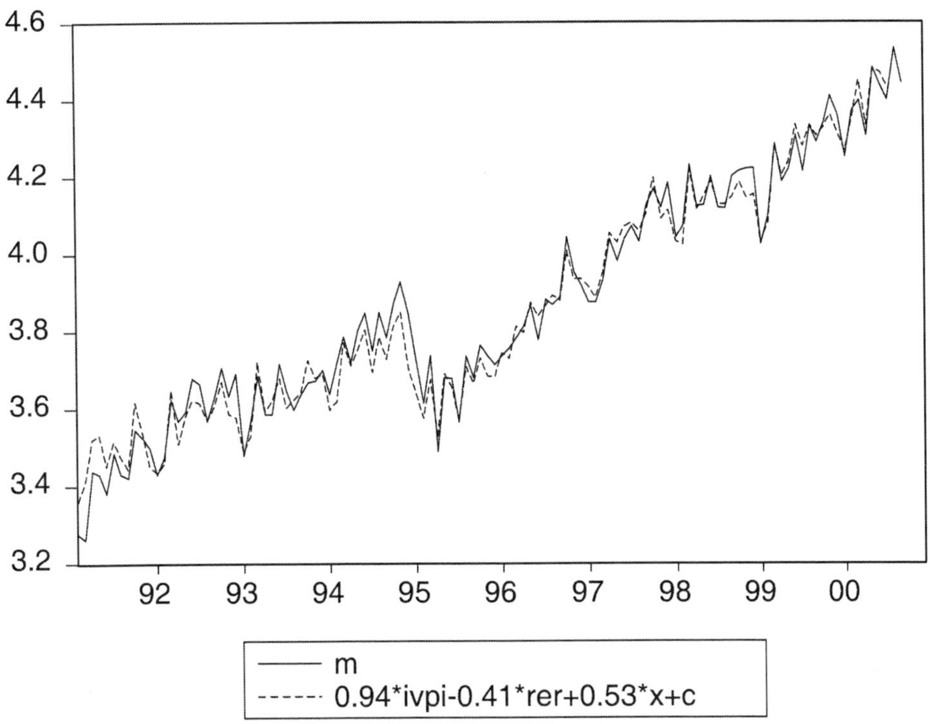

Figure 7. Imports (m) and its Long-Run Level ($0.94ivpi - 0.41rer + 0.53x + c$).

4. Extending the Analysis to Disaggregate Data

The results for exports and imports could be affected by either the shortened sample, the level of aggregation or even the inclusion of oil-related exports, which do not necessarily respond directly to free market forces. To control for all these factors, I estimated and tested the stability of export and import functions for the whole sample and the periods 1980-1989 and 1990-2000. I also disaggregated the data according to some reasonable criteria. Because of the large number of relationships being estimated, I used a single-equation framework. Two methods were used: OLS applied to unrestricted error-correction models and the Fully Modified Least Squares (FM-LS) method proposed by Phillips and Hansen (1990). The latter is more suitable when the normality assumption is not met but in all cases both methods yielded similar results. I first studied the cointegration property for the different types of exports and imports in each subsample and then I checked the stability properties with the Hansen (1992) tests in the cases where a long-run function was found.

4.1. Existence of Long-Run Relationships in Disaggregate Data

This section presents separately the results of cointegration tests based on the ECM statistic for disaggregate data on exports and imports. The p-values in the tables were obtained from the Ericsson and MacKinnon (1999) program. I divided exports in maquila ($x^{\{Q\}}$), oil-related ($x^{\{O\}}$) and the rest ($x^{\{-QO\}}$). Imports are disaggregated in consumer goods ($m^{\{c\}}$), capital goods ($m^{\{k\}}$) and intermediate goods ($m^{\{i\}}$). I also considered imports of intermediate goods for maquila ($m^{\{iq\}}$) and the rest ($m^{\{i-q\}}$). For each category I estimated unrestricted error correction models in each subsample.

4.1.1. Cointegration Tests for Disaggregate Exports

Table 4 reports only the cases where there was evidence of cointegration for the different types of exports. Because the estimates of the unrestricted cointegration vectors are very similar to the ones obtained by FM-LS, shown in table 6, I do not present the corresponding equations.

Several parameters are needed to run the test. Column 3 gives the number of variables in the cointegration relationship k. Column 4 gives the number of deterministic components d. Column 5 contains the sample size T and column 6 the number of total regressors h. Column 7 contains the ECM statistic (which is the t-statistic for the level of the lagged dependent variable). The final column provides the p-value for each ECM statistic generated by the Ericsson and McKinnon (1999) program. Each case is interesting in itself.

Table 4. ECM Tests for Exports

Variable	Period	No. of variables in Coint. Vect. k	No. of Determ. Variables d	Sample Size T	No. of Regressors h	ECM Statistic t	p-value* p
x	90-2000	3	1	127	7	-6.38	0.00
$x^{\{-QP\}}$	80-2000	3	1	234	7	-3.67	0.04
	80-89	3	1	107	7	-3.38	0.07
	91-2000	3	1	114	7	-4.80	0.00
$x^{\{Q\}}$	80-89	2	1	107	6	-3.90	0.01
	91-2000	2	1	113	6	-4.88	0.00

*Critical values and p-values herein were obtained using the response surfaces in Ericsson and MacKinnon (1999), as implemented in the program ECMtest.xls (version 1.0).

For total exports (x) I could find cointegration only for the period 1990-2000 (p-value=0.0) and not for the whole sample. The analysis of the case of maquila exports ($x^{\{Q\}}$) can explain the situation. First of all, the cointegration relationship excludes the real exchange rate (therefore $k = 2$). Second, for the whole sample the ECM statistic is not significant (-2.72 with p-value=0.15); however, for each subsample the ECM statistic is significant. This illustrates a likely structural break (as I will show, the cointegration vector is very different for each subsample) of the type suggested by Gregory and Hansen (1996), where a structural change hides the existence of a long relationship among $I(1)$ variables.[1] These characteristics of the maquila exports explain the problem of finding cointegration for total exports. The case of nonoil-nonmaquila exports ($x^{\{-QO\}}$) shows cointegration for the three periods and the cointegrating variables are the same as the ones for total exports.

4.1.2. Cointegration Tests for Disaggregate Imports

Table 5 shows that for total imports there is cointegration only for the period 1990-2000. For this category, the cointegrating variables are the Mexican index of industrial production, the real exchange rate and exports (so $k = 4$). The same cointegrating variables appear in the case of imports of intermediate goods, but exports are not in the equations of imports of capital goods and consumption goods (so $k = 3$).

Table 5. ECM Tests for Imports

Variable	Period	No. of variables in Coint. Vect. k	No. of Determ. Variables d	Sample Size T	No. of Regressors h	ECM Statistic t	p-value* p
m	91-2000	4	1	113	8	-5.46	0.00
$m^{\{cap\}}$	80-2000	3	1	243	6	-6.00	0.00
	80-89	2	1	116	6	-4.02	0.01
	91-2000	3	1	114	6	-6.85	0.00
$m^{\{cons\}}$	80-2000	3	1	234	8	-3.93	0.02
	80-89	3	1	107	8	-3.71	0.03
	91-2000	3	1	114	8	-5.20	0.00
$m^{\{int\}}$	91-2000	3	1	113	6	-6.37	0.00
$m^{\{int_Q\}}$	91-2000	3	1	113	9	-4.81	0.00
$m^{\{int\_Q\}}$	80-2000	3	1	245	7	-3.38	0.07
	91-2000	3	1	113	7	-6.82	0.00

*Critical values and p-values herein were obtained using the response surfaces in Ericsson and MacKinnon (1999), as implemented in the program ECMtest.xls (version 1.0).

The case of imports of capital goods ($m^{\{cap\}}$) is remarkable because the existence of cointegration for the whole sample hides the presence of a structural change of a special kind. It shows cointegration in the three periods but the cointegrating vectors for the two subsamples contain a different number of components: $k = 3$ for the 1990-2000 sample and

[1] I applied their tests and the results, available upon request, were coincident with the ones I present. It was interesting to observe that their ADF* test had the tendency to reject the hypothesis of cointegration. The other two tests performed more in accordance with what I report.

$k = 2$ for the 1980-89 period. In the latter case, the variable absent from the cointegration relationship is the Mexican index of industrial production. This case of structural change, however, was detected by the stability tests I report below. For imports of consumption goods ($m^{\{cons\}}$) I find cointegration for the three samples and the same number of variables appear in each case. However, as I will show, there is also evidence of a structural break.

For intermediate goods ($m^{\{int\}}$) I only found cointegration for the 1991-2000 period. As this is by far the most important component of Mexican imports, this property is passed on to the total. Dividing this category between those that go to maquila (m^{intQ}) and the rest ($m^{\{int-Q\}}$) I find similar results.

4.2. Stability of the Long-Run Relationships of Disaggregate Data

In this section I tested the stability of the long-run relationships found above. For the same categories of imports included in table 4, I estimated cointegration coefficients with the method of Fully Modified Least Squares (FM-LS) and applied the three stability tests for $I(1)$ variables proposed by Hansen (1991). The three tests have constant cointegration coefficients for the whole sample as the null hypothesis; however, the first two (LC and mean-F) consider a random walk for the coefficients as the alternative hypothesis while the alternative for the third test (sup-F) is a one-time break at an unknown date.[2]

4.3. Stability Tests for Disaggregate Exports

Columns 3 to 5 of table 6 contain the FM-LS estimates of the long-run coefficients and standard errors for each of the cointegrating variables and a constant. Columns 6 to 8 contain the statistics and p-values to test stability.[3]

The first thing to notice is that the long-run elasticities for total exports calculated with FM-LS are quite similar to those obtained with the Johansen method and to the ones obtained with an unrestricted error-correction model. The stability tests confirm the result obtained in section 3 that showed no evidence of instability in the long-run relationship: the p-value of each test statistics is above 0.20.

For nonoil-nonmaquila exports ($x^{\{-QP\}}$) I found a long-run relationship for the three periods; however, for the whole sample, the test statistics detect instability. For each of the two subsamples the cointegration vectors differ mostly in the coefficient for the real exchange rate. Actually, for the whole period and the first subsample, the real exchange rate has very low significance and probably should be excluded. The stability tests do not detect problems within each period. In this case there seems to be a structural break but not so drastic as to hide the existence of a long-run relationship.

[2] See Hansen (1991) for a full description of these tests.

[3] All of the calculations for this table were generated with the program that B. Hansen wrote in Gauss code.

Table 6. Stability of the Long-Run Relationships for Exports

Variable	Period	Cointegrating Variables*			Stability Test**		
		ivusa	*rer*	*C*	*LC*	*Mean F*	*Sup F*
x	90-2000	2.867 (0.070)	0.234 (0.070)	-11.890 (0.656)	0.321 p=0.200	5.090 p=0.107	7.680 p=0.200
$x^{\{-QP\}}$	80-2000	3.597 (0.105)	0.069 (0.100)	-14.756 (1.046)	0.884 p=0.010	10.759 p=0.010	20.371 p=0.010
	80-89	2.917 (0.302)	0.163 (0.123)	-12.595 (1.351)	0.479 p=0.111	5.382 p=0.088	13.884 p=0.082
	91-2000	2.945 (0.0712)	0.702 (0.067)	-17.077 (0.608)	0.258 p=0.200	5.003 p=0.114	10.460 p=0.200
$x^{\{Q\}}$	80-89	4.564 (0.199)	. .	-18.974 (0.889)	0.772 p=0.018	7.560 p=0.010	12.105 p=0.055
	91-2000	3.279 (0.074)	. .	-12.706 (0.353)	0.176 p=0.200	1.831 p=0.200	4.897 p=0.200

*Standard errors between parentheses
**p-value

Maquila exports present the case where the structural break hides the existence of a long-run relationship. For the whole sample I could not find any reasonable cointegration vector but for each subsample I did find one. The real exchange rate does not enter in either vector, and the elasticity of the US index of industrial production is higher in the first subsample. For the first subsample the statistics detect instability but that problem does not appear in the second period.

4.4. Stability Tests for Disaggregate Imports

Table 7 presents the corresponding results for imports. The number of columns for the cointegrating variables and constant is now four. The interpretation is the same as in table 6.

For total imports I found a cointegration only vector for the 1991-2000 period. It is very similar to the one I obtained in section 3, and the stability tests agree with the evidence of instability shown by figure 6. For imports of capital goods it was possible to find a cointegration vector for each period. The one for the whole sample and that for the first period show instability but the second subsample seems very stable. For this category of imports, as well as for those of consumption goods, the level of exports does not enter in the long-run relationship, which is intuitively sound. Interestingly enough, the scale variable (the Mexican index of industrial production) did not enter into the first subsample. This is a case where a possible structural change does not hide the existence of a long-run relationship. The case for imports of consumption goods also shows an unstable cointegration vector for the whole sample, but the ones corresponding to the two subsamples are stable, especially that for the second period.

Table 7. Stability of the Long-Run Relationships for Imports

Variable	Period	Cointegrating Variables*				Stability Test**		
		ivpi	*rer*	*x*	*C*	*LC*	*Mean F*	*Sup F*
m	91-2000	1.124 (0.131)	-0.286 (0.061)	0.461 (0.043)	-0.676 (0.922)	0.863 p=0.020	12.054 p=0.010	24.897 p=0.010
$m^{\{cap\}}$	80-2000	2.217 (0.151)	-1.570 (0.141)	. .	5.141 (1.623)	1.518 p=0.010	9.624 p=0.010	22.547 p=0.010
	80-89	. .	-1.966 (0.237)	. .	18.300 (2.082)	0.762 p=0.019	5.561 p=0.025	11.455 p=0.071
	91-2000	1.966 (0.077)	-0.734 (0.068)	. .	-0.927 (0.728)	0.173 p=0.200	2.658 p=0.200	9.215 p=0.200
$m^{\{cons\}}$	80-2000	3.506 (0.376)	-2.277 (0.350)	. .	4.720 (4.039)	0.962 p=0.010	9.488 p=0.010	17.121 p=0.023
	80-89	5.324 (1.571)	-2.188 (0.402)	. .	-4.095 (8.802)	0.696 p=0.035	5.818 p=0.066	14.974 p=0.054
	91-2000	1.753 (0.150)	-1.160 (0.132)	. .	3.30677 (1.411)	0.086 p=0.200	1.537 p=0.200	7.990 p=0.200
$m^{\{int\}}$	91-2000	. .	-0.476 (0.048)	0.908 (0.017)	4.261 (0.399)	0.331 p=0.200	4.806 p=0.129	10.862 p=0.200
$m^{\{int_Q\}}$	91-2000	. .	-0.206 (0.071)	1.224 (0.026)	-0.181 (0.592)	0.567 p=0.067	10.247 p=0.010	20.327 p=0.010
$m^{\{int\_Q\}}$	80-2000	2.549 (0.502)	-0.719 (0.186)	0.036 (0.182)	-2.833 (2.923)	1.388 p=0.010	11.626 p=0.010	19.623 p=0.264
	91-2000	1.200 (0.158)	-0.146 (0.074)	0.323 (0.053)	-2.523 (1.118)	1.000 p=0.010	10.014 p=0.010	15.524 p=0.113

*Standar Errors between parentheses
**p-value

For imports of intermediate goods I only found cointegration for the second subsample. The cointegration vector, which was very stable, does not include the Mexican index of industrial production and the relevant scale variable is the level of exports. In fact, disaggregating this category further, I found that imports for the maquila industry only show a cointegrating relationship for the second subsample and this is unstable. For intermediate imports for nonmaquila industries I found cointegration for the two subsamples but not for the whole period. The stability of these vectors is not obvious since the results of the tests are contradictory (one of them suggests stability while the other two reject that hypothesis).

After analyzing the stability properties for the export and import functions at disaggregate levels some conclusions can be drawn. First, for the whole period 1980-2000 it is not possible to find a cointegration relationship for each of the types of exports and imports I analyze; however, for most of the categories I did find stable long-run relationships for the 1990-2000 period. The only exceptions seem to be the very disaggregate data for imports of intermediate goods. This is probably the source of the instability suggested by figure 6 for total imports.

5. Error-Correction Models

In this section I analyze the statistical properties of the error-correction models associated with the long-run relationships for the 1990-2000 period. The error-correction terms are constructed with the coefficients from tables 6 and 7. The tables show the estimates for the short-run parameters and, at the bottom, several statistical tests. The variable with superscript $x^i = x, x^{\{-QP\}}, x^{\{Q\}}$ indicates that the explanatory variable should be understood as being specific to a given equation.

5.1. Error-Correction Models for Disaggregate Exports

Table 8 contains the result for exports. The coefficients of speed of adjustment are all negative and quite significant, reinforcing the hypothesis of the existence of a long-run relationship. It is in all cases quite high, indicating that the adjustment process does not take a long time to complete. There are several lags of the dependent variable, mostly negative, that produce an oscillating adjustment process. In the case of total exports, the short-run coefficient of the change in the US economic activity is very high. The short-run effect of changes in the exchange rate appears only in the equation for nonoil-nonmaquila exports.

Table 8. Error Correction Models for Exports

Variables	Models		
	dx	dx^{-QP}	$dx^{\{Q\}}$
$Cex_{t-1}^{\{i\}}$	-0.314 (0.077)	-0.271 (0.085)	-0.592 (0.123)
$dx_{t-1}^{\{i\}}$	-0.420 (0.085)	-0.483 (0.081)	-0.444 (0.102)
$dx_{t-2}^{\{i\}}$	-0.237 (0.078)	-0.358 (0.073)	-0.303°° (0.082)
$dx_{t-4}^{\{i\}}$	-0.231 (0.075)		
$dx_{t-5}^{\{i\}}$	-0.294 (0.077)		
$dx_{t-8}^{\{i\}}$	0.225 (0.072)		
$dx_{t-10}^{\{i\}}$			-0.161 (0.062)
$dx_{t-11}^{\{i\}}$		0.304 (0.075)	
$dx_{t-12}^{\{i\}}$	0.245 (0.071)	0.358 (0.069)	0.214 (0.062)
$drer_t$		0.417 (0.121)	

Table 8. Error Correction Models for Exports (Continued)

Variables	Models		
	dx	dx^{-QP}	$dx^{\{Q\}}$
$dipi_{t-5}^{\{USA\}}$	2.222 (0.897)		
ECM Statistic	-6.380	-4.800	-4.880
R^2	0.769	0.713	0.839
$\overline{R}^2$	0.728	0.679	0.812
S.E	0.045	0.053	0.051
Asym. Coeff.	0.154	0.226	-0.072
Kurtosis Coeff.	3.472	3.583	2.656
Jarque-Bera Stat.	1.68	2.587	0.662
LM(12) AR	1.387	0.728	0.771
LM(12) ARCH	1.970**	0.627	0.786
White Test	1.502*	0.03	1.019
RESET	0.002	0.013	0.4744
Chow B (94:01)	1.016	0.793	1.901**
Chow Pred.(94:01)	1.224	0.839	0.967

$$Cex_{t-1} = x_{t-1} - 2.867ipi_{t-1}^{USA} - 0.234rer_{t-1}$$

$$Cex_{t-1}^{\{-QP\}} = x_{t-1}^{\{-QP\}} - 2.945ipi_{t-1}^{USA} - 0.702rer_{t-1}$$

$$Cex_{t-1}^{\{Q\}} = x_{t-1}^{\{Q\}} - 3.279ipi_{t-1}^{\{USA\}}$$

All of the the ECM statistics (obtained with an unrestricted model) are significant at the 1% level. The measures of goodness of fit are very good. There are no problems with the normality of the residuals and only the equation for total exports shows some evidence of ARCH effects. The Chow tests for structural break and prediction failure for January 1994 (the date of the beginning of NAFTA) are all nonsignificant with the exception of one case. I introduced a dummy variable that was equal to one from the beginning of 1994 (used by some authors as a proxy for the institutional change brought about by NAFTA) and it was strongly nonsignificant. Figure 8 shows the recursive analysis of the ECM for total exports.

The first panel shows the sum of squares, which approaches a straight line; the second panel shows that the sequence of one-step residuals crosses the confidence band in just one month; the next panel shows the one-step Chow statistics that only detect three obvious cases of outliers; the last two panels show the n-step down and up Chow statistics of structural breaks. In both cases the sequence stays below the significance level of 5%. Figure 9 shows the sequence of recursive coefficients for the same ECM. Notice that the sequences for the seasonal dummy variables are also included. It can be seen that the short-run coefficients are constant. From these results it can be concluded that the short-run model does not seem affected by structural changes either.

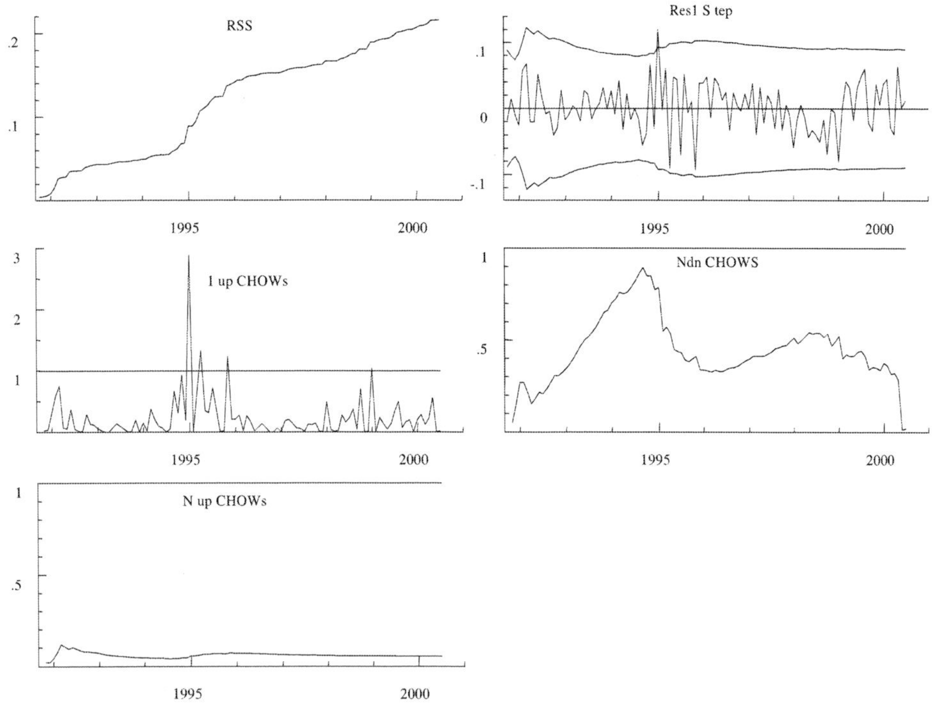

Figure 8: Recursive Stability Tests for Total Exports ECM.

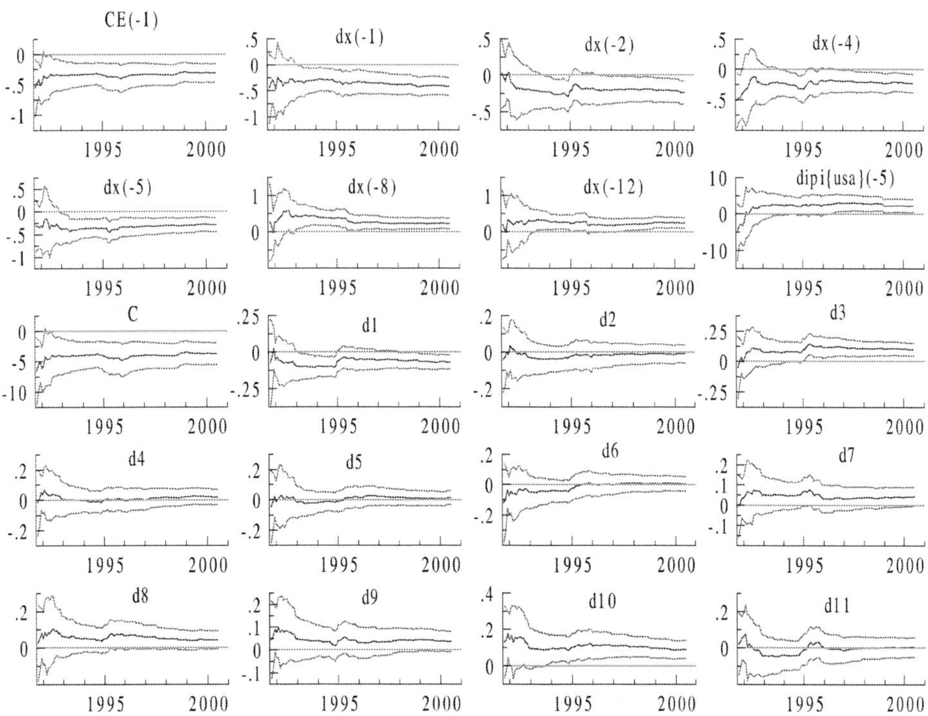

Figure 9: Recursive Coefficients for Total Exports ECM.

Table 9. Error Correction Models for Imports

Variables	Models					
	dm	dm^{cap}	dm^{cons}	dm^{int}	dx^{int_Q}	$dx^{int_{-Q}}$
$Cem_{t-1}^{\{i\}}$	-0.246 (0.057)	-0.343 (0.076)	-0.323 (0.063)	-0.313 (0.069)	-0.277 (0.080)	-0.331 (0.064)
$dm_{t-1}^{\{i\}}$	. .	-0.214 (0.067)	. .	. .	-0.440 (0.082)	. .
$dm_{t-2}^{\{i\}}$	. .	. .	. .	. .	-0.447 (0.089)	. .
$dm_{t-3}^{\{i\}}$	. .	. .	. .	. .	-0.374 (0.093)	. .
$dm_{t-4}^{\{i\}}$	. .	. .	. .	. .	-0.263^{oo} (0.078)	. .
$dm_{t-5}^{\{i\}}$	. .	. .	. .	. .	-0.195 (0.064)	. .
$dm_{t-7}^{\{i\}}$	0.101 (0.035)	. .	. .	. .	. .	. .
$dm_{t-10}^{\{i\}}$	-0.139 (0.037)	. .	-1.888 (0.060)	-0.130 (0.044)	. .	. .
dx_t	0.783^{oo} (0.043)	. .	. .	0.914 (0.048)	1.006^{oo} (0.088)	0.510 (0.054)
$divpi_t$	0.670 (0.091)	1.605 (0.201)	1.772 (0.205)	. .	. .	1.221 (0.122)
$drer_t$	. .	. .	-0.487 (0.156)	. .	. .	. .
$drer_{t-1}$	-0.199 (0.057)	-0.412 (0.161)	. .	-0.218 (0.076)	. .	-0.370 (0.077)
rer_{t-2}	. .	. .	. .	. .	. .	0.175 (0.072)
$drer_{t-3}$	. .	. .	. .	. .	0.342 (0.101)	. .
ECM Statistic	-5.460	-6.850	-5.200	-6.370	-4.810	-6.820
R^2	0.942	0.740	0.813	0.903	0.901	0.892
$\overline{R}^2$	0.932	0.705	0.787	0.888	0.881	0.875
S.E.	0.023	0.067	0.069	0.029	0.040	0.031
Asym. Coeff.	-0.095	0.056	0.239	-0.335	-0.103	-0.427
Kurtosis Coeff.	3.617	2.890	3.484	3.514	2.440	3.144
Jarque-Bera Stat.	1.959	0.130	2.430	3.390	1.691	3.537
LM(12) AR	1.555	1.533	0.839	0.695	1.042	1.106
LM(12) ARCH	0.701	0.779	0.888	1.096	0.919	0.540
White Test	1.065	0.956	1.459	1.169	1.570*	0.72
RESET	0.074	2.453	0.033	0.089	2.456	2.452
Chow B (94:01)	2.113**	1.183	1.201	2.209**	1.913**	1.850**
Chow Pred(94:01)	1.782*	0.533	0.625	0.938	1.271	0.999

$$Cem_{t-1} = m_{t-1} - 1.124ivpi_{t-1} + 0.283rer_{t-1} - 0.461x_{t-1}$$

$$Cem_{t-1}^{int} = m_{t-1}^{int} + 0.476rer_{t-1} - 0.908x_{t-1}$$

$$Cem_{t-1}^{\{int_Q\}} = m_{t-1}^{\{int_Q\}} + 0.206rer_{t-1} - 1.224x_{t-1}$$

$$Cem_{t-1}^{\{cap\}} = m_{t-1}^{\{cap\}} - 1.966ivpi_{t-1} + 0.734rer_{t-1}$$

$$Cem_{t-1}^{cons} = m_{t-1}^{\{cons\}} - 1.753ivpi_{t-1} + 1.160rer_{t-1}$$

$$Cem_{t-1}^{\{int\_Q\}} = m_{t-1}^{\{int\_Q\}} - 1.200ivpi_{t-1} + 0.146rer_{t-1} - 0.323x_{t-1}$$

5.2. Error-Correction Models for Disaggregate Imports

Table 9 shows the results for imports. The ECM statistics are all very high (significance level is above 1%). The measures of goodness of fit are similar to those found for exports. There are no problems with the residuals.

The RESET test is easily passed by each equation; however, only the equations for consumption goods and capital goods pass both Chow tests of structural change for the beginning of NAFTA. Nevertheless, the rejection of stability with both tests occurs only with total imports.

Figure 10 completes the analysis of the ECM for total imports. The panels show the same recursive statistic as in the case of total exports (figure 8).

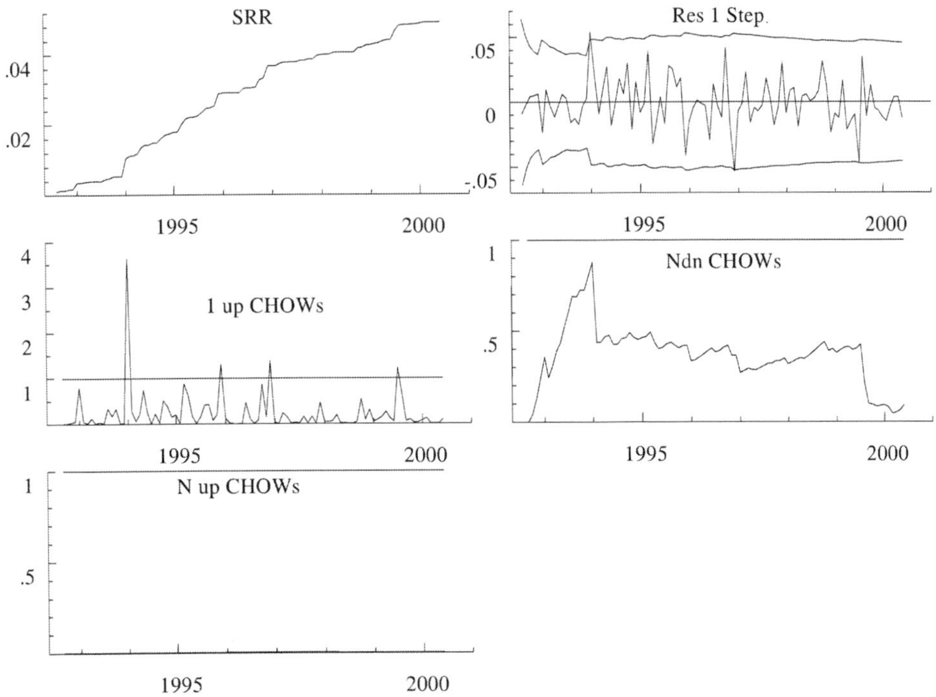

Figure 10: Recursive Stability Tests for Total Imports ECM.

The sum of square residuals also approaches a straight line. The one-step residuals always stay within the bands except in one month. The one-step Chow sequence shows more outliers than in the case of exports but the n-step Chow statistics for structural change (up and down) do not show any problems since in no case do the sequences cross the 5% significance level. To complete the analysis, figure 11 shows the sequences of recursive statistics for the same ECM. The parameters seem to be constant throughout the sample period. The short-run model for imports does not seem to have serious stability problems in spite of the result for the long-run relationship.

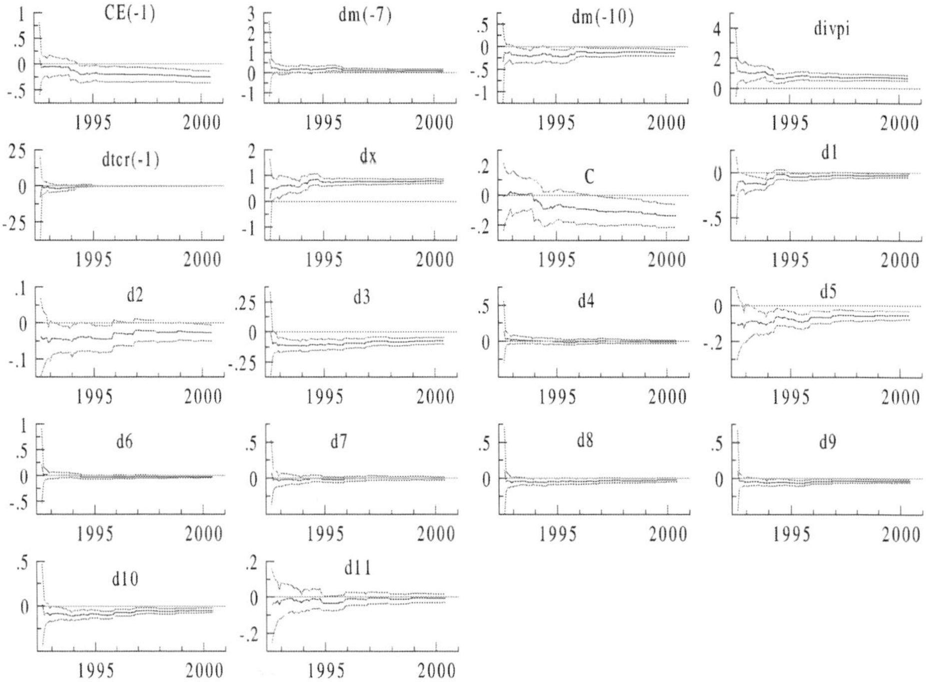

Figure 11: Recursive Coefficients for Total Imports ECM.

6. Conclusions

Mexican Exports tripled their rate of growth from 1994 to 2000. Because this strong performance started around the time when NAFTA took place, it is rather common to interrelate both facts. I estimated long-run demand functions for exports and imports for the period 1990-2000 and obtained coefficients which are correctly signed and of reasonable magnitude. I found that the equation for exports is very stable for that period and, therefore, NAFTA cannot account for the surge in foreign trade between Mexico and the US. The equation for imports demand, on the other hand, shows instability for the same period although it fits the data very well, even without considering seasonality and short-run dynamics.

I also used disaggregate data and extended the analysis for the period 1980-2000 and found cointegration for the whole sample only in a few categories of exports and imports. For each of the categories, I found a stable cointegration vector for the 1990-2000 period. Interestingly enough, the instability detected in the equation for total imports for the 1990-2000 subsample does not carry on to the equations with disaggregate data. In most cases a cointegration vector was also found for the 1980-1989 subsample, although those vectors do not show the stability found for the rest of the sample. I also obtained the error-correction models for the 1990-2000 period and found that they were stable and constant. These results confirm that a structural change in the demand for Mexican exports caused by NAFTA is extremely unlikely. The historical expansion of the American economy was by far the most important reason for the growth of Mexican exports.

A structural change probably occurred during the eighties and for that reason it is not possible to find long-run stable relationships for the whole period (1980-2000). This change is probably linked to the abandonment of the trade policy as a stabilization tool and the opening up of the economy when Mexico joined the GATT. This was quite important for Mexican exporters who depend heavily on the imports of intermediate and capital goods. This is the most likely reason for the lack of evidence of the effects of NAFTA on Mexican trade flows: most of the essential changes that helped Mexico to become an export powerhouse had already taken place as early as the mid eighties.

References

Ericsson, Neil R. and James G. MacKinnon, "Distributions of Error Correction Tests for Cointegration," International Finance Discussion Paper No. 655, Board of Governors of the Federal Reserve System, 1999.

Gould, David M., "Has NAFTA Changed North America Free Trade," *Economic Review*, Federal Reserve Bank of Dallas, First Quarter 1998.

Gruben, W.C. (2001) "Was NAFTA Behind Mexico's High Maquiladora Growth?," *Economics and Financial Review*, Third Quarter, Federal Reserve Bank of Dallas.

Hansen, B.E. (1992) "Tests for Parameter Instability in Regressions with I(1) Processes," *Journal of Business and Economic Statistics*, **10**, 321-335.

Krueger, A. O., (1999) "Trade Creation and Trade Diversion Under NAFTA," *NBER Working Paper* No. **7429**, December 1999.

Kwiatkowski, D., P. Phillips, P. Schmidt and Y. Shin (1992): Testing the Null Hypothesis of Stationarity Against the Alternative of a Unit Root, *Journal of Econometrics* **54**, 159-178.

Phillips, P.C.B. y Bruce E. Hansen (1990), "Statistical Inference in Instrumental Variables Regression With $I(1)$ Processes," *Review of Economic Studies*, **57**, 99-125.

Reinhart, C., 1995, "Devaluation, Relative Prices, and International Trade", *IMF Staff Papers*, vol.42, No 2.

Rose, A., 1991, "The Role of Exchange Rates in Popular Models of International Trade: Does the Marshall-Lerner Condition Hold?" *Journal of International Economics*, vol. 30, 301-16.

Senhadji, A. (1998), "Time Series Estimation of Structural Import Demand Equations: A Cross-Country Analysis", *IMF Staff Papers*, vol. 45, June.

Senhadji, A. and C. Montenegro (1998), "Time Series Analysis of Export Demand Equations: A Cross-Country Analysis", *IMF Working Paper*, **98/149**, October.

In: Mexico: Economic, Political and Social Issues
Editors: Maria L. Castro and Irene P. Navarro
ISBN: 978-1-60456-847-9

Chapter 2

MEXICO

Charles B. Vertos

TRADE SUMMARY

The U.S. goods trade deficit with Mexico was $64.1 billion in 2006, an increase of $14.3 billion from $49.7 billion in 2005. U.S. goods exports in 2006 were $134.2 billion, up 11.5 percent from the previous year. Corresponding U.S. imports from Mexico were $198.3 billion, up 16.5 percent. Mexico is currently the 2nd largest export market for U.S. goods.

U.S. exports of private commercial services (i.e., excluding military and government) to Mexico were $20.6 billion in 2005 (latest data available), and U.S. imports were $14.7 billion. Sales of services in Mexico by majority U.S.-owned affiliates were $8.9 billion in 2004 (latest data available), while sales of services in the United States by majority Mexico-owned firms were $1.2 billion.

The stock of U.S. foreign direct investment in Mexico in 2005 was $71.4 billion, up from $63.5 billion in 2004. U.S. FDI in Mexico is concentrated largely in the manufacturing, banking and finance sectors.

North American Free Trade Agreement

The North American Free Trade Agreement (NAFTA), signed by the United States, Canada and Mexico, entered into force on January 1, 1994. This free trade agreement progressively eliminates tariffs and non-tariff barriers to trade in goods; improves access for services trade; establishes rules on investment; strengthens protection of intellectual property rights; and creates an effective dispute settlement mechanism. The NAFTA is accompanied by supplemental agreements that provide for cooperation to enhance and enforce labor standards and to encourage environmentally friendly practices and bolster environmental protection in North America.

Import Policies

Tariffs and Market Access

Under the terms of the NAFTA, Mexico eliminated tariffs on all remaining industrial and most agricultural products imported from the United States on January 1, 2003. As of January 1, 2006, Mexico applies tariffs or tariff-rate quotas on corn, sugar, dry beans, orange juice, chicken leg quarters, high fructose corn syrup (HFCS) and milk powder. All tariffs and tariff-rate quotas are scheduled to be eliminated on January 1, 2008. (See the section on agriculture below for additional details on HFCS and chicken leg quarter actions.)

Trade growth in agricultural products has been balanced since the NAFTA entered into force, with U.S. exports to Mexico having increased by $7.3 billion from 1993 to 2006, and U.S. imports from Mexico having increased by $7.5 billion. The statistics are less balanced, however, when considering nonagricultural trade. U.S. non-agricultural imports from Mexico grew $188 billion compared with U.S. export growth to Mexico of $123 billion from 1993 to 2006.

A number of U.S. exports, both agricultural and non-agricultural, are subject to antidumping duties that limit access to the Mexican market. Products subject to these duties currently include beef, hydrogen peroxide, epoxidized soy oil, apples, liquid caustic soda, ammonium sulfate, polyvinyl chloride, bond paper, industrial fatty acids, stearic acid, ethylene glycol monobutyl ether, and carbon steel pipe and tube. In 2006, Mexico terminated antidumping duties on rice.

Agricultural Products

The United States exported $10.9 billion in agricultural products to Mexico in 2006, compared to $9.4 billion in 2005. Since 2004, Mexico has become the United States' second-largest agricultural market.

During the past year, Mexico's Secretariat of Economy (SECON) issued a number of decisions relating to antidumping cases affecting U.S. agricultural products. In January 2006, SECON officially announced the resolution of the investigation of dumping charges it had filed on behalf of the Mexican Pork Council against importers and exporters of U.S. pork, deeming that there was not sufficient evidence to impose antidumping duties.

In April 2006, SECON decided to continue antidumping duties on U.S. beef and beef by-products after completing a sunset review investigation. On April 24, 2006, SECON announced that it would continue to apply the antidumping duties imposed on imports of U.S. beef and beef by-products from certain U.S. exporters and producers for another five years. In addition, Mexico's modification of the beef dumping duties in 2004 in response to the findings of a NAFTA Chapter 19 panel, which determined that SECON did not sufficiently demonstrate that U.S. beef imports had damaged Mexico's beef industry, is still pending the Chapter 19 panel's approval. Mexican policies in this area have reduced the number of U.S. suppliers and altered product trading patterns. Industry representatives assert that $100 million to $500 million in revenue is lost each year due to antidumping duties in the beef sector.

On September 11, 2006, SECON published the final resolution of Mexico's antidumping investigation on U.S. long-grain white rice. Mexico undertook the investigation after the December 2005 World Trade Organization (WTO) ruling that Mexico had not properly conducted its previous investigation that had resulted in SECON's June 5, 2002 finding that assessed compensatory duties against U.S. rice exporters. In the September 2006 final resolution, SECON terminated the measures, concluding that the imports during the reference period did not constitute price discrimination and thus did not cause damage to the domestic rice sector.

SECON continues to assess antidumping duties on U.S. imports of red and golden delicious apples. On December 29, 2004, SECON suspended the application of the 46.58 percent antidumping duty on U.S. red and golden delicious apples exported by members of the Northwest Fruit Exporters (NFE) and established a reference price system for NFE members. In February 2005, a Mexican court nullified the reference price system, and on May 26, 2005, in response to an order from a Mexican court, SECON announced the elimination of the 46.58 percent antidumping duty for NFE members and the beginning of a new antidumping investigation on U.S. red and golden delicious apples exported by NFE members. On November 2, 2006, SECON announced the final results of its investigation and imposed final duties ranging from 6.4 percent to 47.05 percent on red and golden delicious apples from NFE members. The original antidumping duty of 46.58 percent still applies to red and golden delicious apples from exporters who are not NFE members.

In July 2003, Mexico put in place an industry-negotiated NAFTA safeguard on U.S. chicken leg quarters that will remain in effect until December 31, 2007. The safeguard takes the form of a tariff-rate quota (TRQ) on chicken leg quarters. The TRQ preserves market access for U.S. exporters at levels achieved in recent years. Pursuant to the NAFTA, Mexico agreed to provide compensation to the United States, including a commitment not to impose any additional import restrictions on U.S. poultry products and to eliminate certain sanitary restrictions on U.S. poultry products.

On December 22, 2006, the Mexican Congress approved legislation repealing the 20 percent tax on certain beverages or products made with sweeteners other than cane sugar, including HFCS (beverage tax). Mexico had imposed the beverage tax on January 1, 2002. As a result of the tax, HFCS sales fell dramatically and industry estimated that the annual cost of the beverage tax was roughly $944 million in lost U.S. HFCS sales, in addition to sizeable investment losses. The Mexican Congress had renewed the beverage tax each year since 2002, including for 2006. The new legislation repealed the beverage tax effective January 1, 2007. Mexico agreed to eliminate the tax in response to findings by a WTO panel and the Appellate Body that vindicated the U.S. position that the beverage tax was inconsistent with Mexico's WTO obligations.

On July 27, 2006, the United States and Mexico concluded an agreement on market access for sweeteners through January 1, 2008, when, under the NAFTA, all remaining duties on agricultural goods will be eliminated. The sweeteners agreement provides Mexico duty-free access to the U.S. market for 250,000 metric tons raw value of raw or refined sugar in Fiscal Year (FY) 2007 and at least 175,000 metric tons raw value of raw or refined sugar for the first three months of FY 2008 (October 1, 2007 through December 31, 2007). Under the agreement, Mexico will provide reciprocal access for U.S. HFCS: 250,000 metric tons in FY 2007 and at least 175,000 metric tons for the first three months of FY 2008 (October 1, 2007 through December 31, 2007). Mexico will also provide, for the first time, duty-free access for

U.S. sugar of not less than 7,258 metric tons raw value for each of the marketing years 2006, 2007 and 2008. Mexico had previously opposed the establishment of such a quota due to the longstanding trade dispute over sugar.

On August 18, 2006, Mexico removed duties that had initially been placed on imports of several U.S. agricultural products on August 18, 2005. Tariffs ranging from 9 percent to 30 percent had been imposed on chewing gum, other confectionaries, certain fortified milk products and certain wines. However, on September 14, 2006, SECON announced the imposition of a 110 percent tariff on dairy blends for a period of 48 calendar days, from September 14, 2006 to October 31, 2006. Mexico took these actions based on its view that the United States had failed to comply with a WTO recommendation that the Continued Dumping and Subsidy Offset Act (CDSOA), known as the "Byrd Amendment," be brought into conformity with U.S. WTO obligations. The President signed legislation in February 2006 to repeal the CDSOA. The duties were ended on November 1, 2006.

Sanitary and Phytosanitary Issues

In recent years, Mexican sanitary and phytosanitary measures have created barriers to exports of certain U.S. agricultural goods, including grains, seed products, apples, stone fruit, pork, beef, poultry, citrus, wood and wood products, dry beans, avocados, potatoes and eggs. In addition, procedural requirements regarding sanitary and phytosanitary inspections at port of entry do not always reflect agreements reached between U.S. Department of Agriculture officials and the Mexican Secretariat of Agriculture, resulting in unnecessary delays at border points of entry, seaports and airports. While this situation improved during 2006, significant quantities of U.S. agricultural goods were still subject to rejection or delays at the Mexican border.

Mexico banned imports of U.S. beef in December 2003, following the detection of a positive case of Bovine Spongiform Encephalopathy (BSE) in Washington state. In March 2004, Mexico announced that it would accept U.S. boneless beef from cattle less than 30 months of age and it subsequently lifted restrictions on a number of offals and processed boneless beef products. In early 2006, Mexico lifted its ban on U.S. bone-in beef and in October 2006 the United States and Mexico reached an agreement allowing the import of U.S. dairy breeder cattle into Mexico. Mexico currently bans or restricts U.S. exports of some live cattle, ground beef and certain offals. The United States is working intensively to reopen the market as quickly as possible.

In June 2004, despite the lack of a protocol for returning live animals or adequate inspection facilities in Mexico, the Mexican Congress approved a measure requiring that the inspection of imported live animals take place in Mexico. The lack of adequate inspection facilities has hampered the importation of live animals. While Mexico's Congress appears to agree that the law should be changed, the provision remains in place pending agreement upon other modifications to the Animal Health Law.

In September 2005, Mexico's Secretariat of Health implemented a rule regulating the meat sector, establishing a zero-tolerance for the presence of salmonella in raw meat. This standard could lead to unnecessary product recalls and export restrictions for U.S. meat exporters.

In October 2005, Mexico lifted its Low Pathogenic Avian Influenza (LPAI) restrictions on poultry imports from nine U.S. states, but restrictions on eleven counties in Texas remain in place following a 2004 detection of High Pathogenic Avian Influenza. In August 2006, Mexico briefly closed its border to poultry shipments from the state of Michigan due to a LPAI finding in wild birds, but swiftly removed the restriction after receiving additional information from U.S. officials demonstrating that there was no danger to commercial poultry operations. U.S. officials continue to work with Mexican officials to ensure that no unnecessary measures or restrictions are taken.

Administrative Procedures and Customs Practices

U.S. exporters continue to be concerned about Mexican customs administrative procedures, including: insufficient prior notification of procedural changes; inconsistent interpretation of regulatory requirements at different border posts; and uneven enforcement of Mexican standards and labeling rules. There have been relatively few specific complaints, however, and Mexican customs has been putting procedures in place to address issues of non-uniformity at border ports of entry. Agricultural exporters note that Mexican inspection and clearance procedures for some agricultural goods are long, burdensome, nontransparent, and unreliable. Customs procedures for express packages continue to be burdensome, although Mexico has raised the *de minimis* level from $1 to $50. However, Mexican regulations still hold the courier 100 percent liable for the contents of shipments. U.S. exporters have highlighted the benefits if the hours of customs operation on the U.S. and Mexican sides of the border were harmonized. Similarly, they cite the delays stemming from the lack of pre-clearance procedures, which the Mexican government claims are not permitted under current law.

To be eligible to import well over 400 different items, including agricultural products, textiles, chemicals, electronics and automotive parts, Mexican importers must apply to the Secretariat of Finance and Public Credit and be listed on a special industry sector registry. U.S. exporters complain that registering is bureaucratically difficult, and this requirement sometimes causes costly customs clearance delays when new products are added to the list of subject items with immediate effect, thereby denying importers sufficient notice to apply. They also report that certain importers have been summarily dropped from the registry without prior notice or subsequent explanation, effectively preventing U.S. exporters from shipping goods to Mexico.

Mexico requires import licenses for a number of commercially sensitive products. It also uses estimated prices for customs valuation of a wide range of products imported from the United States and other countries, including apples, milled rice, beer, distilled spirits, chemicals, wood, paper and paperboard products, textiles, apparel, toys, tools and appliances.

Since October 2000, the Mexican government has imposed a burdensome guarantee system for goods subject to estimated prices. Importers cannot post bonds to guarantee the difference in duties and taxes if the declared value of an entering good is less than the official estimated price. Instead they must deposit the difference in cash at a designated Mexican financial institution or arrange one of two alternative sureties (a trust or line of credit). The cash deposit is not returned for three months and is only returned if the Mexican government has not initiated an investigation and if the supplier in the country of exportation has provided an invoice certified by its local chamber of commerce. Mexican banks charge as much as $500 to open an account for this purpose and $50 for each transaction, making this a burdensome and costly regulation for businesses on both sides of the border. The governments of the United States and Mexico are discussing an exchange of customs data that would result in the elimination of the estimated pricing regime.

Standards, Testing, Labeling and Certification

Under the NAFTA, Mexico is required to recognize conformity assessment bodies (i.e., certification bodies or testing laboratories) in the United States and Canada on terms no less favorable than those applied to conformity assessment bodies in Mexico. Mexico claims that there must be a need for additional bodies before it will recognize additional bodies. In January 2005, Mexico published a *convocatoria* (formal announcement, or "call") stating that one or more Mexican government agencies are requesting applications from certification bodies for recognition with respect to electrical goods and electronics.

Applications by two U.S. certification bodies for accreditation by the Entidad Mexicana de Acreditacion (EMA), the body responsible for accrediting conformity assessment bodies for Mexican Official Standards, are still pending. The publication of the *convocatoria* was a positive first step, suggesting a willingness on the part of the Mexican government to consider additional certification bodies in the electrical and electronics sectors. Unfortunately, EMA has strongly resisted entry by non-Mexican certification bodies, both prior to and since the publication of the *convocatoria.* If U.S. certification bodies were able to certify products for the Mexican market, the potential increase in U.S. exports could be significant. There are estimates that the two U.S. companies with pending applications could generate $2 million to $3 million each annually in the product certification business in the electrical and electronic sectors.

In the telecommunications sector, Mexico initially indicated that it could be ready to begin implementation of Phase I of the Inter-American Telecommunications Commission's (CITEL) Mutual Recognition Agreement (MRA) by June 2006 and possibly implementation of Phase II by March 2008. Phase I of the CITEL MRA provides for the mutual acceptance of test results while Phase II provides for the mutual acceptance of certifications concerning conformity of equipment with technical regulations. Mexico's implementation of Phase I would allow recognized U.S. testing laboratories to test equipment for compliance with Mexican technical requirements, whereas implementation of Phase II would allow recognized U.S. certification bodies to certify equipment as meeting Mexican technical requirements. Mexico, however, did not meet the June 2006 goal and now estimates that it will not be ready to implement Phase I until the second quarter of 2007. Mexican implementation of Phase I and II of the CITEL MRA remains a key issue for U.S. testing and certification bodies, as well as for U.S. exports to Mexico, and the United States will continue to push the Mexican government on this issue.

Mexico has over 700 technical regulations called Normas Oficiales Mexicanas (NOMs) issued by a number of different agencies, each with its own conformity assessment procedures. While the Secretariat of Economy, the Secretariat of Agriculture (for a limited sub-set of its NOMs), the Secretariat of Communications and Transport (for one of its

NOMs), and the Secretariat of Environment and Natural Resources have published some of the conformity assessment procedures, they have not published others.

On January 17, 2006, in Washington, D.C., then U.S. Trade Representative Portman and Mexican Secretary of Economy Sergio García de Alba signed an agreement on trade in tequila. Under the agreement, exports of tequila from Mexico to the United States will continue without interruption. Key elements include: a prohibition on restrictions of bulk tequila exports to the United States; a prohibition on Mexican regulation of tequila labeling or marketing outside of Mexico; a prohibition on Mexican regulation of the labeling, formulation, and marketing of products containing tequila outside of Mexico; creation of a "tequila bottlers registry" that identifies approved bottlers of tequila; continuation of current practice with respect to addressing Mexican concerns regarding the bottling of tequila in the United States; and establishment of a working group to monitor the implementation of the agreement. The working group met on November 15, 2006 to review the operation of the agreement.

Government Procurement

Mexico's efforts to make its government procurement regime more transparent through policy reform and the application of technology have resulted in increased competition as well as savings for the government. The Mexican government has established several "e-government" Internet sites to increase transparency of government processes and establish guidelines for the conduct of government officials. "Compranet" allows on-line processing of government procurement and contracting. While implementation has been successful, there is still a need for further regulatory and technological improvements throughout the Mexican government.

As of January 1, 2003, NAFTA limits the total value of contracts that Mexico's parastatal petroleum and electricity monopolies, PEMEX and the Federal Electricity Commission, respectively, may remove from coverage under NAFTA. Mexico provides an annual notice of the set-aside calculation, along with the methodology used in the calculation, to the United States and Canada. The 2006 value of the set aside for these entities was $380 million.

Intellectual Property Rights (IPR) Protection

Under NAFTA and the WTO Agreement on Trade-Related Aspects of Intellectual Property Rights (TRIPS), Mexico is obligated to implement certain standards and procedures for the protection of intellectual property, including procedures and penalties to be applied in certain cases of copyright piracy and trademark counterfeiting. Despite a fairly extensive set of IPR laws and an increase in the number of seizures and arrests during 2005 and 2006, the extent of IPR violations in Mexico remains dramatic. Monetary sanctions and other penalties, when imposed, are minimal and largely targeted at the bottom-tier of the piracy chain, for example, the small-scale vendors of infringing materials, who are numerous and easily replaced. In 2005, seizures of pirated goods increased 19 percent over 2004 (from 108.8 million articles seized to 129.5 million), and the number of articles seized in 2006 rose another 155 percent over 2005 to a total of 331 million articles seized. However, in 2005, only four people were sentenced to imprisonment for IPR violations. Three were sentenced to three years in prison, and another to one and a half years. In 2006, only one person was sentenced to prison for IPR crimes. Unfortunately, pirates and counterfeiters are often released and return to their illegal activities. The United States remains concerned about the continuing high levels of piracy and counterfeiting in Mexico. It closely monitors how the Mexican government is addressing these problems. Mexico was taken off the Special 301 "Watch List" in 2000, but returned to the list in 2003, where it has remained to date due to enforcement deficiencies.

A concerted intelligence and enforcement effort to target organized crime, which is increasingly behind commercial piracy and counterfeiting in Mexico, is necessary to deter large-scale infringement activity, which is facilitated by the proliferation of Mexico's informal economy. Well-known markets selling pirated and counterfeit goods, such as Tepito in Mexico City, San Juan de Dios in Guadalajara, and some others in Monterrey and San Luis Potosi, continue to operate openly. Currently, it is estimated that six out of every ten new jobs generated in Mexico are in the informal sector. In 2003, the Procuratorate General of the Republic (PGR) created a dedicated IPR unit, which combines federal prosecutors and police, to make the enforcement regime more effective and efficient. In 2004, PGR authorized its Organized Crime Division to investigate cases of piracy and counterfeiting. In September 2006, PGR took the first step in combating organized crime related to intellectual property infringement by apprehending eight leaders of criminal gangs.

In June 2006, several Mexican federal agencies, one state government, civil society groups and concerned industries signed a National Agreement in which all committed to cooperation in combating intellectual property infringement. The Calderón administration is expected to adopt the National Agreement's principles and put in place a Policy of State to combat intellectual property crimes.

On the legislative front, an initiative to give PGR the power to prosecute intellectual property crimes without first receiving a complaint from intellectual property holders or legal representatives has remained stalled in the Mexican Congress for more than two years. In May 2006, a law approved by the Legislative Assembly of the Federal District that would have allowed local authorities to close commercial establishments selling pirated or counterfeit goods was vetoed by Mexico City's mayor.

Copyright Protection

Copyright piracy remains a major problem in Mexico, with U.S. industry loss estimates growing each year. Although enforcement efforts by the Mexican government seem to be improving, piracy levels continue to rise, resulting in closures of legitimate copyright-related businesses, according to industry sources. Pirated sound and motion picture recordings are widely available throughout Mexico, where piracy has shifted from traditional formats to optical discs (CD, DVD, CD-ROM). The International Intellectual Property Alliance estimates that trade losses due to copyright piracy in Mexico totaled $1.3 billion in 2005, with pirated products taking 65 percent of the total music market; 64 percent of the business software market; 62 percent of the motion picture market; and 75 percent of the entertainment software market. In July 2003, the Mexican Congress amended the 1996 Mexican copyright law, and in September 2005 published the implementing regulations, thereby bringing the law into effect. Industry associations and Indautor, the Mexican government agency that regulates copyrights, claim that, in general, the new legislation brings Mexico into compliance with its obligations under the NAFTA IPR Chapter and the WTO TRIPS Agreement. Industry associations remain concerned, however, about exclusive rights to the public performance and exhibition of audio-visual works; Mexican contract formalities that could restrict the exercise of rights; and the requirement that publishing contracts include certain obligations (e.g., the number of editions; the number of copies or reproductions of each edition; whether the material delivery is or is not exclusive; and the remuneration that the author or copyright holder should receive). The amendment also did not raise the minimum amount that an infringer has to pay to a rights holder to compensate for the injury caused by infringement. The law provides that the indemnification for moral and economic damages cannot be lower than 40 percent of a work's sale price.

Patent, Trademark, Pharmaceutical and Agricultural Chemical Data Protection

Patents and trademarks are under the jurisdiction of the Mexican Institute of Industrial Property (IMPI), an independent agency that operates under the auspices of the Secretariat of Economy.

U.S. pharmaceutical and agricultural chemical companies are concerned about the lack of coordination between IMPI and other Mexican agencies with regard to government procurement of unauthorized copies of patented pharmaceuticals. In 2003, the Secretariat of Health modified Mexican health regulations to require that, starting with purchases scheduled for delivery on January 1, 2003, IMSS (Mexican Social Security Institute) and ISSSTE (Social Security Institute for Government Workers) would purchase only legitimate versions of products patented in Mexico. Unfortunately, it appears the new regulations are not being fully implemented because of financial constraints at IMSS and ISSSTE.

In September 2003, the Secretariats of Health and Economy implemented a Presidential decree regarding cooperation between the two agencies. According to the decree, IMPI is required to publish a list of pharmaceuticals covered by a patent in Mexico. A company applying to the Secretariat of Health for safety and health registrations for sale of pharmaceutical products must show proof of patent and proof that test data was obtained in a legitimate matter. According to the regulation, failure to present proof of patent and test data will result in denial of the registration. Also, if a company provides false information, it is now subject to both civil and criminal proceedings. Implementation remains weak, however. U.S. industry reports that the Federal Commission for Protection from Sanitary Risks, which handles drug registration, still continues to authorize the manufacture of pharmaceutical products by unauthorized companies. Stricter compliance with the 2003 decree would also help eliminate unauthorized copies of patented pharmaceuticals from the supply chain for IMSS and ISSSTE.

Mexico took a step forward when it published a Presidential decree in May 2006 that amends the Mexican Health Law and the Mexican Penal Code to raise to the felony level the act of selling, distributing, or transporting counterfeit pharmaceuticals, or fostering the forgery, of or tampering with, pharmaceuticals, medicines, active ingredients, raw materials, or additives used in products for human consumption. This law also applies felony status to committing or fostering the forgery of, or tampering with, the packaging of such products, as well as to the selling, distributing, or transporting of such forged or tampered packaging.

U.S. companies holding trademarks in Mexico have cited problems with trademark enforcement and administration. Although Mexican federal administrative actions are supposed to be completed within four months, actions related to trademark enforcement often take as long as 18 months. The time can be lengthened by jurisdictional and procedural disputes within the Mexican government, as well as by internal coordination problems within the Mexican Institute of Industrial Property (IMPI) and between IMPI and the Procuratorate General of the Republic.

Border Enforcement of Intellectual Property Rights (IPR)

NAFTA Article 1718 and Article 51 of the TRIPS Agreement obligate Mexico to allow U.S. IPR holders to apply to Mexican authorities for suspension of release of counterfeit trademark or pirated copyright goods. IPR holders seeking to use the procedure must obtain an order from IMPI that directs customs officials to detain the merchandise. Companies requesting such actions generally report positive outcomes. However, U.S. industry has sought increased cooperation and communication between IMPI and Mexican customs in order to prevent the release of counterfeit goods into the Mexican market.

Services Barriers

Telecommunications

The 2005-2006 Global Information Technology Report's Networked Readiness Index of 115 nations ranked Mexico number 55, up from 60 the year before, on a scale measuring the degree of information and communication technology development. Mexico ranked well in the readiness and usage indices, but poorly in the environment component index, earning especially low scores in the effectiveness of lawmaking bodies and burden of government regulation. The report cites the Mexican government's passivity in dealing with this sector and Mexico's consequent lack of competitiveness in telecommunications. It calls for a more independent Federal Telecommunications Commission (COFETEL) to foster increased competition. An October 2006 OECD report entitled *ICT Diffusion to Business: Peer Review Country Report Mexico* singled Mexico out as being the second most expensive country as far as residential telephone rates are concerned, and the most expensive for business charges, due to the continuing low levels of competition in the domestic telephony market. The report recommended that the regulatory environment in communications be strengthened in order to allow markets to operate more effectively, thereby helping to reduce communications prices and improve services.

Promoting competitiveness in the telecommunications market continues to be an enormous challenge for Mexico. Although the Fox Administration initially identified this as a priority goal for Mexico, virtually no progress was made in its six years in office, and hopes that the new administration can do better are high.

Telmex dominates the market and is perceived to exercise influence over the legislative process, the courts, governmental policy departments (in particular the Secretariat of Communications and Transport, or SCT), and the telecommunications regulatory agency COFETEL. (For example, Telmex successfully lobbied SCT for several years to deny cable television operators concessions to enter the telephone business until SCT assured Telmex that it would have the right to also provide video services).

In March 2006, Mexico's Congress passed the Radio and Television Law, which, among other things, granted COFETEL stronger regulatory powers (see television below regarding other effects of the law). COFETEL subsequently underwent a complete change in commissioners in July 2006. These enhanced powers are welcome, but it remains to be seen whether COFETEL will have the political muster to use them. The United States will monitor to see whether COFETEL will be able, and willing, to use such enhanced powers to improve the competitive environment in the Mexican telecommunications market.

The recent debate over the "Convergence Accord," SCT's proposal to allow telecommunications companies to provide so-called triple-play services (voice, data and video), highlighted the degree to which COFETEL and the Federal Competition Commission (COFECO) are asserting their independence with regard to concerns over Telmex's market dominance. Soon after SCT released its "convergence" plan, COFECO voiced support for the claims of cable companies that the accord would unfairly advantage Telmex. COFETEL also voiced opposition, asserting that "triple play" was already possible under existing legislation. The final version of the Convergence Accord, published on October 3, 2006, took into account some of the concerns raised and did impose some limits on Telmex's ability to use its market dominance for anticompetitive purposes. For example, it establishes a committee to ensure that Telmex complies within 200 days with the requirements that it guarantee interconnection, interoperability, and number portability before allowing Telmex to change its concession to allow video services. It also gives power to COFETEL and Hacienda (Mexico's finance ministry) to determine whether Telmex should pay a fee to modify its license to provide video services. The provisions of the published accord also allow mobile phone companies, radio communications systems and satellite TV providers to expand their portfolio of services.

After an almost two year delay, in September 2006 COFETEL attempted to take a first step in resolving a dispute between fixed and mobile carriers by announcing termination rates for fixed-to-cellular calls. This was also designed to pave the way to implement a long distance "calling party pays" ("CPP") system for wireless services that will shift all interconnection charges to the company (and ultimately the customer) from whence calls originate. The announced rates were set to start (retroactively) from 2005 at 1.71 pesos/minute (about 16 U.S. cents) and gradually decreased to .90 pesos/minute (about 8 U.S. cents) by 2010. COFETEL claims that the rates, plus rounding and billing fees, are cost-oriented, although it has not responded to the U.S. Government request for information on the basis used for calculating the per minute rates. The announced rates, however, have not taken effect due to injunctions filed against COFETEL, both by Telcel asserting that the rates are too low and by long-distance carriers asserting the opposite. In the meantime, Telcel and some fixed and wireless companies notified COFETEL that they had reached an agreement on a termination rate of 1.54 pesos/minute (14 U.S. cents) for 2006. COFETEL accepted this arrangement, and the CPP system for international calls entered into effect on November 4, 2006. Several carriers have already negotiated rates through 2010, with only a handful not yet having agreed to implement CPP. There are U.S. industry estimates that the higher interconnection rates agreed upon between the companies will cost U.S. industry and consumers hundreds of millions of dollars.

U.S. companies who form joint ventures with Mexican partners to obtain authorizations (called "concessions" under Mexican law) to provide public network and satellite-based services routinely face delays in obtaining their authorizations, with time frames extending far beyond the four-month period established in COFETEL's Satellite Communication Regulations. The lack of clarity regarding the roles of COFETEL and the SCT in granting the authorizations makes it difficult for the companies to seek help in resolving delays.

COFETEL has made headway on approving the petition of the Federal Electronics Commission to allow data service to be provided over electric lines ("broadband over powerline").

Television and Radio

As in telecommunications, there are concerns that the two dominant television companies, Televisa and TV Azteca, who share duopoly status in the sector, continue to exercise influence over Mexican legislative, policy, and regulatory bodies to prevent competition. The Radio and Television Law passed in March 2006 (mentioned above with regard to telecommunications) has been criticized as catering to the interests of dominant industry players by imposing permanent disadvantages on new entrants as compared to the current dominant duopoly.

U.S. firms remain unable to penetrate the Mexican television broadcast market, despite the fact that both Televisa and TV Azteca benefit from access to the U.S. market. TV Azteca has used the Mexican legal system against a U.S. firm trying to enter this sector. Such actions have included TV Azteca personnel directing a raid, with the support of Mexico City auxiliary police, on production facilities to stop production of a show in Mexico and thereby hinder or discourage additional work. Mexico's television advertising market is estimated to be worth in excess of $2.5 billion annually.

Competition

Mexico passed a new competition law in June 2006 that gave COFECO additional authority to regulate market concentration and anticompetitive behavior in both the private and public sectors. There have been calls, including by key members of the Calderon transition team, to open up sectors of the Mexican economy currently dominated by monopolies or duopolies, though doubts remain over whether the new law and the new administration will be able to make these sectors truly competitive.

Investment Barriers

Ownership Reservations

Mexico's oil and gas policy is highly restrictive with regard to private equity investment. The sector remains closed to foreign investment, with the exceptions of the Liquefied Natural Gas sector and in the marketing of petroleum products. Only Mexican nationals may own gas stations.

The Mexican constitution mandates state ownership of hydrocarbons and provides that no concessions or other types of production-sharing agreements or risk contracts shall be granted in regard to hydrocarbon exploitation.

Mexico was able to meet its energy needs for many years under this restriction. Recently, the Mexican government has explored ways of allowing additional foreign investment in the energy sector that are consistent with its constitution, hoping to attract capital that will strengthen the highly-leveraged national oil company, Pemex. So far the reform efforts have had little success.

Other laws limit participation in certain sectors or activities (e.g., forestry exploitation) to Mexican nationals. Investment restrictions prohibit foreign ownership of residential real property within 50 kilometers of the nation's coasts and 100 kilometers of its land borders. However, foreigners may acquire the effective use of residential property in the restricted zones through trusts administered by Mexican banks. A national foreign investment commission reviews foreign investment in Mexico's restricted sectors, as well as investments in non-restricted sectors that exceed a 49 percent share of an investment with a value greater than $150 million (as adjusted each year for growth in Mexico's nominal GDP). All of these restrictions are incorporated into the NAFTA.

In: Mexico: Economic, Political and Social Issues
Editors: Maria L. Castro and Irene P. Navarro ISBN: 978-1-60456-847-9

Chapter 3

MEXICO-U.S. RELATIONS: ISSUES FOR CONGRESS*

Colleen W. Cook, Rebecca G. Rush and Mark P. Sullivan

ABSTRACT

The United States and Mexico have a close and complex bilateral relationship, with extensive economic linkages as neighbors and partners under the North American Free Trade Agreement (NAFTA). Bilateral relations are generally friendly, although the U.S. enactment of border fence legislation in October 2006 caused some tension in the relationship. Drug trafficking issues are prominent in relations since Mexico is the leading transit country for cocaine, a leading supplier of methamphetamine and heroin, and the leading foreign supplier of marijuana to the United States.

In October 2007, the United States and Mexico announced the Mérida Initiative to combat drug trafficking, gangs, and organized crime in Mexico and Central America. The Administration requested $500 million in FY2008 supplemental assistance for Mexico as part of a $1.4 billion, multi-year aid package for the Initiative. In legislative action on H.R. 2642, the second FY2008 supplemental appropriations measure, the House approved $400 million for Mexico on May 15, 2008, while the Senate approved $350 million on May 22; the measure will now go to conference. Both versions have human rights conditions. In other action, a bill that would authorize $1.1 billion for Mexico over three years under the Mérida Initiative, H.R. 6048, was approved by the House Foreign Affairs Committee on May 14, 2008. The Administration has also requested an additional $450 million for Mexico under the Mérida Initiative in its FY2009 budget request.

Shortly after taking office in December 2006, President Felipe Calderón of the conservative National Action Party (PAN) launched operations against drug cartels in nine Mexican states. Since early 2008, he has sent more than 25,000 soldiers and federal police to drug trafficking "hot-spots." Calderón has increased extraditions to the United States, and has demonstrated an unprecedented willingness to reach out for counternarcotics assistance from the United States while also calling for increased U.S. efforts on arms trafficking and a reduction in the U.S. demand for illicit drugs.

Migration, border security, and trade issues also have dominated the bilateral relationship in recent years. Comprehensive immigration reform was debated early in the

* This report is excerpted from CRS Report RL32724, Dated May 23, 2008

110th Congress, but the issue was put aside following a failed cloture motion in the Senate on the Comprehensive Immigration Reform Act of 2007 (S. 1348). In September 2006, Congress approved the Secure Fence Act of 2006 (P.L. 109-367) to authorize the construction of a border fence and other barriers along 700 miles of the U.S.-Mexico border. Since 1994, NAFTA institutions have been functioning, trade between the countries has tripled, and allegations of violations of labor and environmental laws have been considered by the trilateral institutions. The Bush Administration argues that NAFTA has had modest positive impacts on all three member countries, but Mexican farmers have strongly criticized the effects of NAFTA. Notable bilateral trade disputes relate to trucking, tuna, sweeteners and anti-dumping measures.

Most Recent Developments

On May 22, 2008, the Senate approved its version of a second FY2008 supplemental appropriations measure, H.R. 2642 (Edward), that includes $450 million for the Mérida Initiative, with $350 million for Mexico and $100 million for Central America, Haiti, and the Dominican Republic. The House approved its version of the bill on May 15, which would provide $461.5 million for the Mérida Initiative, with $400 million for Mexico and $61.5 million for Central America, Haiti, and the Dominican Republic. Both versions have human rights conditions requiring that vetting procedures be in place to ensure that members and units of the military and police forces of the recipient countries that receive assistance have not been involved in human rights violations or corrupt acts. (See "The Mérida Initiative Proposal" below.)

On May 14, 2008, the House Foreign Affairs Committee approved H.R. 6028 (Berman), which would authorize $1.6 billion over three years, FY2008-FY2010, for the Mérida Initiative. Of that amount, $1.1 billion would be authorized for Mexico, $405 million for Central America, and $73.5 million for activities of the U.S. Bureau of Alcohol, Tobacco, Firearms, and Explosives (ATF) to reduce the flow of illegal weapons from the United States to Mexico.

In May 2008, Mexico experienced a surge in drug-related violence. Early in the month, four senior police officers were killed, among them, Edgar Millán Gómez, one of Mexico's top federal policemen in the fight against drug cartels. Millán had orchestrated the arrest of 13 drug traffickers in Sinaloa on May 1, 2008, which triggered the shootings of 12 policemen, allegedly carried out by the Sinaloa cartel. Other high ranking officials killed in this time period include the head of the Organized Crime Department at the Federal Secretariat of Public Security, the director of the Public Security Secretariat general staff, a police captain in Ciudad Juárez, a former commander of Mexico's anti-kidnapping unit, and the second-in-command of the Ciudad Juárez police force. The police chief of Ciudad Juárez resigned on May 18, and will be replaced by a retired army officer; seven police commanders in the city have been killed over the last several months. As of May 20, more than 1,300 people were killed in drug gang violence.

On April 8, 2008, President Calderón proposed to the Mexican Congress some limited measures to allow Mexico's state-oil company, *Petróleos Mexicanos* (Pemex), to contract out to foreign companies to help with exploration and allow private companies to build and operate refineries, pipelines, and storage facilities. The proposal, which was dubbed a "light reform" by industry analysts, prompted strong political resistence from Mexico's leftist opposition, led by Andrés Manuel López Obrador of the Party of the Democratic Revolution

(PRD), that blockaded Mexico's Congress, paralyzing its work for two weeks. The opposition successfully won a period of 71 days, from May 13th to July 22nd, to conduct a national debate on the energy reforms.

On March 6, 2008, Mexico's Senate approved reform legislation that would amend Mexico's Constitution to create a system of public, oral trials and establish the presumption of innocence. Mexico's Chamber of Deputies approved the legislation in February 2008. The judicial reform bill still must be approved by at least 16 of Mexico's 31 states and signed into law by Mexico's President.

On March 1, 2008, the Colombian military bombed a Revolutionary of the Armed Forces (FARC) camp in Ecuador, killing at least 25 people, among them, four Mexican students visiting the camp.

On February 27, 2008, the Bush Administration announced delays in the construction of the initial phase of the virtual fence along 28 miles of the U.S.-Mexico border. The pilot, known as Project 28 (P-28), is the first phase of the Secure Border Initiative network (SBInet). In April 2008, the Department of Homeland Security announced that most of the P-28 system will be replaced by new equipment because the original design was not compatible with Border Patrol needs.

On January 1, 2008, the full implementation of NAFTA began with the lifting of remaining tariff protections on various agricultural products, including beans, corn, sugar, and powdered milk, were lifted.

U.S.-Mexico Relationship

Political Developments

Felipe Calderón of the conservative National Action Party (PAN) was sworn in as President on December 1, 2006 in an unusually brief inauguration ceremony due to fears that members of the Party of the Democratic Revolution (PRD) congressional delegation would interrupt the ceremony. President Calderón has called increasing drug violence in Mexico a threat to the Mexican state, and in December, reorganized the two federal law enforcement agencies to address this issue by placing them under a single commander.[1] In his first year in office, President Calderón emphasized law and order through initiatives to combat drug cartels and has launched a job creation initiative to both further Mexican development and reduce emigration to the United States. While the PAN, along with the leftist PRD, made significant gains in congressional elections, the PAN failed to win a majority in either house. President Calderón will have to forge alliances with other parties in order to achieve some of his campaign platforms, particularly his proposal for energy reform.

President Calderón is continuing the progress made in bilateral relations under President Fox, but is emphasizing the need for U.S. support of Mexican efforts to combat drug cartels and drug trafficking rather than immigration reform. President Calderón has displayed an unprecedented willingness to increase narcotics cooperation with the United States. This willingness led to the proposed Mérida Initiative, a multi-year $1.4 billion effort to combat drug trafficking and organized crime, discussed in more detail below. He urged the U.S. Congress to approve funding to support the Mérida Initiative. President Calderón has been particularly vocal in requesting U.S. efforts to reduce U.S. drug demand, money laundering, and arms trafficking to Mexico.

Drug trafficking and violence, immigration, and border security dominate the bilateral relationship. Felipe Calderón made his first official visit to the United States as President-elect in early November 2006, after first visiting Canada and several Latin American countries. During his visit, Calderón criticized the recent authorization of 700 miles of fencing along the U.S.-Mexico border and noted that it complicated U.S.-Mexico relations. He asserted that job-creation and increased investment in Mexico would be more effective in reducing illegal migration from Mexico than a border fence. Calderón signaled a shift in Mexican foreign policy when he noted that while immigration is an important issue in the bilateral relationship, it is not the only issue, as trade and economic development are also important. He reiterated these concerns during President Bush's March 2007 visit to Mexico.

Since taking office in December 2006, President Calderón has made combating drug cartels and drug violence a top priority of his administration. President Calderón has called increasing drug violence in Mexico a threat to the Mexican state, and has sent more than 25,000 soldiers and federal police to drug trafficking "hot-spots" throughout Mexico. The operations boosted Calderón's approval ratings to over 60%. During President Bush's March 2007 visit to Mexico, President Calderón called for U.S. assistance in combating drug and weapons trafficking. Specifically, Calderón promised to continue his efforts to combat drug trafficking and called for U.S. efforts to reduce the demand for drugs stating, "while there is no reduction for demand in your territory, it will be very difficult to reduce the supply in ours."[2]

Heightened Violence in Mexico [3]

The rivalries and turf wars among Mexico's drug cartels fueled an increase in violence within the country, particularly along the Southwest border region that the United States shares with Mexico. In an effort to control the most lucrative drug smuggling routes in Mexico, rival drug cartels are launching attacks on each other, the Mexican military, and police personnel. This heightened violence is posing a serious challenge to Mexico's security forces.

By May 20, 2008, there were over 1,300 drug-related killings in Mexico, a higher rate of killings than in 2006 and 2007. During the first 10 days of May 2008 alone, Mexico experienced one of the most significant surges in violence. Four senior police officers were killed, among them, Edgar Millán, Mexico's acting federal police chief. Millán had orchestrated the arrest of 13 drug gansters in Sinaloa on May 1, 2008, which triggered the shootings of 12 policemen in Sinaloa, allegedly carried out by the Sinaloa cartel. Other high ranking officials killed in this time period include the head of the Organized Crime Department at the Federal Secretariat of Public Security, the director of the Public Security Secretariat general staff, a police captain in Ciudad Juárez, a former commander of Mexico's anti-kidnapping unit, and the second-in-command of the Ciudad Juárez police force. The police chief of Ciudad Juárez resigned on May 18, and will be replaced by a retired army officer; seven police commanders in the city have been killed over the last several months.

The spike in violence has increased pressure on the Calderón government, and some fear that it could erode public support for the government. Mexican officials maintain, however, that the government will "not take even a pace back in its battle against organized crime."[4]

Economic Conditions

Mexico is the second leading market for U.S. exports after Canada, and is the third most important source of U.S. imports after Canada and China. The United States is Mexico's most important customer by far, receiving about 80% of Mexico's exports, including petroleum, automobiles, auto parts, and winter vegetables, and providing about 50% of Mexico's imports. The United States is the source of over 60% of foreign investment in Mexico, and the primary source of important tourism earnings. Mexico is also the leading country in Latin America in terms of U.S. investment, with the total stock of U.S. investment being about $85 billion in 2006.

With some 80% of the country's exports going to the United States, Mexico's economy is strongly affected by the U.S. business cycle. Mexico's economy grew 4.8% in 2006, the last year of the Fox's presidency, which was the highest of his administration. Economic growth slowed to 3.3% in 2007, the first year of Calderón's administration. Slower growth is anticipated for 2008 due to declining demand in the United States, declining oil production, and slow growth in remittances sent by Mexicans abroad.[5] After years of high growth, remittances only grew by 1% in 2007, possibly due to slower growth in the U.S. economy. This decline is in sharp contrast to the 17.1% increase in remittances the year before. Remittances declined by 2.8% in the first two months of 2008 as compared to the same time period in 2007, and most analysts expect to see little or no rise in remittances for the remainder of the year.[6]

During the Fox Administration (2000-2006), the pace of economic growth slowed, in large part because of the effects of the slowdown in the United States following the terrorist attacks. Mexico's economy contracted 0.8% in 2001, and grew only 0.9% in 2002 and 1.3% in 2003, but it revived strongly in 2004 with a 4.4% growth rate. Economic growth in 2005 was 3% with a record 750,000 jobs created. The earlier meager growth results under Fox contrasted with economic growth averaging over 5% in the previous six years. Under the circumstances, President Fox was forced to operate under austere budgets in 2001, 2002, 2003, and 2004, reducing the funding for promised health and education programs. Lacking majority support in Congress, Fox was unable to obtain approval of major legislation, including a proposed tax reform and a proposed energy reform that would permit greater private participation in the hydrocarbon and electricity sectors, although Congress did pass a social security reform in July 2004. Calderón, like his predecessor, lacks a majority in Congress, meaning that he will need to make alliances with members from other parties to pass key fiscal and energy sector reforms.

Until the early 1980s, Mexico had a closed and statist economy and its independent foreign policy was often at odds with the United States. Beginning under President Miguel de la Madrid (1982-1988), and continuing more dramatically under President Carlos Salinas de Gortari (1988-1994) and President Ernesto Zedillo (1994-2000), Mexico adopted a series of economic, political, and foreign policy reforms. It opened its economy to trade and investment, adopted electoral reforms that leveled the playing field, and increased cooperation with the United States on drug control, border issues, and trade matters. Cooperation under the North American Free Trade Agreement (NAFTA) and the annual cabinet-level meetings of the Binational Commission are the clearest indications of the close and increasing relationships between the countries.

Socio-Economic Conditions

Mexico is a middle-income country of approximately 107 million people. According to the United Nations Economic Commission for Latin America and the Caribbean (ECLAC) nearly 31.7% of Mexicans lived in poverty in 2005 and just under 9% of Mexicans lived in extreme poverty or indigence. This represents a significant improvement from 2000 when 41% of Mexicans lived in poverty and 15% were indigent. Nevertheless, income inequality appears to be worsening in Mexico. ECLAC considered Mexico a nation with an average level of income inequality from 2000 to 2002 but changed its categorization to that of a highly unequal country for the period from 2003 to 2005.[7]

Mexico's main program to reduce the effects of poverty is the Opportunities program (Oportunidades, formerly known as Progresa). The program began under President Ernest Zedillo (1994-2000) and expanded under President Vicente Fox (2000-2006) to benefit 5 million families throughout Mexico. The program seeks to not only alleviate the immediate effects of poverty through cash and in-kind transfers, but to break the cycle of poverty by improving nutrition and health standards among poor families and increasing educational attainment. This program provides cash transfers to families in poverty who demonstrate that they regularly attend medical appointments and can certify that children are attending school. The government provides educational cash transfers to participating families. The program also provides nutrition support to pregnant and nursing women and malnourished children. Monthly benefits are a minimum of $15 with a cap of about $150. The majority of households receiving Opportunities benefits are in Mexico's six poorest states: Chiapas, Mexico State, Puebla, Veracruz, Oaxaca, and Guerrero.[8] Mexico also has programs to expand the development potential of remittances which are discussed in more detail below.

Remittances

Remittances are often discussed as a potential tool to combat poverty. Mexico is the third leading recipient of remittances after India and China, accounting for just over 11% of global remittance flows in 2007.[9] Its nationals received $23 billion in 2006 and just under $24 billion in 2007. While Mexico receives the largest amount of remittances in Latin America, it is a comparatively small share of Mexican national income, accounting for about 3% of Mexico's GDP in 2007.[10] The rate of remittance growth slowed dramatically in 2007, accounting for a nominal 1% increase, much less than the 17% increase recorded the year before. From 2003 to 2006 remittance flows increased an average of 19% annually. The cause of the lower growth rate is still uncertain, but possible explanations include the rise of anti-immigrant sentiment in the United States, increased deportations of illegal immigrants, and the slow down of the U.S. construction market. Some observers doubt these explanations because remittances to Central America continue to grow at higher rates, and it is unclear why Mexican workers would be more affected by immigration enforcement or the decline in construction jobs than Central American workers. Another explanation is that remittance growth rates to Mexico were exaggerated as improved accounting and reporting mechanisms were implemented and, now that those mechanisms are in place, the financial system is more accurate in reporting changes in remittance flows.[11]

The pattern of remittance flows to Mexico suggests potential limitations to the use of remittances to reduce poverty and inequality. Mexican states receiving the most remittances are those with traditionally high rates of migration, which do not represent the poorest states in Mexico. In 2006, roughly 55% of remittances sent to Mexico went to 7 of Mexico's 32 states. These states are Michoacán, Guanajuato, Jalisco, Mexico, the Federal District, Veracruz, and Puebla. The impoverished states of Oaxaca, Guerrero, and Chiapas received less than 14% of remittances sent to Mexico in the first half of 2007.

The effect of remittances on poverty in Mexico remains unclear, though there is evidence to suggest that remittances improve household income. It is estimated that 80-90% of remittances in Mexico are used to cover consumer needs, including food and utilities. Another 10% is spent on investment, most likely housing. Home town associations (HTAs) from the state of Zacatecas pioneered efforts to increase the development impact of remittances. Beginning in 1993, the state of Zacatecas and the Mexican federal government agreed to allocate one dollar for every dollar Zacatecan HTAs spend on local development programs. In 1999, municipal governments agreed to match donations dollar for dollar, making what is now known as the "3-for-1" program, which triples HTA donations. President Fox extended the program nationwide in 2002. Through 2005, HTAs, municipal, state, and federal governments spent $230 million on 5,000 local development projects in partnership with HTAs.[12] While this is a significant amount of money, it amounts to just 1% of remittances sent to Mexico in 2006. U.S. assistance to improve Mexico's financial sector, administered by USAID, includes small grants to help microfinance institutions increase products and services, including remittance-related services.

Foreign Policy Challenges

President Calderón has sought to pursue an independent foreign policy with closer ties to Latin America. He has tried to mend relations with Cuba and Venezuela. Relations with both countries became tense under the administration of President Vicente Fox (2000-2006). In September 2007, Mexican and Venezuelan ambassadors presented credentials to the respective governments, restoring full relations for the first time since November 2005 when President Fox expelled Venezuela's ambassador to Mexico. A Cuban ambassador to Mexico also presented his credentials to President Calderón in September 2007. In May 2004, President Fox recalled Mexico's ambassador to Cuba, ambassadors were later restored, but relations between the two countries remained tense through the remainder of the Fox administration. Migration is likely to be an issue in Mexico-Cuba relations, with Cubans increasingly preferring to emigrate to the United States via Mexico rather than by sea.

Under President Fox, Mexico pursued a more activist and diversified foreign policy, with greater involvement in UN activities, and stronger ties to Latin America and Europe. He promoted the so-called Puebla-Panama Plan, which promotes cooperative development efforts among the Central American countries and the southeastern states of Mexico. He attempted to revive the G-3 group trade preferences (Colombia, Venezuela, and Mexico), however Venezuela formally withdrew from the group in November 2006 after joining the Common Market of the South (Mercosur). Fox also sought better ties with Mercosur countries in South America. He attempted to expand trade with the European Union under the EU-Mexico free trade agreement that went into effect in July 2000, and with Japan under the Mexico-Japan free trade agreement that entered into force in April 2005. Mexico held a temporary seat on the U.N. Security Council in 2002 and 2003 and expressed support for continuing diplomatic efforts under United Nations auspices to achieve the disarmament of Iraq, leading to expressions of disappointment from the Bush Administration.

President Fox encouraged strong relations with the United States, and he called for greater cooperation under NAFTA and for a bilateral migration agreement that would regularize the status of undocumented Mexicans in the United States. Relations became strained during the debate on immigration reform in the United States. After President Bush approved the Secure Fence Act of 2006, Mexico, with the support of 27 other nations, denounced the proposed border fence at the Organization of American States. Mexico also indicated that it will challenge the border fence before the United Nations. (See *Migration/Border Issues* below for more detail).

BILATERAL ISSUES FOR CONGRESS

U.S. Assistance to Mexico

Mexico, a middle income country, traditionally has not been a major recipient of U.S. foreign assistance, which may change depending on what action Congress takes regarding the Administration's request for funding to support the Mérida Initiative aimed at helping Mexico and Central America combat drug trafficking and other criminal organizations (see "The Mérida Initiative Proposal" below). In FY2008, the Administration is spending an estimated $50.6 million in regular foreign assistance funding, while it requested $500 million in supplemental funding through the INCLE account to support the Mérida Initiative. For FY2009, the Administration requested some $501 million in foreign aid to Mexico, including some $450 million requested through the INCLE account to support the Mérida Initiative.

Table 1. U.S. Assistance to Mexico FY2004-FY2009

Account	FY2004	FY2005	FY2006	FY2007	FY2008 (Est.)	FY2008 Supp. Req.	FY2009 (Req.)
CSH	3.70	3.23	3.99	3.72	2.68	--	2.50
DA	17.28	15.06	11.36	12.28	8.22	--	14.00
ESF	11.43	13.39	11.39	11.35	11.90	--	--
FMF	--	--	--	--	--	--	2.00
IMET	1.27	1.25	.01	.06	.37	--	.83
INCLE	37.00	39.68	39.60	36.68	26.55	500.00	477.82
NADR	--	.29	.63	1.30	.92	--	3.85
Peace Corps	.99	1.22	1.31	--	--	--	--
TOTAL	**71.67**	**74.12**	**68.29**	**65.39**	**50.64**	**500.00**	**501.00**

Accounts

ACI	Andean Counterdrug Initiative
CSH	Child Survival and Health
DA	Development Assistance
ESF	Economic Support Fund
FMF	Foreign Military Financing
IMET	International Military Education and Training
INCLE	International Narcotics Control and Law Enforcement

NADR Non-proliferation, Anti-terrorism, Demining and Related Programs

Migration/Border Issues

Nature of the Immigration Problem

Widely cited demographers at the Pew Hispanic Center estimated in March 2006 that there were 6.2 million undocumented Mexican migrants residing in the United States in 2005, accounting for 56% of the total estimated illegal alien population of 11.5 to 12 million.[13] The United States' Mexican-born population increased from 4 million in 2000 to 7 million in the first quarter of 2007.[14] Mexico takes the view that the migrants are "undocumented workers," making the point that since the U.S. market attracts and provides employment for the migrants, it bears some responsibility. Mexico regularly voices concern about alleged abuses suffered by Mexican workers in the United States, and for the loss of life and hardships suffered by Mexican migrants as they utilize increasingly dangerous routes and methods to circumvent tighter border controls. Mexico benefits from illegal migration in at least two ways: (1) it is a "safety valve" that dissipates the political discontent that could arise from higher unemployment in Mexico; and (2) it is a source of remittances by workers in the United States to families in Mexico, estimated at $24 billion in 2007.

In June 2007, the U.S. Senate voted against cloture on the Comprehensive Immigration Reform Act of 2007 (S. 1348). The measure has not been considered since that vote. The bill would improve border security, establish a temporary worker program, and normalize the status of most illegal immigrants in the United States. Mexico has long lobbied for such reforms and is cautiously watching debate on this measure. Immigration reform legislation was introduced in the House of Representatives in March 2007, but debate has not been scheduled. The House measure, the Security Through Regularized Immigration and Vibrant Economy Act of 2007 (H.R. 1645), would set border and document security benchmarks that must be met before normalizing the status of illegal immigrant or the creation of a guest worker program. A variety of other migration-related legislative initiatives have been introduced in the 110th Congress. (See *Legislation in the 110th Congress* below for more detail.)

In February 2006, the Mexican Congress approved a concurrent resolution on migration and border security in which Mexico acknowledges that Mexican workers will continue to emigrate until there are more opportunities in Mexico. Mexico also accepts the need to revisit its migration policies to consider enforcement of its northern and southern borders, enforcement of Mexican immigration laws that respects the human rights of migrants, and the need to combat human trafficking. Perhaps most significantly, the Mexican resolution states that the Mexican government does not promote illegal migration and calls for the development of a guest worker program in the United States under the principle of shared responsibility. The resolution commits Mexico to enforcing legal emigration "if a guest country offers a sufficient number of appropriate visas to cover the biggest possible number of workers and their families, which, until now cross the border without documents because of the impossibility of obtaining them."[15]

The 109th Congress considered competing measures for comprehensive immigration reform and increased border security, including the enactment of the Secure Fence Act of 2006 which authorizes construction of barriers along 700 miles of the U.S. border with

Mexico. Mexico has stated that the border fence will cause difficulties in the bilateral relationship and goes against the trend of increased cooperation on border security matters. The 109th Congress did not enact comprehensive immigration reform because of disagreement over key provisions of House and Senate proposals (see the section titled Legislation Relating to Mexico in the 109th Congress for more detail).

Congress last enacted major immigration reform in 1986 and 1996. Main provisions of the Immigration Reform and Control Act of 1986 (P.L. 99-603) included civil and criminal penalties for U.S. employers who knowingly hire undocumented workers; increased border control and enforcement measures; anti-discrimination safeguards; provision for legalization of illegal aliens who resided continuously in the United States before 1982; and a special legalization for farm workers previously employed on American farms. In 1996, two laws relating to immigration were enacted, the Illegal Immigration Reform and Immigrant Responsibility Act of 1996 (IIRIRA, P.L. 104-208) and the Personal Responsibility and Work Opportunity Reconciliation Act of 1996 (P.L. 104-193). The first measure sought to control illegal immigration by adding 1,000 Border Patrol agents per year for five years (FY1997-FY2001), along with additional personnel, equipment, and procedures. The IIRIRA increased penalties for unlawful presence and created the expedited removal program.[16] Individuals who depart the United States after more than 180 days of unlawful presence now face either a three or 10 year bar to admission to the United States, depending on the total period of unlawful presence. Both measures aimed to reduce the attractiveness of immigration by restricting the eligibility of aliens for federal programs.[17]

Executive Initiatives

A number of initiatives have been launched in recent years to improve border security and the economic competitiveness of NAFTA member countries. President Bush has also proposed comprehensive immigration reform, and the 110th Congress is currently considering various proposals.

Human Smuggling

The Operation Against Smuggling Initiative on Safety and Security (OASISS) is a bilateral effort to combat human smuggling established in August 2005. The program was initially limited to the area between San Diego, California and Yuma, Arizona, but was extended to El Paso, Texas in April 2006. In August 2007, the United States and Mexico agreed to extend the program to the Mexican state of Coahuila and the area between El Paso and Eagle Pass, Texas. From its inception through FY2007, OASISS has led to the prosecution of 660 individuals in Mexico on smuggling or trafficking charges. Over 300 individuals were presented for prosecution in Mexico during FY2007.[18]

In October 2007, U.S. Customs and Border Protection announced the creation of "Operation Lifeguard," an extension of OASISS in the El Paso Border Patrol Sector. The objectives of the new operation are to reduce migrant deaths and prosecute human smugglers. In FY2007, migrant deaths fell 24% in the El Paso sector, from 33 to 25.[19]

Border Security

U.S. and Mexican authorities are also increasing joint efforts to combat crime and increase border security. U.S. and Mexican border governors announced plans to share crime data in August 2006. In April 2006, the U.S. Consul to Nuevo Laredo, Tamaulipas and the Mexican Consul to Laredo, Texas announced a joint-effort to increase cooperation among the police forces to more effectively combat crime in the Laredos. On February 19-20, 2004, Department of Homeland Security Secretary Tom Ridge met with Mexican Government Secretary Santiago Creel in Mexico City to review progress under the U.S.-Mexico Border Partnership. The two leaders signed the U.S.-Mexico Action Plan for Cooperation and Border Safety for 2004, as well as a Memorandum of Understanding on the Safe, Orderly, Dignified and Humane Repatriation of Mexican Nationals. They also committed to develop six new Secure Electronic Network for Traveler's Rapid Inspection (SENTRI) lanes for pre-screened, low-risk individuals, and to develop five new Free and Secure Trade (FAST) lanes for pre-cleared cargo. Six SENTRI lanes opened in FY2006 at San Ysidro, California; Calexico, California; Nogales, Arizona; and Brownsville, El Paso, and Hidalgo, Texas.

On November 2, 2005, Homeland Security Secretary Chertoff launched the Secure Border Initiative (SBI), a comprehensive, multi-year plan to secure U.S. borders, and to reduce illegal immigration. The Department of Homeland Security planned to achieve these objectives through increased detention and removal, including an end to the "catch and release" of illegal immigrants; increased personnel at borders and ports of entry; increased enforcement of immigration laws in the U.S. interior, including worksite inspections; technological upgrades to assist in border enforcement; and improved infrastructure. Increased funding was approved by Congress in early October 2005 in the Department of Homeland Security Appropriations Act (H.R. 2360/P.L. 109-90). DHS submitted its SBI strategic plan to Congress in November 2006, including estimates of the cost of the technology and infrastructure component referred to as SBInet. DHS indicated that SBInet will allow the Department to gain operational control of the U.S. southern border by 2011 and will cost an estimated $7.6 billion. According to the plan DHS would have control of some 345 miles of the 2,000 mile U.S.-Mexico border by the end of FY2007. Some criticized the plan for shifting the date of operational control of the southern border to 2011 from 2008. The DHS Inspector General cautioned in November 2006 testimony before House Homeland Security Subcommittee on Management, Integration, and Oversight that DHS lacked sufficient staff to manage the contract awarded to Boeing to implement SBInet and stated that costs could rise to as much as $30 billion.

U.S. Customs and Border Protection completed 76 miles of fencing along the Southwest border in FY2007 as part of SBI. As of April 2008, 172 miles of pedestrian fencing were complete, and a projected total of 370 miles of pedestrian fencing under SBI is to be completed by December 2008. CBP announced that the 9 relocatable communication, camera, and radar towers were deployed in the Sasabe, Arizona area during FY2007. CBP also reported progress on the use of picture hardware in certain Border Patrol agent vehicles as part of the Project 28 program to implement a virtual fence to secure 28 miles of the U.S.-Mexico border. Congress has been critical of the progress of the SBI program, and Project 28. Project 28 was due to be completed in mid-2007, but the $20 million project has faced technological setbacks. The GAO testified in an October 24, 2007 hearing before the House

Homeland Security Committee that the camera technology was too sensitive and that it misinterpreted items such as moving shrubs as border crossers.[20]

On February 27, 2008, the Bush Administration announced further delays in Project 28. The current design of the project reportedly was not compatible with Border Patrol needs, and in April 2008, Department of Homeland Security officials announced that a large amount of the P-28 system will be replaced by new equipment and software. This delays progress of SBInet, which aimed to put a virtual fence along 100 miles of the U.S.-Mexico border by the end of 2008. In May 2008, a CBP spokesman said that the first phase of P-28 would be finalized with the installation of permanent surveillance towers, which would replace the nine temporary towers. Delays in Project 28 have prompted some Members to question the Department of Homeland Security's ability to secure another 387 miles of the U.S.-Mexico border by December 2008.[21]

Security and Prosperity Partnership.[22]

On March 23, 2005, President Bush, Mexican President Vicente Fox, and Canadian Prime Minister Paul Martin established the trilateral Security and Prosperity Partnership (SPP) of North America. Through the SPP the three nations have sought to advance the common security and prosperity of the countries through expanded cooperation and harmonization of policies. The SPP is not a treaty or agreement and is limited to the existing legal framework relating to the trilateral relationship. The SPP seeks to address security and commercial cooperation at the regulatory level. To operationalize this partnership, the leaders established Ministerial-led working groups to develop measurable and achievable goals in the specified areas. In August 2006, the SPP working groups submitted their second report to SPP leaders outlining completed initiatives and proposing new initiatives to ensure common security and prosperity. The working groups established an Avian and Human Pandemic Influenza Coordinating Body and a North American Competitiveness Council.

Cooperation under the SPP has increased security cooperation on port security and border security. In April 2007, the United States and Mexico signed an agreement to detect and prevent the smuggling of nuclear and radioactive materials.

Under the Megaports agreement, the U.S. Department of Energy's National Nuclear Security Administration and Mexican customs will install radiation detection devices at four Mexican seaports. These ports account for 90% of container traffic in Mexico. The three countries are also working to more efficiently determine the risk of cargo at seaports. Mexico has implemented the Sea Cargo Initiative which allows gathers data electronically before loading at a port of origin. Earlier completed initiatives included measures to facilitate trade, such as the signing of a Framework of Common Principles for Electronic Commerce,[23] and border security through, among other measures, an agreement between the U.S. and Mexico to create an Alien Smuggler Prosecution Program along the common border.

At an SPP leaders' meeting held in New Orleans, Louisiana in April 2008 President Bush, President Calderón, and Canadian Prime Minister Stephen Harper commended the success of NAFTA, which they say tripled trade between the three countries to a projected $1 trillion in 2008. They also reevaluated the five priority areas that were identified in a ministerial meeting held in Los Cabos, Mexico in February 2008. The three leaders decided that their Ministers should renew and focus their work on 1) increasing the competitiveness of business and economies by making regulations between the countries more compatible and strengthening intellectual property strategies; 2) making the borders between the countries more secure by coordinating infrastructure plans, strengthening technological advancements, and investigating new customs procedures; 3) fortifying energy security and environmental protection initiatives by exchanging information and collaborating on new projects; 4) improving citizen access to safe food, and health and consumer products by deepening regulatory and inspection programs; and 5) improving response to emergencies by updating bilateral agreements.[24] The next SPP leaders' meeting is scheduled to be hosted in Mexico in 2009.

Drug Trafficking Issues

Mexico remains a major supplier of heroin, methamphetamine, and marijuana, as well as the major transit point for cocaine sold in the United States. Although U.S.-Mexico counternarcotics efforts have been marked by distrust at times in the past, with criticisms mounting in March of each year when the President was required to certify that drug producing and drug transit countries were cooperating fully with the United States, relations improved during the Fox administration (2000-2006) and cooperation has continued under President Calderón. Reforms to the drug certification process enacted in September 2002 have helped improve bilateral relations on drug cooperation. The revised procedures require the President to make a report, not later than September 15 of each year, identifying the major drug transit or major illicit drug producing countries. At the same time, the President is required to designate any of the named countries that has "failed demonstrably," during the previous 12 months, to make substantial efforts to adhere to international counter-narcotics agreements (defined in the legislation) and to take other counter-narcotics measures.[25] In the late 1990s, Congress acted to strengthen Border Patrol and international interdiction efforts along the Southwest Border, and it passed the Foreign Narcotics Kingpin Designation Act (P.L. 106-120), which strengthened the President's authority under the International Emergency Economic Powers Act (IEEPA) to block the assets in the United States of designated international drug traffickers.[26]

According to the State Department's March 2008 International Narcotics Control Strategy Report (INCSR), Mexico is a major foreign supplier of marijuana and methamphetamine to the United States, and although it accounts for only a small share of worldwide heroin production, it is a major supplier of heroin consumed in the United States. The State Department estimates that 90% of cocaine entering the United States transits Mexico. Despite Mexico's major role as a producing and transit country in 2007, the Calderón Administration was credited with carrying out unprecedented efforts to eradicate and seize illicit drugs. Mexican authorities seized more than twice the amount of cocaine in 2007 than it did in 2006 and over $200 million in cash from a methamphetamine precursor operation. The report praised the Mexican government for its efforts to implement regulations that will ban the import of products containing methamphetamine precursors in 2008 and will ban the commercial sale of products containing methamphetamine precursors in 2009.[27]

Until 2006, Mexico refused to extradite criminals facing the possibility of life without parole to the United States. However, two recent decisions by the Mexican Supreme Court may facilitate extraditions to the United States. In November 2005, in a partial reversal of its

October 2001 ruling, the Court found that life imprisonment without the possibility of parole is not cruel and unusual punishment. The Mexican Supreme Court ruled in January 2006 that U.S. extradition requests only need to meet the requirements of the 1978 bilateral treaty, not the general law on international extradition.[28] President Felipe Calderón has indicated that he will use extradition as a major tool to combat drug traffickers. In 2007, Mexico extradited a record 83 alleged criminals to the United States, including the alleged head of the Gulf Cartel, Osiel Cárdenas. These extraditions surpassed a record 63 extraditions in 2006.

Counternarcotics cooperation improved significantly during the Fox administration, and President Calderón has indicated that combating drug cartels will be a priority of his administration, citing drug violence as a major threat to the Mexican state.[29] In December 2007, President Calderón reorganized the two federal police agencies — the Federal Investigations Agency (AFI) and Federal Preventative Police (PFP) — by placing them under a single commander. Shortly after taking office, President Calderón launched offensives against drug cartels and drug violence in several states. Since December 2006, the Mexican government has deployed over 36,000 soldiers and federal police to combat cartels in drug trafficking "hot-spots." Soldiers and law enforcement officials have been tasked with arresting traffickers, establishing check points, burning marijuana and opium plants, and interdicting drug shipments along the Mexican coast. This offensive has been criticized by some as being ineffective, and some are concerned about the militarization of Mexican law enforcement. The Calderón Administration, however, maintains that it must use the military due to the corruption of state and local police by the cartels. Additionally, a high-ranking member of the Mexican armed forces has stated that the military has to be involved in fighting drug traffickers because the police force cannot compete with the type of heavy weaponry that the drug cartels are now using.[30]

Corruption of state and local police is a significant problem in Mexico. In January 2007, the federal government temporarily seized weapons from Tijuana police to run ballistics checks to determine if the guns were used in any drug crimes. In April 2007, over 100 state police officers in the northern state of Nuevo León were suspended due to corruption concerns. In June 2007, President Calderón purged 284 federal police commanders, including federal commanders of all 31 states and the federal district. These commanders were suspended and subjected to drug and polygraph tests. The Mexican government immediately named replacements for the 284 dismissed commanders. The new commanders all successfully passed an array of examinations designed to weed out corrupt officers, including financial checks, drug testing, and psychological and medical screening. These tests are to be repeated on a regular basis.[31] On May 6, 2008, the state solicitor in Baja California fired 162 state policemen after a military commander named a horde of senior law enforcement personnel involved in receiving bribes from drug gangs.[32] Other police officers, acting out of fear, are reportedly resigning and fleeing for safer cities or asking for asylum in the United States.

There have been several significant developments on drug trafficking issues since 2006. The U.S. Coast Guard captured Tijuana cartel leader Francisco Javier Arellano Felix in August 2006. After negotiating a plea agreement in September 2007, he pled guilty to running a criminal enterprise and money laundering, which spared him the death penalty. He was sentenced to life in prison without the possibility of parole in November 2007. His brother, Francisco Rafael Arellano Felix, was extradited to the United States in September 2006. In June 2007, Francisco Rafael Arellano Felix pled guilty to conspiracy to distribute cocaine and intent to distribute based on a 1980 drug bust. He escaped prosecution in the 1980s when he fled to Mexico after he was released on bond. Francisco Rafael Arellano Felix was sentenced to six years in federal prison in September 2007. Hector Palma Salazar, the former head of the Sinaloa cartel, was extradited to the United States in 2007 and was sentenced to 16 years imprisonment for cocaine trafficking in February 2008.

The Mérida Initiative Proposal.[33]

The United States and Mexico issued a joint statement on October 22, 2007, announcing a multi-year plan for $1.4 billion in U.S. assistance to Mexico and Central America to combat drug trafficking and other criminal organizations. The Mérida Initiative, named for the location of a March 2007 meeting between Presidents Bush and Calderón, expands bilateral and regional cooperation to combat organized crime, drug cartels, and criminal gangs. The Administration requested $500 million for Mexico and $50 million for Central American countries in a FY2008 supplemental appropriations request. In the FY2009 foreign aid request, the Administration requested another $550 million for the Mérida Initiative – $450 million for Mexico and $100 million for Central American countries.[34]

The stated objective of the Mérida Initiative, according to the October 2007 joint statement, is to maximize the effectiveness of our efforts to fight criminal organizations – so as to disrupt drug-trafficking (including precursor chemicals), weapons trafficking, illicit financial activities, and currency smuggling, and human trafficking.[35] The joint statement highlights current efforts of both countries, including Mexico's 24% increase in security spending in 2007, and U.S. efforts to reduce weapons, human, and drug trafficking along the Mexican border. Although the statement did not announce additional funding for U.S. domestic efforts, it cited several examples of such efforts to combat drugs and crime that are already in place. Those examples included the 2007 Southwest Border Counternarcotics Strategy, the 2008 National Drug Control Strategy, and the 2007 U.S. Strategy for Combating Criminal Gangs from Central America and Mexico.

All proposed funding for the Mérida Initiative is designated for the International Narcotics Control and Law Enforcement (INCLE) account, administered by the Department of State's Bureau of International Narcotics and Law Enforcement Affairs (INL). There are four categories of assistance in the Mérida Initiative request. The largest category for "Counternarcotics, Counterterrorism, and Border Security" would fund equipment and technology infrastructure improvements for the Mexican military and law enforcement agencies. The category of "Public Security and Law Enforcement" would fund such items as inspection scanners, x-ray ions, computer equipment, and security equipment. A third category would fund "Institution Building and Rule of Law" projects, while the final category of assistance would fund program support. (See Table 2 for a breakdown of these categories for the Mexico portion of the Mérida Initiative request.)

In legislative action on the Mérida Initiative, the House Committee on Foreign Affairs approved a bill, H.R. 6028, on May 14, 2008, that would authorize $1.6 billion over three years, FY2008-FY2010, for both Mexico and Central America, $200 million more than originally proposed by President Bush. Of that amount, $1.1 billion would be authorized for Mexico, $405 million for Central America, and $73.5 million for activities of the U.S. Bureau of Alcohol, Tobacco, Firearms, and Explosives (ATF) to reduce the flow of illegal weapons from the United States to Mexico. Among the bill's various conditions on providing the assistance, the measure requires that vetting procedures are in place to ensure that members or units of military or law enforcement agencies that may receive assistance have not been involved in human rights violations.

In terms of appropriations legislation, FY2008 supplemental funding for the Mérida Initiative is being considered as part of a broader FY2008 Supplemental Appropriations Act, H.R. 2642. The May 15, 2008 House-amended version of the bill would provide $461.5 million, with $400 million for Mexico and $61.5 million for Central America (with $5 million of this going to Haiti and the Dominican Republic, both outside of the Central American region). The amount provided for Mexico is $100 million less than the Administration requested. As approved by the House, the bill also includes human rights conditions requiring vetting procedures be in place to ensure that members and units of the military and police forces of the recipient countries that receive assistance have not been involved in human rights violations or corrupt acts.

The Senate version of H.R. 2642, as amended on May 22, 2008, would provide $450 million for the Mérida Initiative, with $350 million for Mexico under the INCLE account; and $100 million for Central America, Haiti, and the Dominican Republic under the INCLE and ESF accounts (with $5 million for Haiti, $5 million for the Dominican Republic, and $40 million in ESF through the U.S. Agency for International Development for an Economic and Social Development Fund for Central America). As with the House version, the Senate version has human rights conditions requiring that vetting procedures be in place to ensure that members and units of the military and police forces of the recipient countries that receive assistance have not been involved in human rights violations or corrupt acts.

Table 2. Proposed Mérida Initiative Funding for Mexico, FY2008-FY2009 ($ in millions)

Category	FY2008 (Supp. Req.)	FY2009 (Req)
Counternarcotics, Counterterrorism, and Border Security	306.3	238.3
Public Security and Law Enforcement	56.1	158.5
Institution Building and Rule of Law	100.6	30.7
Program Support	37.0	22.5
Total	**500.0**	**450.0**

Source: Department of State Briefing Paper distributed to Capitol Hill offices.

Trade Issues[36]

Trade between Mexico and the United States has grown dramatically in recent years under the North American Free Trade Agreement (NAFTA) between the United States, Mexico, and Canada. Total U.S. trade with Mexico more than tripled from $82 billion in 1993 to a high of $347 billion in 2007, but the balance of U.S. trade with Mexico has shifted from a surplus of $1.3 billion in 1994 to a generally growing deficit of $74.3 billion in 2007 (exports of $136.5 billion; imports of $210.8 billion). High oil prices and growth in the factory sector explain much of the increase in the trade deficit. This change in the trade balance has caused some Members of Congress to question the benefits of NAFTA. Despite the deficit, Mexico is one of the fastest growing export markets for the United States in recent years, and it became the second most important trading partner after Canada in 1999.

The NAFTA agreement was negotiated in 1991 and 1992, and side agreements on labor and environmental matters were completed in 1993. The agreements were approved by the respective legislatures in late 1993 and went into force on January 1, 1994. Under the agreements, trade and investment restrictions are being eliminated over a 15-year period, with most restrictions eliminated in the early years of the agreement. Over the years, spokesmen from the Clinton and Bush Administrations have argued that NAFTA has been successful in increasing U.S. exports to Mexico, particularly in heavily protected areas such as agricultural products, and in promoting job creation and investment in both countries.

Functioning of NAFTA Institutions

Several NAFTA institutions mandated by the agreements have been functioning since 1994. The tripartite Commission on Environmental Cooperation (CEC) was established in Montreal, Canada; and the Commission for Labor Cooperation (CLC) was established in Dallas, Texas. In addition, the bilateral Border Environment Cooperation Commission (BECC), located in Ciudad Juarez, Mexico; and the North American Development Bank (NADBank), headquartered in San Antonio, Texas, were created to promote and finance border environment projects along the U.S.-Mexico border. Following up on a March 2002 agreement by Presidents Bush and Fox in Monterrey, Mexico, to broaden the mandate of the NADBank, Congress agreed in March 2004 to permit the NADBank to make grants and nonmarket rate loans for environmental infrastructure along the border, and the measure (H.R. 254) was signed into law (P.L. 108-215) on April 5, 2004.

The NAFTA institutions have operated to encourage cooperation on trade, environmental and labor issues, and to consider nongovernmental petitions under the labor and environmental side agreements.

Recent Trade Disputes

Major trade disputes between the countries have involved the access of Mexican trucks to the United States, the access of Mexican sugar, tuna, and avocados to the U.S. market, and the access of U.S. sweeteners to the Mexican market.

Trucking

With respect to trucking issues, the Mexican government objected to the Clinton Administration's refusal, on safety grounds, to allow Mexican trucks to have access to U.S. highways under the terms of NAFTA. A NAFTA dispute resolution panel supported Mexico's position in February 2001. President Bush indicated a willingness to implement the provision, but the U.S. Congress required additional safety provisions in the FY2002 Department of Transportation Appropriations Act (P.L. 107-87). On November 27, 2002, with safety inspectors and procedures in place, the Administration announced that it would begin the process that will open U.S. highways to Mexican truckers and buses, but environmental and labor groups went to court in early December to block the action. On January 16, 2003, the U.S. Court of Appeals for the Ninth Circuit ruled that full environmental impact statements were required before Mexican trucks would be allowed to operate on U.S. highways, but the U.S. Supreme Court reversed that decision on June 7, 2004.

On September 22, 2004, the House approved 339-70 an amendment to the Transportation-Treasury Appropriations (H.R. 5025) that would prohibit implementation of a rule allowing Mexican and Canadian truck operators an additional two years to bring their trucks into compliance with U.S. safety provisions, and this was eventually incorporated into the Consolidated Appropriations Act for FY2005 (H.R. 4818/P.L. 108-447) that was approved by the Congress and the President in November-December 2004. In October 2006, officials from the Department of Transportation indicated that the Department is prepared to ensure that Mexican trucks meet U.S. and Canadian safety provisions. The head of the Federal Motor Carrier Safety Administration, John Hill, indicated that a pilot project could be implemented to allow a limited number of Mexican companies access to the United States at some point in the future, but noted that there are "no immediate plans" to open the border to Mexican trucks beyond the 20-mile commercial limit.[37]

In February 2007, the Administration announced a pilot project to grant Mexican trucks from 100 transportation companies full access to U.S. highways. The Administration announced a delay in the program in April 2007, likely in response to critics who contended that Mexican trucks do not meet U.S. standards. The Iraq War Supplemental (P.L. 110-28), enacted May 25, 2007, mandates that any pilot program to give Mexican trucks access beyond the border region cannot begin until U.S. trucks have similar access to Mexico. Before a pilot project can begin, the Department of Transportation (DOT) must meet certain reporting and public notice requirements. The DOT's Inspector General must prepare a report to Congress to verify that the DOT has established mechanisms to ensure that Mexican truck comply with U.S. federal motor carrier safety laws. The report must also verify that Mexican trucks meet the safety provisions of P.L. 107-87, mentioned above. The DOT must also publish a Federal Register notice and allow for public comment on pre-audit inspection data and plans to protect the health and safety of Americans.

In September 2007, the Department of Transportation launched a one-year pilot program to allow approved Mexican carriers beyond the 25-mile commercial zone, with a similar program allowing U.S. trucks to travel beyond Mexico's commercial zone. As of early January 2008, 57 trucks from 10 Mexican companies had received permission to operate in the United States and 41 trucks from 4 U.S. companies received permission to operate in Mexico. Department of Transportation data reportedly shows that U.S. carriers have made twice as many trips to Mexico as Mexican carriers have to the United States from the time the program was launched until early January 2008. The Consolidated Appropriations Act (P.L. 110-161) includes a provision prohibiting the use of FY2008 funding for the establishment of a pilot program. The Department of Transportation determined that it can continue with the pilot program because it had already been established. A coalition of unions and environmental groups filed suit in the 9th Circuit Court of Appeals to end the pilot program. The court heard arguments on the case in February 2008, but a decision is still pending.[38]

In March 2008, the DOT issued an interim report on the cross-border trucking demonstration project to the Senate Committee on Commerce, Science, and Transportation. The report makes three key observations: 1) The Federal Motor Carrier Safety Administration (FMCSA) plans to check every participating truck each time it crosses the border to ensure that it meets safety standards; 2) There is less participation in the project than was expected;

and 3) The FMCSA has implemented methods to assess possible adverse safety impacts of the project and to enforce and monitor safety guidelines.[39]

Sugar and High Fructose Corn Syrup

The United States and Mexico recently resolved a long standing trade dispute involving sugar and high fructose corn syrup. Mexico argued that the sugar side letter negotiated under NAFTA entitled it to ship net sugar surplus to the United States duty free under NAFTA, while the United States argued that the sugar side letter limited Mexican shipments of sugar. Mexico also complained that imports of high fructose corn syrup (HFCS) sweeteners from the United States constituted dumping, and it imposed anti-dumping duties for some time, until NAFTA and WTO dispute resolution panels upheld U.S. claims that the Mexican government colluded with the Mexican sugar and sweetener industries to restrict HFCS imports from the United States.

In late 2001, the Mexican Congress imposed a 20% tax on soft drinks made with corn syrup sweeteners to aid the ailing domestic cane sugar industry, and subsequently extended the tax annually despite U.S. objections. In 2004, USTR initiated WTO dispute settlement proceedings against Mexico's HFCS tax, and following interim decisions, the WTO panel issued a final decision on October 7, 2005, essentially supporting the U.S. position. Mexico appealed this decision, and in March 2006, the WTO Appellate Body upheld its October 2005 ruling. In July 2006 the United States and Mexico agreed that Mexico would eliminate its tax on soft drinks made with corn sweeteners no later than January 31, 2007. The tax was repealed, effective January 1, 2007.

The United States and Mexico reached a sweetener agreement in August 2006. Under the agreement, Mexico can export 500,000 metric tons of sugar duty free to the United States from October 1, 2006 to December 31, 2007. The United States can export the same amount of HFCS duty free to Mexico during that time. NAFTA provides for the free trade of sweeteners, which began January 1, 2008. The House and Senate sugar caucuses expressed objections to the agreement, questioning the Bush Administration's determination that Mexico is a net-surplus sugar producer to allow Mexican sugar duty free access to the U.S. market.[40]

Tuna

On tuna issues, the Clinton Administration lifted the embargo on Mexican tuna in April 2000 under relaxed standards for a dolphin-safe label in accordance with internationally agreed procedures and U.S. legislation passed in 1997 that encouraged the unharmed release of dolphins from nets. However, a federal judge in San Francisco ruled that the standards of the law had not been met, and the Federal Appeals Court in San Francisco sustained the ruling in July 2001. Under the Bush Administration, the Commerce Department ruled on December 31, 2002, that the dolphin-safe label may be applied if qualified observers certify that no dolphins were killed or seriously injured in the netting process, but Earth Island Institute and other environmental groups filed suit to block the modification. On April 10, 2003, the U.S. District Court for the Northern District of California enjoined the Commerce

Department from modifying the standards for the dolphin-safe label. On August 9, 2004, the federal district court ruled against the Bush Administration's modification of the dolphin-safe standards, and reinstated the original standards in the 1990 Dolphin Protection Consumer Information Act. That decision was appealed to the U.S. Ninth Circuit Court of Appeals, which ruled against the Administration in April 2007, finding that the Department of Commerce did not base its determination on scientific studies of the effects of Mexican tuna fishing on dolphins.

Avocados

In February 2007, the U.S. Department of Agriculture (USDA) authorized the importation of Mexican avocados. The California Avocado Commission (CAC) disagrees with this decision. In April 2007, the CAC sued the U.S. Department of Agriculture for allowing the importation of Mexican avocados containing armored scaled insects, which has reportedly deterred shipment of avocados from Mexico because growers there are concerned about future market access.

Other Trade Disputes

On other issues, in early October 2002, the U.S.-Mexico working group on agriculture dealt with major agricultural issues, including Mexico's recent anti-dumping decisions on apples, rice, swine, and beef, and safeguard actions on potatoes. In January 2003, the countries agreed to permit Mexican safeguard measures against U.S. imports of chicken legs and thighs, and in July 2003, these safeguard measures were extended until 2008, with tariffs declining each year. In September 2006, Mexico revoked anti-dumping duties imposed on U.S. rice imports in 2002 following rulings by the WTO and WTO Appellate Body in 2005 which found that the duties were contrary to WTO rules. Mexico banned beef imports from the United States in December 2003 following the discovery of one cow infected with mad cow disease in Washington state. Mexico resumed importation of boneless beef in early March 2004, and bone-in beef in February 2006 in response to improved beef cow screening.

Political and Human Rights Issues

Concerns over Elections and Political Rights

Mexico has become increasingly democratic, and effectively ended 71-years of one party rule by the Institutional Revolutionary Party (PRI) in 2000 when Vicente Fox of the conservative National Action Party (PAN) was elected president. Mexico has concentrated on developing its political institutions and election agency. The Federal Elections Institute (IFE) and Federal Electoral Tribunal (TEPJF) were well-regarded going into the 2006 presidential and congressional elections. The July 2, 2006, presidential race was extremely close and final results were not announced until September 5 when TEPJF completed adjudication of all the challenges. TEPJF rulings may not be appealed. According to the final vote count, Calderón won just under 36% of the vote, defeating PRD candidate Andrés Manuel López Obrador by less than 234,000 votes. Voter turnout was 59%.[41]

After the vote, Andrés Manuel López Obrador led a campaign of civil disobedience, including the blockade of Mexico City's principal avenue, Paseo de la Reforma, until mid-September. The blockade reportedly cost Mexico City businesses over $500 million in revenue. On September 1, 2006, PRD members of congress prevented President Fox from delivering the state of the union address at the Mexican congress. López Obrador rejected the election tribunal's September 5 ruling and was named the "legitimate president" of Mexico at a democratic convention of his supporters held on September 16 at the Zocalo, Mexico City's main square. He swore himself in as the "legitimate president" on November 20. It is not clear how this parallel government will operate or how much support it has. In mid-September PRD founder Cuahtémoc Cárdenas criticized López Obrador's tactics as undemocratic and criticized him for surrounding himself with advisors who helped to orchestrate what many believe to be Carlos Salinas de Gortari's fraudulent defeat of Cuahtémoc Cárdenas in the 1988 elections.[42]

Allegations of Human Rights Abuses

According to the State Department's 2007 human rights report, issued in early March 2008, the Mexican government generally respected human rights during 2007, but many problems remained. It recognized the Mexican government's efforts to reform and professionalize the police force, although it highlighted that corruption and impunity, particularly at the state and local levels, remain endemic problems. The conduct of state law enforcement officials in response to protests in Oaxaca and Michoacán was of particular concern in 2006, but these situations stabilized in 2007. However, no progress was made during 2007 concerning the allegations of state abuses and killings during these 2006 protests. Additionally, during 2007, there were reports of the police sometimes torturing suspects to force confessions, which were sometimes used in prosecution despite a constitutional prohibition. While the government took action against some improper behavior by law enforcement personnel, including firing some 250 federal police commanders and 34 regional police coordinators, many officers committed crimes with impunity and without fear of prosecution.

Violence among drug cartels was of particular concern during 2007. Approximately 2,470 people were killed by drug cartels, including some 300 police officers and 27 soldiers. Narcotics-related killings and violence increased, and there were credible reports that some individual local, state, and federal police, immigration, and customs officials were involved in facilitating drug trafficking, according to the human rights report. Despite various judicial reforms, lengthy pretrial detentions, lack of due process, and judicial inefficiency and corruption persisted.

Human rights conditions in Oaxaca were of concern in 2006, due to significant political unrest from May to December 2006. The unrest was initially due to the violent repression of a peaceful teachers union strike, but expanded to include other parties and broader political interests. A central goal of the protesters was the removal of Oaxacan governor Ulises Ruiz of the Institutional Revolutionary Party (PRI). The protests, led by the Popular Assembly of the People of Oaxaca (APPO), resulted in what amounted to a blockade of the historic city center, with millions of dollars in lost tourist revenue. At least nine people were killed in the violence, including American independent journalist Bradley Will. The Mexican Congress has the power to remove the governor, but did not. Ruiz remains in his post.

On December 11, 2006, thousands of protesters demanded Governor Ruiz's resignation and the withdrawal of federal police from the city. Federal troops withdrew from Oaxaca on December 16, and the city has been relatively calm since then. Human rights activists criticized the arrest of over 100 protesters in November and December 2006. Many were released toward the end of the year, but APPO leader Flavio Sosa remains in custody in a high security prison outside Mexico City. APPO insists that the conflict is not over and has protests planned for January 2007 and is considering a march on January 27 calling for the Oaxacan governor's resignation. On January 4, Oaxacan officials confirmed that the federal prosecutor is investigating the deaths of APPO supporters. In May 2007, Mexico's National Human Rights Commission determined that federal authorities were responsible for the abuse and torture of some protestors. The Commission also determined that federal police were responsible for the killing of at least one protestor.[43]

Former President Fox pledged to investigate and prosecute those responsible for human rights violations, including the "Dirty War" period from the 1960s to 1980s. Human rights activists are critical of what they view as lukewarm efforts by his administration to improve human rights in Mexico and to address past violations.

The National Commission on Human Rights presented a report to President Fox, on November 27, 2001, that documented human rights abuses and disappearances of persons in the 1970s and early 1980s, and President Fox named legal scholar Ignacio Carrillo as a Special Prosecutor to investigate these and other cases on January 4, 2002. In April 2006, the Fox administration announced that the special prosecutor's office would be disbanded. In November 2006, Ignacio Carrillo presented his final report on the repressive era from the late 1960s to 1982. The report found that the repression was a matter of state policy and led to the summary execution of over 700 Mexicans; torture; and the razing of villages.

The report was praised by some as an acknowledgment of state responsibility for the repression that can be used to prosecute those responsible for human rights violations. Others remain critical, as no one has been convicted of charges relating to these alleged crimes. Only one of the three presidents from this period, Luis Echeverria (1970-1976), is still alive. President Echeverria faced genocide charges for his role in the repression of a 1968 student protest that left dozens dead when he was interior minister. Echeverria tried to evade prosecution by claiming the 30-year statute of limitations had expired. A judge rejected this argument and reinstated the arrest order in November 2006 after he determined that the statute of limitations did not go into effect until Echeverria left public office in December 1976. In July 2007, the Criminal Tribunal absolved Echeverria of any responsibility of the 1968 killings.

The unsolved murders of over 400 women killed and disappeared in Ciudad Juárez and other parts of the northern state of Chihuahua since 1993 remain a concern to human rights activists who maintain that the lack of prosecutions and inadequate investigations demonstrate the level of impunity in Mexico and a lack of official accountability to Mexican citizens. In February 2006, the Fox administration closed the special prosecutors office charged with coordinating federal and state investigations into the murders and folded it into an office responsible for crimes against women throughout Mexico. The Mexican government also announced in February 2006 that it found no evidence of serial killings in Ciudad Juárez.

Nineteen women were reportedly murdered in Ciudad Juárez in 2007, and nine suspects were arrested and four are under investigation.

Over 90 Members of Congress signed a letter from Representative Hilda Solis to President Felipe Calderón in August 2007. The letter commends the Calderón Administration for enacting a federal ban on violence against women, and calls on the Mexican federal government to encourage states to enact similar legislation. The letter also suggests that Mexico reform its penal codes to increase penalties for violence against women. The Members also expressed concern that Mexico's 14-year statute of limitations meant that the families of women killed in 1993 will no longer have legal options to seek justice in their daughters' deaths. The letter requested that President Calderón encourage state and local authorities to prioritize cases that are about to expire under the statute of limitations.

Drug violence contributed to a hostile environment for journalists in 2007. Two journalists and three media assistants were killed and three disappeared, reportedly due to their reporting on drug trafficking and organized crime. Self-censorship among journalists who fear reprisals for their work is reported to be common in Mexico. According to the Committee to Protect Journalists (CPJ), Mexico is the fourth most dangerous country for journalists — tied with Colombia, Pakistan, and Russia. In 2006, CPJ reports that two journalists were killed as a result of their work, including American Bradley Will, who was killed during civil unrest in Oaxaca. The Deputy Attorney General for Organized Crime is responsible for crimes against journalists committed by drug traffickers, terrorists, and human traffickers.

Legislation and Legislative Initiatives in the 110th Congress

Enacted Legislation

P.L. 110-161, Consolidated Appropriations Act of 2008

The Consolidated Appropriations Act, signed into law on December 26, 2007, makes appropriations for the Department of State, foreign operations, and other programs for the fiscal year ending September 30, 2008. Relating to Mexico, the joint explanatory statement prohibits funding for the establishment of a Department of Transportation (DOT) NAFTA trucking pilot program, under which a limited number of Mexican cargo trucks can deliver goods within the United States. The joint explanatory statement also noted the administration's request for $500 million in the FY2008 Supplemental Appropriations request to fund the proposed Mérida Initiative, but stated that the Department of State failed to adequately consult with Congress prior to submitting the budget amendment.

P.L. 110-53, Implementing the 9/11 Commission Recommendations Act of 2007

Section 701 of P.L. 110-53, signed into law August 3, 2007, requires that the Secretaries of State and Homeland Security, with the Director of National Intelligence, and heads of other relevant agencies, submit a report to Congress, no later than 270 days after the bill's enactment, on the status of U.S. efforts to collaborate with allies and international partners to improve border security, global document security, and to exchange terrorist information.

Section 511 of the measure calls for the Secretary of Homeland Security to make it a priority to assign personnel from U.S. Immigration and Customs Enforcement (ICE), U.S. Customs and Border Protection (CBP), and the U.S. Coast Guard to regional, state, and local intelligence fusion centers in order to enhance land and maritime border security and to improve dissemination of information amongst the myriad of jurisdictions in border areas.

P.L. 110-28, U.S. Troop Readiness, Veterans' Care, Katrina Recovery, and Iraq Accountability Appropriations Act of 2007

Section 6901 of P.L. 110-28, singed into law on May 25, 2007, mandates that a pilot program to give Mexican trucks access beyond the border region cannot begin until U.S. trucks have similar access to Mexico. Before a pilot project can begin, the Department of Treasury must meet certain reporting and public notice requirements. The Transportation Department's Inspector General must prepare a report to Congress to verify that the Department of Transportation has established mechanisms to ensure that Mexican trucks comply with U.S. federal motor carrier safety laws. The report must also verify that Mexican trucks meet the safety provisions of P.L. 107-87. The Department of Transportation must also publish a *Federal Register* notice and allow for public comment on pre-audit inspection data and plans to protect the health and safety of Americans.

Additional Legislative Initiatives

S. 9 (Reid), Comprehensive Immigration Reform Act of 2007

Introduced January 4, 2007, S. 9 expresses the sense of Congress that both the House and Senate should pass immigration reform that acknowledges the United States' immigrant heritage, creates more effective border enforcement, prevents illegal immigration, and reforms the legal immigration process. The measure was referred to the Senate Committee on the Judiciary. While this measure does not specifically address Mexico, Mexico is the leading source of both legal and illegal immigrants to the United States, thus any immigration reform in the United States would likely affect Mexico.

S. 132 (Allard), Methamphetamine Trafficking Enforcement Act of 2007

Introduced January 4, 2007, S. 132 expresses the sense of Congress that efforts to reduce the trafficking of methamphetamine and its precursor chemicals should be included in all bilateral and multilateral negotiations of the U.S. Trade Representative, the Secretary of State, the Secretary of Homeland Security, and the Attorney General. Section Four also expresses the sense of Congress that the Drug Enforcement Administration should collaborate with law enforcement officials from countries that are known to traffic in methamphetamine and its precursor chemicals and calls for education, training, and information sharing on the international trafficking and use of methamphetamine. Mexico is a leading foreign source of methamphetamine.

S. 575 (Domenici) / H.R. 2431 (Cuellar), Border Infrastructure and Technology Modernization Act of 2007

S. 575 was introduced February 13, 2007, while H.R. 2431 was introduced May 22, 2007. Section 8b permits funds authorized in this act to be used for the implementation of projects described in the Declaration on Embracing Technology and Cooperation to Promote the Secure and Efficient Flow of People and Commerce across our Shared Border between the United States and Mexico, agreed to March 22, 2002, Monterrey, Mexico (commonly known as the Border Partnership Action Plan).

S. 844 (Feinstein) Unaccompanied Alien Child Protection Act of 2007

Introduced March 12, 2007, S. 844 addresses the care and custody of unaccompanied alien children and directs immigration officers who find such children at U.S. land borders or ports of entry to permit them to withdraw their applications for admission and return to their country of nationality or last habitual residence. In the majority of cases, it gives the Office of Refugee Resettlement at the Department of Health and Human Services (HHS) jurisdiction over the care and custody of those unaccompanied alien children under the age of 18 who have not committed a federal crime or pose a threat to national security. This measure would affect all illegal immigrants, including Mexicans. It has been referred to the Senate Judiciary Committee.

S. 1007 (Lugar), United States-Brazil Energy Cooperation Pact of 2007

Introduced March 28, 2007, S. 1007 would establish a Western Hemisphere Energy Cooperation Forum to strengthen relationships between the United States and Western Hemisphere countries, particularly the countries of Brazil, Canada, Mexico, and Venezuela, through cooperation on energy issues. Regarding Mexico, the bill would direct the Secretary of Energy to work with Mexico to conduct a technical analysis of the Mexican oil and gas production status, future technological and investment needs, and recommendations for maintaining and increasing hydrocarbon production.

S. 1216 (Domenici), Laser Visa Extension Act of 2007

Introduced April 25, 2007, S. 1216 would permit a national of Mexico to travel up to 100 miles from the international border between Mexico and New Mexico if the person possesses a valid machine-readable biometric border crossing identification card issued by a Department of State consular officer, enters New Mexico through a port of entry where such card is processed using a machine reader, has successfully completed any required background check, and is admitted into the United States as a nonimmigrant tourist or business visitor. This bill has been referred to the Senate Judiciary Committee.

S. 1269 (Inhofe), Engaging the Nation to Fight for Our Right to Control Entry Act of 2007

Introduced May 2, 2007, S. 1269 would direct the Commissioner of the United States Customs and Border Protection (USCBP) to establish a National Border Neighborhood Watch Program to allow retired law enforcement officers and civilian volunteers to assist in carrying out such a program and establish a Border Regiment Assisting in Valuable Enforcement Force (BRAVE Force), which would consist of retired law enforcement officers, who would be employed to carry out the Program. Introduced by Senator Inhofe of Oklahoma, this bill has been referred to the Senate Judiciary Committee.

S. 1348 (Reid), Comprehensive Immigration Reform Act of 2007

Introduced May 4, 2007, S. 1348 would significantly reform the U.S. immigration system. The measure would establish a temporary worker program; normalize the status of illegal immigrants; reduce the backlog of pending family- and employment-based immigration petitions; enhance border security; and introduce a point-based immigration system to replace the current emphasis on family reunification. Issues under debate include the size of a temporary worker program; changes to the family-based immigration system; and the normalization of status of illegal immigrants. With regard to illegal immigrants, some oppose any normalization of immigration status. Others question the proposed amount of time for illegal immigrants to "touch back" in their native country before applying for permanent residence. The proposed point system is also controversial. Some critics disagree with the priority given to employment qualifications over family. Critics from within the business community fear the new system will be too rigid to meet their needs. This measure is not specific to Mexico, but Mexico has been lobbying for a temporary worker program since 2001, and has long sought the normalization of status of Mexican illegal immigrants in the United States.

This measure also calls for increased cooperation between the United States, Canada, and Mexico to improve security in North America. The measure would require annual reports to Congress on the status of information sharing between the United States, Mexico, and Canada in areas such as security clearances and document integrity; visa policy; terror watch lists; and money laundering. The measure would seek to improve the security of Mexico's southern border through a review of assistance needed to secure the borders of Guatemala and Belize. The bill also calls for improved coordination between the United States and Mexico to improve border security and to reduce: drug trafficking, human trafficking, gang membership, domestic violence, and crime. The bill includes a provision to improve circular migration between Mexico and the United States. This last provision could include development assistance to create employment opportunities in Mexico. In June 2007, the U.S. Senate voted against cloture on S. 1348. The measure has not been considered since that vote.

S. 2348 (Cornyn), Emergency Border Security Funding Act of 2007

Introduced November 13, 2007, S. 2348 would direct the President, no later than two years after enactment of the bill, to ensure that operational control of the U.S.-Mexico border will be met, the Border Patrol will have 23,000 full-time agents, specified barriers will be installed along such border, and specified detention capacities will be met.

H.R. 98 (Dreier), Illegal Immigration Enforcement and Social Security Protection Act of 2007

Introduced January 4, 2007, H.R. 98 seeks to curtail the hiring of unauthorized workers by modifying social security cards to include a machine readable strip and the creation of an employment eligibility database by the Department of Homeland Security. Employers would be required to verify potential employee's eligibility to work in the United States before allowing the individual to commence employment. The bill was referred to the House Committees on Judiciary, Homeland Security, Education and Labor, and Ways and Means. This measure would affect all immigrants attempting to work illegally, including Mexicans.

H.R. 133 (Gallegly), Citizenship Reform Act of 2007

Introduced January 4, 2007, H.R. 133 would deny citizenship to children born in the United States whose parents are not U.S. citizens or permanent residents. The measure has been referred to the House Committee on the Judiciary. This measure would apply to all nationalities, including children born to Mexicans in the United States who are not citizens or permanent residents.

H.R. 305 (Pearce)

Introduced January 5, 2007, H.R. 305 would amend the Immigration and Nationality Act to prohibit the parole into the United States of aliens who become ill at a port of entry or who seek emergency medical assistance from a Department of Homeland Security agent at, or near, the border. This measure has been referred to the House Committee on the Judiciary. It is likely that this measure would most often apply at the U.S.-Mexican and U.S.-Canadian borders.

H.R. 371 (Berman), AgJOBS Act of 2007

Introduced January 10, 2007, H.R. 371 reforms the H-2A, temporary agricultural worker provisions of the Immigration and Nationality Act and creates a temporary agricultural worker program, called "blue card," that includes derivative status for spouses and children and allows for eligible blue card holders to adjust status to permanent residents within seven years of the legislation's enactment. This measure was referred to the House Committee on the Judiciary. While not specific to Mexico, Mexican agricultural workers could potentially benefit from the proposed program.

H.R. 502 (Cuellar), Prosperous and Secure Neighbor Alliance Act of 2007

Introduced January 17, 2007, H.R. 502 would amend the Foreign Assistance Act of 1961 to provide assistance to improve security and economic development in Mexico by professionalizing its law enforcement personnel, providing personnel with technology, strengthening the judicial branch, supporting anti-corruption programs, and reducing poverty through targeted funding.

H.R. 1645 (Gutierrez), Security Through Regularized Immigration and a Vibrant Economy Act of 2007

Introduced March 22, 2007, H.R. 1645 would normalize the status of eligible illegal immigrants and establish a guest worker program. These programs could not be created until certain border and document security requirements had been met and the implementation of the first phase of an employment verification system. This bill was referred to the House Committees on the Judiciary and Homeland Security.

H.R. 2642 (Edwards), Supplemental Appropriations Act of 2008

Originally introduced June 11, 2007 as the FY2008 Military Construction and Veterans Affairs Appropriations Act, this bill subsequently became the vehicle for the second FY2008 supplemental appropriations measure. As amended by the House on May 15, 2008, the bill would provide $461.5 million for Mexico and Central America for funding the Administration's proposed Mérida Initiative, with $400 million for Mexico and $61.5 million for Central America (with $5 million of this going to Haiti and the Dominican Republic outside of Central America). Instead of restricting Mérida Initiative funding to the INCLE account, as proposed by the Administration, the House version would provide funding under the INCLE, Economic Support Funds (ESF), and Foreign Military Financing (FMF) accounts. As approved by the House, the bill also includes human rights conditions requiring that vetting procedures be in place in the recipient countries for members of the armed forces and law enforcement agencies to ensure that they have not been involved in human rights violations or corrupt acts.

The Senate version of H.R. 2642, as amended on May 22, 2008, would provide $450 million for the Mérida Initiative, with $350 million for Mexico under the INCLE account; and $100 million for Central America, Haiti, and the Dominican Republic under the INCLE and ESF accounts, with $5 million for Haiti, $5 million for the Dominican Republic, and $40 million of ESF through the U.S. Agency for International Development for an Economic and Social Development Fund for Central America. As the House version, the Senate version also has human rights conditions requiring that vetting procedures be in place in the recipient countries for members of the armed forces and law enforcement agencies to ensure that they have not been involved in human rights violations or corrupt acts.

H.R. 3270 (Filner), Visitors Interested in Strengthening America (VISA) Act of 2007

Introduced August 1, 2007, H.R. 3270 would waive certain entry documentary requirements for a non-immigrant child (unmarried and under the age of 16) who is a citizen or national of Mexico and accompanying parent or adult chaperone in instances of medical visits, student groups, and/or special community events. This bill was referred to the House Subcommittee on Immigration, Citizenship, Refugees, Border Security, and International Law.

H.R. 3531 (Brown-Waite), Accountability in Enforcing Immigration Laws Act of 2007

Introduced September 14, 2007, H.R. 3531 would make illegal immigration a felony as opposed to a violation of administrative law. It would also require select airport security screeners to undergo immigration status checks. It also addresses local and state authority issues, including the reimbursement of state and local jurisdictions any detention costs of illegal aliens who are apprehended by state or local law enforcement officers, upholding authority of state and local law enforcement personnel to assist in immigration enforcement while carrying out their routine duties, establishing an immigration-related training manual for state and local law enforcement personnel, and providing financial assistance to state and local law enforcement agencies for immigration enforcement assistance. In Sec. 106, Congress expresses condemnation of rapes by smugglers along the international land border of the United States and strongly advocates that the Government of Mexico work in coordination with United States Customs and Border Protection to take immediate action to prevent such incidents from occurring. This measure would affect all illegal immigrants present within the United States, including Mexicans. This bill has been referred to the House Judiciary and Homeland Security Committees.

H.R. 4065 (Sensenbrenner), Border Enforcement, Employment Verification, and Illegal Immigration Control Act of 2007

Introduced November 1, 2007, H.R. 4065 would amend the Immigration and Nationality Act to strengthen enforcement of the immigration laws and enhance border security. It would provide mandatory minimum sentences on smuggling convictions and for aliens convicted of reentry after removal, make illegal U.S. presence a crime, and increase penalties for improper U.S. entry and marriage fraud. It would also revise passport, visa, and immigration fraud provisions and expand the institutional removal program (IRP) to all states. The bill would require the mandatory detention of illegal aliens apprehended along the borders, create a National Crime Information Center database to list immigration violators, and makes an unlawful alien deportable for driving while intoxicated. It is likely that these measures would most often apply at the U.S.-Mexican and U.S.-Canadian borders. This bill was referred to the House Subcommittee on Border, Maritime, and Global Counterterrorism.

H.R. 4088 (Shuler), SAVE Act of 2007

Introduced November 6, 2007, H.R. 4088 would provide immigration reform by securing America's borders, clarifying and enforcing existing laws, and enabling a practical employer verification program. The bill sets forth provisions for increasing border patrol, recruiting former military personnel, using Department of Defense equipment along the border, aerial surveillance, and mandatory use of the E-verify system. In March 2008, a motion was filed to discharge the Committees on Homeland Security, Judiciary, Ways and Means, Education and Labor, Oversight and Government Reform, Armed Services, Agriculture, and Natural Resources from consideration of this bill.

H.R. 4192 (Tancredo), Optimizing Visa Entry Rules and Demanding Uniform Enforcement Immigration Reform Act of 2007

Introduced November 15, 2007, H.R. 4192 would establish new terms of birth right citizenship to make it unlawful to obtain citizenship or nationality for a person born in the United States unless one parent is a U.S. citizen or a lawful permanent resident. It also provides criminal penalties for unlawful presence in the United States; document, benefit or citizenship fraud; and for employer hiring violations. Electronic fingerprinting for U.S. passports and electronic birth and death registration systems would also be established. The bill would also address local and state authority issues, which would allow local and state law enforcement personnel to have the inherent authority to apprehend, arrest, detain, or transfer aliens in the United States to federal custody. Most significantly, the bill would eliminate federal reimbursement of emergency health services provided to undocumented aliens after FY2007 and coverage of Mexicans with border crossing cards. Introduced by Representative Tancredo of Colorado, this bill was subsequently referred to the Committee on the Judiciary, in addition to the Committees on Armed Services, Homeland Security, Oversight and Government Reform, Ways and Means, Education and Labor, Foreign Affairs, and Energy and Commerce.

H.R. 4329 (Kaptur), NAFTA Accountability Act of 2007

Introduced December 6, 2007, H.R. 4329 provides that, unless the specified conditions set forth in the bill are met, Congress would withdraw its approval of the North American Free Trade Agreement (NAFTA) effective October 1, 2009 and that the President, not later than April 1, 2009, would provide written notice of withdrawal to the governments of Canada and Mexico. It also expresses the sense of Congress that the President should not engage in negotiations to expand NAFTA to include other countries and that trade promotion authority should not be renewed with respect to the approval of any such NAFTA expansion.

H.R. 4987 (Jones, Walter B. Jr.), Fence By Certain Date Act of 2008

Introduced November 16, 2007, H.R. 4987 would require construction of fencing and security improvements in the border area from the Pacific Ocean to the Gulf of Mexico, which would include the U.S.-Mexican border area. Specifically, it would ensure construction of at least 2 layers of reinforced fencing, and the installation of additional physical barriers, roads, lighting, cameras, and sensors to be completed by May 2008. Representative Jones of North Carolina introduced the bill, which has been referred to the House Subcommittee on Border, Maritime, and Global Counterterrorism. It was referred to the Subcommittee on Border, Maritime, and Global Counterterrorism.

H.R. 5863 (Cuellar); H.R. 5869 (Rodriguez); S. 2867 (Bingaman), Southwest Border Violence Reduction Act of 2008

H.R. 5864 and H.R. 5869, introduced April 22, 2007, and S. 2867, introduced April 15, 2007, would authorize additional resources to identify and eliminate illicit sources of firearms smuggled into Mexico for use by violent drug trafficking organizations. It would also expand the resources provided for the Project Gunrunner initiative of the Bureau of Alcohol, Tobacco, Firearms, and Explosives to identify, investigate, and prosecute individuals involved in the trafficking of firearms across the international border between the United States and Mexico. It has been referred to the House Committee on the Judiciary, the House Committee on Foreign Affairs, and the Senate Committee on the Judiciary.

H.R. 6028 (Berman), Merida Initiative to Combat Illicit Narcotics and Reduce Organized Crime Authorization Act of 2008

Introduced May 13, 2008, H.R. 6028 would authorize $1.6 billion over three years, FY2008-FY2010, for both Mexico and Central America, to combat drug trafficking and organized crime. Of that amount, $1.1 billion would be authorized for Mexico, $405 million for Central America, and $73.5 million for activities of the U.S. Bureau of Alcohol, Tobacco, Firearms, and Explosives (ATF) to reduce the flow of illegal weapons from the United States to Mexico. The measure requires that vetting procedures are in place to ensure that members or units of military or law enforcement agencies that may receive assistance have not been involved in human rights violations. The bill was introduced May 13, 2008, referred to the Committees on Foreign Affairs and the Judiciary, and approved by the Committee on Foreign Affairs on May 14, 2008.

H.Res. 18 (Goode) and H.Res. 22 (King, Steve)

H.Res. 18 and H.Res. 22, introduced by Representative King of Iowa and Representative Goode of Virginia, respectively, express the House of Representatives disapproval of the Social Security Totalization Agreement signed by Mexico and the United States in 2004, which must still be submitted to the U.S. congress and Mexican Senate for review. Both resolutions were referred to the House Committee on Ways and Means.

H.Res. 499 and S.Res. 239. H.Res (Smith, Sessions)

499 and S.Res. 239 express the sense of Congress that the Administration should rigorously enforce the laws of the United States to substantially reduce the illegal immigration and greatly improve border security. This measure would affect all illegal immigrants, including Mexicans.

H.Res. 1087 (Kaptur)

H.Res. 1087 expresses the sense of Congress that NAFTA must be renegotiated to foster fair trade that truly benefits all Canadian, Mexican, and U.S. citizens.

H.Con.Res. 22 (Goode)

H.Con.Res. 22 expresses the sense of Congress that the United States should withdraw from NAFTA due to increased trade deficits, and potential health and security risks of permitting Mexican trucks to transport goods throughout the United States.

H.Con.Res. 40 (Goode)

H.Con.Res. 40 expresses the sense of Congress that the United States should not engage in the construction of a North American Free Trade Agreement (NAFTA) Superhighway System or enter into a North American Union with Mexico and Canada.

H.Con.Res. 119 (Goode)

H.Con.Res. 119 expresses the sense of the Congress that the President should immediately and unequivocally call for the enforcement of existing immigration laws in order to reduce the threat of a terrorist attack and to reduce the massive influx of illegal aliens into the United States. It is likely that this measure would most often apply at the U.S.-Mexican and U.S.-Canadian borders.

For Additional Reading

Mexico

CRS Report RL34215. *Mexico's Drug Cartels*, by Colleen W. Cook.

CRS Report RS22837. *Merida Initiative: Proposed U.S. Anticrime and Counterdrug Assistance for Mexico and Central America*, by Colleen W. Cook, Rebecca G. Rush, and Clare Ribando Seelke.

CRS Report RS22462. *Mexico's 2006 Elections*, by Colleen W. Cook.

CRS Report RL32934. *U.S.-Mexico Economic Relations: Trends, Issues, and Implications*, by M. Angeles Villarreal.

Immigration and Border Security

CRS Report RL34007. Immigration Fraud: Policies, Investigations, and Issues, by Ruth Ellen Wasem.

CRS Report RL32270. Enforcing Immigration Law: The Role of State and Local Law Enforcement, by Blas Nuñez-Neto, Michael John Garcia, and Karma Ester.

CRS Report RL32657. Immigration-Related Document Fraud: Overview of Civil, Criminal, and Immigration Consequences, by Yule Kim and Michael John Garcia.

CRS Report RL32235. U.S. Immigration Policy on Permanent Admissions, by Ruth Ellen Wasem.

CRS Report RL31381. U.S. Immigration Policy on Temporary Admissions, by Chad C. Haddal and Ruth Ellen Wasem.

CRS Report RS22574. Immigration Reform: Brief Synthesis of the Issue, by Ruth Ellen Wasem.

CRS Report RL32044. Immigration: Policy Considerations Related to Guest Worker Programs, by Andorra Bruno.

CRS Report RL32004. Social Security Benefits for Noncitizens: Current Policy and Legislation, by Dawn Nuschler and Alison Siskin.

CRS Report RL33896. Unaccompanied Alien Children: Policies and Issues, by Chad C. Haddal.

CRS Report RL32861. Farm Labor: The Adverse Effect Wage Rate (AEWR), by William G. Whittaker.

CRS Report RL30395. Farm Labor Shortages and Immigration Policy, by Linda Levine.

CRS Report RL33659. Border Security: Barriers Along the U.S. International Border, by Blas Nuñez-Neto and Michael John Garcia.

Drug Trafficking, Organized Crime, and Criminal Gangs

CRS Report RL34215. *Mexico's Drug Cartels*, by Colleen W. Cook.

CRS Report RL32352. *War on Drugs: Reauthorization and Oversight of the Office of National Drug Control Policy*, by Mark Eddy.

CRS Report 98-958. *Extradition To and From the United States: Overview of the Law and Recent Treaties*, by Charles Doyle.

CRS Report RS22325. *Methamphetamine: Legislation and Issues in the 110th Congress*, by Celinda Franco.

CRS Report RL34317. *Trafficking in Persons: U.S. Policy and Issues for Congress*, by Clare Ribando Seelke and Alison Siski.

CRS Report RL34233. *The MS-13 and 18th Street Gangs: Emerging Transnational Gang Threats?*, by Celinda Franco.

CRS Report RL34112. *Gangs in Central America*, by Clare Ribando Seelke.

Economic Issues

CRS Report RL32934. U.S.-Mexico Economic Relations: Trends, Issues, and Implications, by M. Angeles Villarreal.

CRS Report RS22701. Security and Prosperity Partnership of North America: An Overview and Selected Issues, by M. Angeles Villarreal and Jennifer E. Lake.

CRS Report 98-253. U.S. Agricultural Trade: Trends, Composition, Direction, and Policy, by Charles E. Hanrahan, Beverly A. Banks, and Carol Canada.

CRS Report RL33577. U.S. International Trade: Trends and Forecasts, by Dick K. Nanto, Shayerah Ilias, and J. Michael Donnelly.

CRS Report RL31356. Free Trade Agreements: Impact on U.S. Trade and Implications for U.S. Trade Policy, by William H. Cooper.

CRS Report RL33087. United States-Canada Trade and Economic Relationship: Prospects and Challenges, by Ian F. Fergusson.

REFERENCES

[1] "The Spectre of Rebellion Recedes in Mexico but Calderón Will Still Face Unrest and Violence," *Latin American Security & Strategic Review*, September 2006; Kevin G. Hall and Pablo Bachelet, "Mexico's Calderón Gives Bush an Earful on Immigration," *Miami Herald*, November 10, 2006; Patty Reinert, "Calderón Vows to Help Curb Illegal Immigration," *Houston Chronicle*, November 10, 2006; and, Jerry Kammer, "Calderón will Pursue Other Topics with U.S.," *San Diego Union Tribune*, November 10, 2006.

[2] "Bush Reassures Skeptical Mexico on Immigration," *Reuters*, March 13, 2007.

[3] For more information about Mexico's drug cartels, see CRS Report RL34215, *Mexico's Drug Cartels*, by Colleen Cook.

[4] "Gangs Challenge Government in Mexico," *LatinNews Daily*. May 7, 2008; "Killings in Mexico Hit Record," *Latin American Weekly Report*, May 22, 2008.

[5] Economist Intelligence Unit. "Country Report: Mexico," May 2008.

[6] Ibid; "Mexico's Remittances Down 6 Percent in January Compared to Year Previous," *Associated Press*, March 5, 2008; and "Mexico Remittances Fall at Record Pace in January," *Reuters*, March 4, 2008;

[7] UN Economic Commission for Latin America and the Caribbean, *Social Panorama 2007* and *Social Panorama 2006*.

[8] Santiago Levy, *Progress Against Poverty*, Brookings Institution, 2006.

[9] World Bank, *Migration and Remittances Factbook 2008*.

[10] Inter-American Development Bank, "Remittances in 2007, A Bend in the Road, or a New Direction?" March 2008.

[11] Migration Policy Institute, "Variable Impacts: State-level Analysis of the Slowdown in the Growth of Remittances to Mexico," September 2007; and Manuel Orozco, "Mexican Remittances: Issues and Considerations about its Recent Trend," September 2007.

[12] Richard Lapper, "Village Depends on its Migrants in California," *Financial Times*, May 9, 2007.

[13] Pew Hispanic Center, *The Size and Characteristics of the Unauthorized Migrant Population in the United States*, by Jeffrey Passel, March 7, 2006, data from the March 2005 Current Population Survey (CPS) and monthly CPS through January 2006 conducted by the U.S. Bureau of the Census and the Bureau of Labor Statistics. For more detail and comparisons with earlier years, see CRS Report RS21938, *Unauthorized Aliens in the United States: Estimates Since 1986*, by Ruth Ellen Wasem.

[14] Pew Hispanic Center, "Indicators of Recent Migration Flows from Mexico," May 30, 2007.

[15] "Mexico-U.S.: Migration and Border Security," Embassy of Mexico, February 2006.

[16] For more information on expedited removal, see CRS Report RL33109, *Immigration Policy on Expedited Removal of Aliens*, by Alison Siskin and Ruth Ellen Wasem.

[17] See CRS Report 95-881, *Immigration Legislation in the 104th Congress*, by Joyce Vialet.

[18] U.S. Customs and Border Protection, "Securing America's Borders: CBP 2007 Fiscal Year in Review," November 6, 2007.

[19] U.S. Customs and Border Protection, "U.S. Border Patrol Partners with Agencies to Unveil Operation Lifeguard," October 17, 2007.

[20] Elise Castelli, "Glitches Delay Virtual Fence on Border," *Federal Times*, October 29, 2007.

[21] Ibid; Spencer S. Hsu, "Virtual Fence Along Border to be Delayed," *Washington Post*, February 28, 2008; "Secure Border Initiative to Adjust – Not Terminate," *Penton Business Media*, May 1, 2008; and Congressional Testimony of John P. Hutton, US Government Accountability Office, before the House Committee on Homeland Security, May 8, 2008.

[22] For more information, see CRS Report RS22701, *Security and Prosperity Partnership of North America: An Overview and Selected Issues*.

[23] For more information, see CRS Report RL32934, *U.S.-Mexico Economic Relations: Trends, Issues, and Implications*, by M. Angeles Villarreal.

[24] "Joint Statement by President Bush, and President Calderón, and Prime Minister Harper" April 22, 2008.

[25] U.S. assistance would be withheld from any designated countries unless the President determines that the provision of assistance to that country is vital to the national interest of the United States or that the designated country subsequently made substantial counter-narcotics efforts. Notwithstanding the general suspension of the previous drug certification and sanctions procedures, subsection 706(5)(B) provides that the President may apply those procedures at his discretion. A transition rule provides that for FY2003, the required report was to be submitted at least 15 days before foreign assistance funds are obligated or expended.

[26] See CRS Report 98-174, *Mexican Drug Certification Issues: U.S. Congressional Action, 1986-2002*, by K. Larry Storrs.

[27] Department of State Bureau of International Narcotics and Law Enforcement Affairs, *International Narcotics Control Strategy Report 2008*, March 2008, hereafter INCSR 2008.

[28] Jesus Aranda, "Allana la Corte el Camino para Extraditar a Connacionales a EU," *La Jornada*, February 1, 2006; "Mexico: Court Clears Way for Faster Extraditions to U.S.," *Latin American Weekly Report*, February 7, 2006; and, U.S. Department of State, *INCSR 2006*.

[29] For more information see CRS Report RL34215, *Mexico's Drug Cartels*, by Colleen W. Cook.

[30] U.S. Government Printing Office, "The Mérida Initiative: Guns, Drugs, and Friends," Minority Staff Report to Senate Committee on Foreign Relations, United States Senate, December 21, 2007.

[31] CRS interview with Mexican Embassy officials, October 27, 2006; "Mexico: Congress Summons Defense Minister," *Latin American Weekly Report*, April 19, 2007; "Mexico Shakes Up Federal Police," EFE News Service, June 25, 2007; and, Sam Enriquez, "Mexico Purges Federal Police Chiefs," *Financial Times*, June 26, 2007.

[32] Corchado, Alfredo. "Drug War: Another Police Official Slain in Mexico," *The Dallas Morning News*, May 11, 2008; "Gangs Challenge Government in Mexico," *LatinNews Daily*, May 7, 2008; Roig, Franzia. "Drug Gangs Have Police on the Run; Police Chief

of Mexican Border Town Seeks Asylum in U.S. after Threats," *Vancouver Sun*, April 23, 2008; and Franco Ordoñez. "Army Tries to Confront Violence in Border City; Gangs Battle over Money-Making Drug Routes; Police Outgunned," *Charlotte Observer,* April 6, 2008.

[33] For additional information, see CRS Report RS22837, *Merida Initiative: Proposed U.S. Anticrime and Counterdrug Assistance for Mexico and Central America.* For more on the Central American components of the Mérida Initiative, see CRS Report RL34112, *Gangs in Central America*, by Clare Ribando Seelke.

[34] Joint Explanatory Statement to the Consolidated Appropriations Act of 2008, Division J (P.L. 110-161); "Security: President Bush Offers US$500 Million," *Latin American Regional Report – Mexico and NAFTA*, November 2007 and the U.S. Department of State and Government of Mexico, "Joint Statement on the Merida Initiative," October 22, 2007.

[35] U.S. Department of State and Government of Mexico, "Joint Statement on the Merida Initiative," October 22, 2007.

[36] For more information, see CRS Report RL32934, *U.S.-Mexico Economic Relations*, by M. Angeles Villarreal.

[37] Angela Greiling Keane, "Cracking Open the Border," *Journal of Commerce*, October 23, 2006.

[38] "9th Circuit Considers Injunction to Halt Mexican Truck Pilot Program," *International Trade Daily*, February 13, 2008; Rosalind McLymont, "Long Haul Across the Border," *Shipping Digest*, January 7, 2008; and "Hoffa Blasts Bush Administration's Indifference to NAFTA Harm," *PR Newswire*, March 10, 2008.

[39] Department of Transportation. "Cross-Border Trucking Demonstration Project," March 11, 2008.

[40] "Bush Administration Defends Sugar Deal to Congress," *Inside U.S. Trade*, November 3, 2006; "Grassley, U.S. Industry Welcome Agreement with Mexico on Sugar, HFCS," *International Trade Reporter*, August 3, 2006; and, "U.S., Mexico Reach Agreement on WTO Soft Drink Dispute Compliance Deadline," *International Trade Reporter*, July 13, 2006.

[41] For more information, see CRS Report RS22462, *Mexico's 2006 Elections*, by Colleen W. Cook.

[42] "Mexico: López Obrador Declared 'Legitimate President,'" *LatinNews Daily*, September 18, 2006; and "Critica CCS intolerancia perredista," *La Reforma*, September 14, 2006.

[43] "Mexico Rights Panel: Feds Committed Acts of Torture in Oaxaca," EFE News Service, May 24, 2007; Gerardo Soriano and Paulina I. Valencia, "Investiga PGR Crímenes Cometidos durante Conflicto en Oaxaca," *Notimex*, January 4, 2007; Gerardo Soriano and Paulina I. Valencia, "Asegura APPO que Conflicto en Oaxaca no Ha Terminado," *Notimex*, January 4, 2007; and "Calderón Opts for Ruiz," *Latin American Regional Report - Mexico and NAFTA*, January 2007.

In: Mexico: Economic, Political and Social Issues
Editors: Maria L. Castro and Irene P. Navarro
ISBN: 978-1-60456-847-9

Chapter 4

ARCHITECT OR HOME BUILDER? PRESIDENT GEORGE W. BUSH, MEXICO, AND THE MISUNDERSTOOD EUROPEAN REFERENT

Mark J. Miller
Department of Political Science and International Relations
University of Delaware, DE USA

INTRODUCTION

U.S. immigration policy has largely been viewed as a domestic issue and one where the prerogatives of the Congress prevailed over those of the executive and judicial branches. By the 1970s, however, concerns over growing illegal migration led to the creation of an inter-agency task force to study the phenomenon. During the presidency of Jimmy Carter, the Interagency Task Force on Immigration Policy issued its Staff Report in March 1979, which noted that "In the last twelve years, I.N.S. apprehensions of deportable aliens have increased twenty - fold and the vast majority of those apprehended are Mexican nationals."[1] The work of the Interagency Task Force on Immigration Policy was superseded by the creation of the Select Commission on Immigration and Refugee Policy by Public Law 95 - 412 in 1979. The 16 member Select Commission included four presidential appointees, four cabinet members, four U.S. senators, and four members of the U.S. House. It was led by Father Theodore M. Hesburgh, the President of the University of Notre Dame.

An influx of Haitian entrants and the Cuban government-sanctioned outflow, which included numerous Cubans who had been incarcerated for non-political offenses, hurt Carter's bid for re-election. In Arkansas, a riot by Cubans at a detention center in 1980 was widely seen as costing then Governor Bill Clinton re-election. The stakes of immigration and

---

[1] Interagency Task Force on Immigration Policy, *Staff Report* (Washington, DC: Departments of Justice, Labor and State, 1979).

refugee policies for U.S. presidents were rising. This reflected a broader pattern of politicization and securitization of international migration policies in the transatlantic area.[2]

The Select Commission communicated its report and recommendations to President Ronald Reagan. It recommended a legalization policy, imposition of employer sanctions for unauthorized hiring of aliens, a system of more secure identification for all employees and a slightly modified, "streamlined" H-2 temporary foreign worker program which did "...not exclude a slight expansion of the program."[3] The purpose of the Select Commission was to forge a national consensus concerning reform of immigration policy. However, the vote on the question, "Do you favor employer sanctions with some system of more secure identification?" was eight yes, seven no and one pass.[4] The vote concerning temporary foreign workers was an unambiguous fourteen to two, a major setback to proponents of expanded temporary foreign worker policy. The text voted upon included "The Commission believes that government, employers and unions should cooperate to end the dependence of any industry on a constant supply of H-2 workers."[5]

Bills reflecting the Select Commission's recommendations concerning illegal migration were then submitted to both houses of the U.S. Congress but became mired in a protracted and complex debate.[6] Supporters of expanded temporary foreign worker policy helped prevent passage of legislation until 1986 when Congressman Charles Schumer of New York brokered a deal which would authorize a special legalization program for foreign agricultural workers that ended the legislative logjam. President Reagan signed the Immigration Reform and Control Act (IRCA) into law on November 6, 1986. Meanwhile, all major Democratic Party presidential hopefuls in 1984 had announced their opposition to the imposition of employer sanctions. They viewed employer sanctions as damaging their electoral prospects with Hispanic voters. Polls, however, indicated that Hispanic voters were about evenly split for and against enactment of employer sanctions.

One provision of IRCA authorized the creation of a Commission for the Study of International Migration and Cooperative Economic Development (CSIMCED). This Commission would produce numerous reports and studies which would pave the way to President George H. W. Bush embracing a Mexican proposal to enlarge the free trade agreement signed in 1988 between Canada and the United States to include Mexico. Very significantly, the major research finding of the scores of studies commissioned by the CSIMCED held that trade liberalization would reduce illegal migration from Mexico only in

---

[2] The French presidential election of 1981 witnessed Socialist candidate Mitterand vow his solidarity with the SONACOTRA rent strikers, a protest movement that had begun in 1975. Asylum policy played a key role in the 1982 German elections won by Helmut Kohl. On the concept of securitization, see Barry Buzan, Ole Waever and Jaap de Wilde, *Security: A New Framework for Analysis* (Boulder: Lynne Rienner, 1998).

[3] Select Commission on Immigration and Refugee Policy, *US Immigration Policy and the National Interest*, staff report of April 30, 1981, p.Lii.

[4] Ibid, p. xxxiv.

[5] Ibid, p. Lii.

[6] Mark J. Miller, "Continuities and discontinuities in immigration reform in industrial democracies: The case of the Immigration Reform and Control Act of 1986" in Han Entzinger and Jack Carter, eds. *International Review of Comparative Public Policy*, volume 1, (Greenwich, CT/London: JAI Press, 1989), pp. 131-151. Also see Nancy Humel Montwieler, *The Immigration Reform Law of 1986*, (Washington, DC: The Bureau of National Affairs, 1987).

the long run. Over the short to medium term, it would significantly increase it. Philip L. Martin would later refine this insight into his theory of a migration hump.[7]

President George H. W. Bush, signed the Immigration Act of 1990 into law, which increased legal immigration into the United States by 35 percent. The new law reflected a growing conservative celebration of international migration as economically beneficial. Both of the principal contenders for the presidency in 1992 touted a North American Free Trade Agreement (NAFTA) as a way to reduce illegal migration. President George H. W. Bush, referred Mexican President Carlos Salinas' proposal for the creation of NAFTA to the National Security Council which, according to Mexican immigration specialist Jorge Bustamente, determined that international migration had created such interdependency between the United States and Mexico that any adverse development in Mexico would affect the United States. It recommended U.S. support for the Mexican initiative which dovetailed with many of the recommendations made by the CSIMCED. During the 1992 presidential campaign, the Democratic nominee criticized President Bush's policy of forcibly repatriating Haitians only to reverse his stand shortly before his inauguration.[8]

NAFTA came into effect on January 1, 1994. Later that year, a sharply contested referendum to deny public benefits, such as education to illegally resident alien children, passed by a large margin in California. Proposition 187 had been openly opposed by Mexican government officials who helped organize protests against the measure. Although implementation of the measure was determined to be unconstitutional, as it clearly clashed with the 1982 Plyler versus DOE Supreme Court decision which upheld the right of undocumented children to attend public schools in Texas, the referendum sounded a tocsin in Washington, DC.

The subsequent flurry of legislative proposals to curtail legal immigration to the United States was defeated, however. President Clinton signed into law the Illegal Immigration Reform and Responsibility act of 1996 and thereby largely defused immigration as a campaign issue in the 1996 presidential election. The far-ranging legislation reflected a hardening of views in that it mandated a massive increase in Immigration and Naturalization Service personnel as well as support for enhanced border interdiction, removal of criminal aliens and expedited abjudication of asylum cases. Very significantly, however, the 1996 law did not reflect the recommendations of yet another federal commission, the Commission on Immigration Reform, which had recommended implementation of a secure employee identification system and other measures to bolster lagging enforcement of employer sanctions. President Clinton had endorsed the Commission on Immigration Reforms recommendations, which included reduction in legal immigration.[9] President Clinton repeatedly voiced his opposition to guestworker policy and threatened to veto any measure expanding admissions of unskilled foreign workers.

While immigration issues did not centrally affect the outcome of the 1996 presidential election, they nevertheless were accorded much more significance than had been the case in elections in the 1960s or 1970s. Influential newspapers scrutinized the positions of Senator

---

7 Philip L. Martin and J. Edward Taylor, "Managing Migration: The Role of Economic Policies," in Aristide R. Zolberg and Peter M. Benda, eds., *Global Migrants, Global Refugees*, (New York/Oxford, Berghahn, 2001), pp. 95-120.

8 Eric Schmitt, "Milestones and Missteps on Immigration," *The New York Times*, October 26, 1996, p. 9.

9 Ibid, p.9.

Robert Dole and President Clinton on immigration.[10] Senator Dole supported an amendment which would have denied public education to illegal immigrant children whereas Clinton opposed the amendment. The unsuccessful candidacy of Patrick Buchanan also served to heighten awareness of the principal candidates' stances on immigration. By 2000, George W. Bush would conclude that the anti-immigration overtones of the 1996 GOP candidates had hurt the party's performance in the election.

By the 2000 election, international migration could be viewed in a strategic way. Virtually everyone acknowledged that international migration constituted a key dynamic within globalization which, in turn, was viewed as central to the advancement of U.S. foreign and security interests. (See the article by Oliver in this issue.) Moreover, more ideologically-inclined Republicans took a dim view of governmental regulation in general and found confirmation of the accuracy of their views in the flagging effort of the U.S. government to curtail illegal migration despite the vast increases in resources devoted to that task in the Clinton administrations.

Nevertheless, Republican candidate George W. Bush did not articulate a strategic or architect's vision of international migration policy in overall U.S. foreign and national security policy in the 2000 campaign. It was widely known that he had supported a Southwest Governors' endorsement of expanded admissions of temporary Mexican workers. The Republican candidate was generally not viewed as well-versed in foreign policy matters, save for his knowledge of Mexico. He had some Spanish language facility and kin of Hispanic background. Immigration policy issues, however, did not figure centrally in the 2000 race, although both candidates campaigned for Hispanic votes. Thus, if the Republican contender possessed a strategic vision of international migration in regional or world order, it was kept under wraps. In all probability, any strategic or architect's view of international migration in global and regional order came from Vincente Fox Quesada, elected President of Mexico in July 2000 who, shortly after his election, called for the creation of a North American common market that would allow freer flow of merchandise and workers.[11]

The U.S. – Mexico Migration "Honeymoon"

Perhaps the most remarkable aspect of the initial (pre-9/11) period of the Bush administration's foreign policy involved its relationship with the new Mexican government led by President Vincente Fox. The historic transfer of power in Mexico appeared to set the stage for a new approach. The former Coca Cola executive and U.S.-educated Mexican president was unabashedly pro-American and had promised to make improvement of the lot of Mexican citizens abroad a top priority. President Fox came into office in a bilateral context that had evolved significantly in recent years due in part to the patient work of a bilateral commission on border issues and a web of institutionalized meetings between U.S. and Mexican legislators and governmental counterparts that had fostered considerable mutual understanding. The North American Free Trade Agreement between the United States,

[10] See, for example, Gerald F. Seib, "Backlash Over Immigration Has Entered Mainstream This Year," *The Wall Street Journal*, September 27, 1996, p. A20.

[11] Ginger Thompson, "Victor in Mexico Plans to Overhaul Law Enforcement," *The New York Times*, July 5, 2000, p. A8.

Mexico, and Canada in 1993 profoundly altered the U.S.-Mexico relationship. Its signature bore witness to growing North American socio-economic and political interdependence. However, with one minor exception, immigration issues were pointedly excluded from NAFTA's purview because U.S. and Mexican positions on issues like illegal migration diverged to such a degree that they were deemed unbridgeable. During President Clinton's second term, nevertheless, progress had been made in easing bilateral tensions over migration issues. For instance, the United States acceded to, even welcomed, expanded Mexican consular protection of its citizens within the United States.

In the last year of President Clinton's second term, the AFL-CIO declared its support for a broad legalization or amnesty for Mexican workers and withdrew its support for enforcement of provisions of the 1986 law which made it a punishable offense for U.S. employers to hire aliens ineligible for employment under the U.S.-employer sanctions. The new Mexican administration accurately interpreted the AFL-CIO shift as signaling a possible seachange in the political environment of U.S. immigration policy. It made betterment of the status of Mexican citizens abroad through diplomatic initiatives the centerpiece of the Fox administration's foreign policy.

As expected, President Bush made his first trip abroad to Mexico where he met with President Fox at his home. In the weeks preceding the visit, there was a frenzy of talk and speculation about the possible contours of a U.S.-Mexico migration initiative. Reference was made to a European referent in negotiations over labor mobility in the context of regional integration. The Treaty of Rome of 1957, which created the European Economic Community, contained provisions for freedom of movement for employment within the then six-nation framework. It seemed that the Fox administration perceived the freedom of labor mobility provision as something for possible emulation in the context of North American regional integration. The OECD had several years earlier held a conference on migration, free trade and regional integration in North America which may have encouraged such thinking.[12] At a subsequent summit of the three heads of states of the NAFTA signatories in Ottawa, Canada, however, President Fox could only articulate a vision of greater labor mobility and deeper North American integration as long-term goals. Speculation about opening of borders and freedom of movement for employment in North America proved to be just that. The substance of U.S.-Mexico talks about immigration during the early months of the Bush administration appeared to center chiefly around proposals for expanded temporary foreign worker recruitment and the modalities of a legalization or regularization initiative. This outcome supports interpretation of President Bush's foreign policy as the product of a home builder more so than that of an architect.

Presidents Fox and Bush agreed to establish a high-level (Cabinet) bilateral working group to translate the desire for improved relations into specific policy initiatives. Shortly before the September 11, 2001 violence, President Fox toured areas of the United States and addressed a joint session of Congress. U.S.-Mexico agreement on an immigration-related initiative was announced. But the details of it were not specified. The Mexican President returned home with a face-saving promise without mutually agreed upon content. Moreover, U.S. congressional leaders made it clear that they would exercise their traditional prerogatives. In other words, the U.S. Congress would have to authorize through legislation

[12] Organization for Economic Co-operation and Development, *Migration, Free Trade and Regional Integration in North America*, (Paris: OECD, 1998).

components of a U.S.-Mexico agreement concerning U.S. immigration law. As best as can be discerned, the Bush administration appeared to offer a vague reassurance that it would endeavor to expand temporary foreign worker recruitment perhaps in conjunction with an earned legalization procedure for illegally resident Mexicans in the United States. Interpreting just what was promised or agreed to, however, is challenging because of the vagueness of public declarations. The Bush administration clearly was already backtracking on the bilateral immigration initiative even prior to 9/11. No consensus for either expanded temporary foreign worker policy or legalization emerged in the U.S. Congress or in public policy debates.

The U.S.-Mexico high-level dialogue over migration in the initial period of the George W. Bush presidency appeared quite broad ranging. Mexico unilaterally announced a legalization program for certain illegally resident aliens. And it pledged to cooperate with the United States in suppression of human trafficking. The contours of the improved bilateral cooperation seemed to include measures to prevent illegal entry from the Mexican side in return for legalization of Mexicans illegally residing in the United States and for expanded legal employment opportunities for Mexicans in the United States. Foreign Minister Casteneda made reference to a whole enchilada and, at one point, warned that all the requisite elements of a comprehensive migration initiative had to be in place for Mexico to support it.[13] The Mexican foreign minister also claimed that the bilateral talks were without historical precedent.

Assessing the Honeymoon

The events of 9/11 abruptly ended the honeymoon. By the end of the day, matters like overstaying of visas or document fraud to circumvent immigration law loomed large as they affected everyone's security. The legalization proposal had dropped off the agenda. Several days later, the Bush administration did announce that it intended to respect its commitments pertaining to the U.S.-Mexico migration initiative, but prospects for congressional support for expanded temporary foreign worker recruitment or legalization had dimmed, especially as the economic downturn and unemployment worsened.

In retrospect, several competing interpretations of the honeymoon appear plausible. If one accepts the gloss of U.S. and Mexican proponents of the initiative, it might be viewed as a radical departure in U.S. foreign policy. Migration policy became the priority and there was comprehensive discussion of how it affected U.S.-Mexico relations. Moreover, the U.S. relationship with Mexico became a top priority if not pre-eminent concern. This suggested a fundamental recasting of U.S. foreign policy by the Bush administration, an architect's vision of U.S. foreign policy.

A less generous view derives from skepticism about the Bush administration's foreign policy credentials in general. Seen in this light, the honeymoon betrayed inexperience and diplomatic naiveté. The new administration rushed pell-mell into an embrace of the Fox administration which itself harbored unrealistic expectations for radical departures in U.S. foreign policy, especially within the context of NAFTA. The lack of preparedness and unsophistication of the new U.S. administration overall provided a window of opportunity

[13] Ginger Thompson, "Mexico Takes Small Steps to Improving its US Ties", *The New York Times*, September 5, 2001, p. A6.

which was exploited by a relatively small coterie of diplomats and migration policy advocates to advance their agendas. This resulted in the creation of unrealistic expectations about prospects for a U.S.-Mexico immigration initiative that burst before, not after, the events of 9/11.

A third interpretative narrative would view the honeymoon as a regression to an earlier period in U.S.-Mexico relations. In this perspective, underneath the hoopla and symbolism of the honeymoon lay the reality of Americans and Mexicans negotiating a return to bracero policy, a recurrent feature of U.S.-Mexico relations in the twentieth century. Ever since the unilateral termination of the bracero policy by the United States in 1964, successive Mexican administrations had sought renewal of U.S. authorization for temporary Mexican employment in agriculture and other industries heavily dependent on illegally employed workers. Contrary to appearances, thus, the U.S.-Mexico migration initiative principally involved a turning back of the clock. The Fox administration might aspire to major power status and posture as an equal partner to the United States but this stance had little to do with U.S. and Mexican realities which have proven durable in the face even of skillful public relations. Hence, stripped of its embellishments, the U.S.-Mexico initiative centrally involved renegotiation of a temporary Mexican worker admissions program that would subordinate Mexico once again in a bilateral labor agreement with the economically and diplomatically dominant United States. Was there any reason to believe that the outcome of a renewed bracero policy would differ from the past?

Perhaps the most intriguing aspect of the honeymoon involved the European referent. Both the Mexican media and U.S. media began to buzz with allusions to a coming opening of borders in North America and freedom of labor mobility within the NAFTA bloc. Much of such speculation might best be described as journalistic hyperbole, but the Fox administration and its allies in the United States contemplated a recasting and deepening of NAFTA to become a regional integration framework akin to the European Union. By early February 2001, as Secretary of State Powell journeyed to Mexico to set the stage for President Bush's inaugural trip abroad to Jalisco state, the Bush administration already was pointedly distancing itself from speculation about open borders and freedom of labor mobility within NAFTA.

In fact, NAFTA differed greatly from the European regional project. While it is true that the original proposal floated by then President Salinas was referred to the U.S. National Security Council, which recommended approval on the grounds of U.S.-Mexico interdependence, NAFTA was a free trade agreement without an explicit political project. The origins of the European Union, on the other hand, involved an explicit security policy-driven commitment to the goal of European federation. Supporters of the creation of the European Coal and Steel Community, the forerunner of the European Economic Community and today's European Union, viewed regional integration as imperative to prevention of recurrence of war in Europe.

The Treaty of Rome foresaw eventual implementation of freedom of labor mobility between the signatories. However, with the partial exception of the Italian case, there has been relatively insignificant labor movement within the European regional framework. This was due to continuing barriers to freedom of labor mobility long after the coming into effect of the Treaty of Rome, the rigidities of European labor markets and the underlying socio-economic convergence of the states involved.

More to the point, the European referent speculation or vision seemed to obscure the key fact that the states involved in the European regional integration process had pointedly rebuffed Turkish and Moroccan bids for full membership. The Islamic background of Turkey and Morocco figured in this. But Europeans obviously would not agree to extension of full membership to states and societies that would likely result in large - scale emigration even after a transition period. In other words, the European referent, when construed to suggest that the NAFTA signatories could and should follow the precedent for labor mobility within European regional integration badly missed the mark. It is within the realm of possibility, however, that President Fox's call for a new vision of NAFTA at the Ottawa summit of the NAFTA signatories may still prove prophetic. Some view the integration processes generated by free trade agreements as mechanistically fostering deeper forms of integration, although this did not occur in the history of the European Free Trade Agreement and the world is littered with regional pacts that have gone bust or become moribund. Another clear difference between the North American and European situations arose from U.S. preponderance within NAFTA as compared to the European situation. The predominance of one partner country in African regional integration frameworks has contributed to a pattern of failure of such pacts in Africa.[14]

Another puzzling aspect of the honeymoon arose from the sheer complexity of the bundle of legalization and temporary foreign worker recruitment issues. A series of federal commissions studying U.S. immigration laws and policies had consistently recommended against expansion of temporary foreign worker recruitment. Nevertheless, advocacy of such policy has been persistent and support in Congress for expanded temporary foreign workers admissions had grown although partisans of such an approach often disagree on key features of such a policy. Canada's relatively small admissions program for Mexican agricultural workers was touted as fit for emulation by the United States. In fact, steadily growing numbers of temporary foreign workers, including Mexicans, have been admitted to the United States in recent years.

Advocacy of legalization or regularization policy also has been persistent. But again no consensus emerged amongst advocates as to the scope and nature of the policy. Many Republicans, such as the influential former Republican senator from Texas, Phil Gramm, vociferously oppose legalization on the grounds that it undermines the rule of law and rewards lawbreaking, but favor expanded temporary foreign worker admissions. While Senator Gramm proposed detailed legislation to expand temporary foreign worker admissions, like-minded conservatives often favor administrative transformation of currently illegally employed aliens into legally-admitted temporary foreign workers. However, with an estimated nine million illegal aliens in the United States, transforming a concept into administrative reality is a daunting matter. Would a temporary foreign worker program be available only to Mexican workers? What would be the rights of such workers? Could they qualify for eventual legal residency in the United States with full employment rights after a certain period of employment in the United States? The answers to such questions were not disclosed.

---

[14] Anderanti Andepoju, "Regional Integration, Continuity and Changing Patterns of Intra-Regional Migration in Sub-Saharan Africa," in M.A.B. Siddique, ed., *International Migration into the 21st Century*, (Cheltenham: Edward Elgar, 2001), pp. 50-73.

Advocacy of legalization similarly came in different shapes and sizes. At one end of the spectrum, the U.S. Catholic Conference and the AFL-CIO called for a quite open-ended legalization available to non-Mexicans as well. While several proposed bills before Congress envisage some form of legalization, they differ on scope of eligibility and other all important details. Moreover, the legalizations enacted under the much- decried 1986 law, the Immigration Reform and Control Act, resulted in widespread fraud, especially in the Special Agricultural Workers program. The Bush administration's problem was clear. Even if called regularization and not legalization, the narrower the scope of eligibility and the higher the standards set for eligibility, the less likely it was to address the public policy problem for which it was ostensibly designed to correct. Likewise, the greater the coverage and openendedness of such an initiative, the less likely it was to garner congressional and public support.

More puzzling still, beneath all of the diplomatic fanfare of the honeymoon period lay a domestic political calculation, perhaps constituting the best evidence of an interior decorator reality behind the Bush administration's policy. President Bush apparently viewed a migration initiative with Mexico as a way to garner more electoral support for Republicans like himself amongst Mexican-American voters and perhaps Roman Catholic voters. Similarly, President Fox's initiative towards Mexican expatriates was also calculated to result in additional votes for his National Action Party. To the extent that the honeymoon was motivated by domestic political calculations, President Bush certainly appeared to be gambling as Mexican-Americans vote heavily Democratic. It may be that he viewed the migration initiative as likely to reduce the level of Mexican- American support for Democratic candidates. President Bush also sought a greater constituency amongst Roman Catholic voters and may have viewed the U.S.-Mexico migration initiative as a means to that end even though migration policy matters do not sway Roman Catholic voters to the same extent as abortion or death penalty questions do. In sum, the domestic political calculus on the U.S. side of the honeymoon loomed large but also, at best, was highly dubious. The risk of alienating voters through a migration initiative, including loyal Republicans opposed to legalization, also ran high.

The honeymoon in U.S.-Mexico relations appeared to end in the days prior to September 11, 2001 when President Fox returned home with a promise but no deal. The sheer complexity of bilateral U.S.-Mexico migration issues mitigated against the quick deal sought by the Fox administration in particular against a backdrop of growing economic and political woes in Mexico.[15] The Fox administration staked its prestige on securing improved treatment of Mexicans in the United States and its partnership with the Bush Administration. This created enormous pressure on the Bush administration to fashion policies amenable to Mexico. But, in the end, longstanding differences on policy matters and enduring realities like the socio-economic disparities between Mexico and the United States could not be overcome. Any victory, if a U.S.-Mexico migration initiative could be termed such, was likely to prove pyrrhic over the long run. In the final analysis, a genuine referent to Europe was missing because there was no consideration on the U.S. side of a massive program of investment in Mexican infrastructure and economic assistance to reduce inequalities in Mexico that would reduce incentives for emigration.

[15] Ginger Thompson and Tim Weiner, "Great Expectations of Mexico's Leader Sapped by Reality", *The New York Times*, September 4, 2001, p. A1.

THE U.S. – MEXICO INITIATIVE AFTER SEPTEMBER 11, 2001: FROM HONEYMOON TO LIMBO

An assortment of mainly recent immigrants from the Middle East perpetrated the 1993 attack on the World Trade Center. In late 1999, the arrest of an Algerian who belonged to the Armed Islamic Group and who planned to bomb Los Angeles airport prompted a month-long state of alert. Nevertheless, despite such ominous warnings, securitization of U.S. immigration policy had not occurred prior to September 11, 2001.

The concept of securitization derives from the post-Cold War or new security literature and specifically from writings by Ole Waever and Barry Buzan.[16] Securitization refers to a perception of an existential threat to the ability of a society to maintain and reproduce itself. When this occurs, issues are viewed differently and governments reserve the right to address the threat by extraordinary means. A number of analysts have argued that European migration policies, and particularly asylum/refugee policies, were securitized in the 1990s. In the United States, the Oklahoma City bombing perpetrated by U.S. citizens and the 1993 World Trade Center bombing prompted adoption of a new counter-terrorism and effective death penalty law with significant implications for non-citizens and influenced adoption of the 1996 immigration law. But even key features of the 1996 law motivated in part by security concerns, such as the provision calling for implementation of monitoring system for foreign students studying in the United States, remained stillborn due to intense opposition to the measure.

In the wake of 9/11, however, opposition to implementation of the monitoring system for student visa holders crumbled. The Border Patrol immediately went into a heightened state of alert and much more aggressively patrolled the U.S. borders with Mexico and Canada, which caused enormous backups and considerable economic losses. Both the Canadian and Mexican governments declared their support for the Bush administration's campaign against terrorism and promised full support for bilateral efforts to prevent cross-border movements of political extremists and funding. Some analysts argued in favor of deepening NAFTA area "perimeter defense" through closer cooperation on migration and security issues. But such advocacy ran smack into a long-standing frustration in the United States with Canada's migration policies and its perceived laxity towards militants from Sri Lanka and Algeria in particular. Similarly, cascading revelations about corruption in Mexico's police and civil services did not inspire confidence in "perimeter defense" from the south. Nevertheless, heightened "harmonization" of U.S. migration policies with its neighbors to the North and South in the context of NAFTA has been discussed. The concept resembles the Schengen visa-free zone among participating members of the European Union.

The attacks of 9/11 exacted a large toll in immigrant dead. While incomparable, the economic effects of 9/11 on immigrants also were devastating. Several industries particularly dependent upon immigrant labor experienced mass layoffs. Moreover, it became increasingly difficult to cross into the United States illegally from Mexico or Canada. The heightened prospects for an economic recession made congressional support for legalization and/or temporary foreign worker policy less likely. Overnight, the discourse about U.S. migration policies shifted to prevention of recurrence of 9/11.

---

[16] Barry Buzan, Ole Waever and Jaap de Wilde, *Security: A New Framework of Analysis*, (Boulder: Lynne Reinner, 1998).

Admission of refugees to the United States slowed. U.S. visa policy came under intense scrutiny as most of the airplane hijackers possessed visas, although some had overstayed theirs. In 2000, almost 10 million aliens applied for visas and three-quarters of the applications were approved. About 1,100 consular officers at U.S. embassies and consulates around the world bear the brunt of the visa workload. Most consular officers are young and relatively inexperienced. The Congress chronically underfunds the Department of State and the extremely heavy caseload of individual consular officers has long been a concern.[17]

Most of the 31 million aliens entering the United States temporarily each year, however, do not require visas. They are citizens of 29 countries which have signed reciprocal visa waiver agreements with the United States. At least one suspect arrested in the wake of the attacks had French citizenship and thereby entered the United States visa-free.[18]

The United States also has made special arrangements for Canadian and Mexican citizens living in border areas to receive Border Crossing Cards. There are about 500 million recorded crossings each year at the U.S.-Mexico and U.S.-Canadian borders. The 1996 immigration law authorized creation of a system to track all aliens entering and leaving the United States. But, like the monitoring system for students, the measure generated intense political opposition. Compliance with the new I-94 form requirement for airlines to provide the Immigration and Naturalization Service with records of entry and exit by airline passengers has been incomplete and many aliens exiting by overland routes do not turn in the form.[19]

The work cut out for the newly created Department of Homeland Security headed by former Pennsylvania governor Tom Ridge in the visa area seems enormous. Consular officers currently have no way of knowing who overstays visas and who does not. Nearly half of the estimated 9 million illegally resident aliens in the United States are thought to have overstayed visas.[20] The National Automated Lookout System used by the INS, Customs officials and the Department of State to stymie entry of unwanted persons can be circumvented by changing names or adoption of a false identity. Moreover, access to the information stored in the system is limited.

Interior enforcement of U.S. immigration law also came under renewed scrutiny. Several of the hijackers had obtained valid drivers licenses through fraudulent means. Several states are notorious for the ease of obtaining valid driving licenses by illegally resident aliens. The driving licenses are then used, along with other false documents, to prove eligibility for employment in the United States and thereby circumvent the intent of the 1986 immigration law.[21] The events of 9/11 quickly rekindled discussions of the pros and cons of a national identity card and a more counterfeit-resistant card for resident aliens and temporary visitors. In 1986, the Congress did not adopt a recommendation by the Select Commission on Immigration and Refugee Policy to adopt a counterfeit-resistant employment eligibility document when it made employment of unauthorized aliens illegal and punishable. In so doing Congress all but invited wholesale circumvention of the 1986 law through document fraud. The Commission on Immigration Reform subsequently recommended adoption of a counterfeit-resistant employment eligibility document, but no such provision was adopted in

---

17 Philip Martin and Susan Martin, Immigration and Terrorism: Policy reform challenges, manuscript submitted to *Migration World*, pp. 3-6.

18 Ibid, p. 3

19 Ibid, p. 3

20 Martin and Martin, p. 1

21 Ibid, p. 5

the 1996 immigration law. The events of 9/11, however, seemed to alter the context or policy environment of matters like enforcement of employer sanctions. Suddenly, the germaneness of effective employer sanctions enforcement to a comprehensive response to perceived insecurity could be ascertained. However, it was also clear that whatever steps were taken could not preclude a similar disaster. There is no silver bullet solution to U.S. vulnerability.

Estimates of the Muslim population in the United States vary from two to six million.[22] Most Muslims are of immigrant background. President Bush and many other U.S. officials and local and state government officials spoke of the need to differentiate between a minority of political extremists and Muslims in general. Still, there has been some political violence targeted at foreign-looking persons, such as a Sikh apparently killed in response to 9/11. And many immigrants have reported incidents of harassment. Between seven and eight hundred individuals were detained by law enforcement officials, most of whom appeared to be of immigrant and Muslim background. And a new counter-terrorism law lengthened the time that suspects could be detained without formal charges being brought. Many of those detained were detained for violations of immigration laws.

It is conceivable that the response to 9/11 will jeopardize integration and incorporation of Muslim immigrants. Measures to curb fundraising and financing of terrorism raise important disagreements over what precisely constitutes terrorism.

More broadly, the events of 9/11 raise important questions about the relationship between immigration policies and U.S. foreign policy in general. Several years ago, the influential American Assembly called for more systematic coordination of U.S. immigration and foreign policies.[23] Whereas U.S. unilateralism characterized the initial period of the Bush administration's foreign policy, save perhaps with reference to NAFTA partners, its declared war on terrorism clearly necessitates close cooperation and harmonization of policies with states and international organizations around the world. Inevitably, a campaign against global terrorism must engage the so - called root causes of terrorism. When that happens, the migration and security nexus will come into sharp relief as will the insecurity perceived by so many around the world, inclusive, of course, of the many millions of international migrants driven by adverse circumstances to seek better lives elsewhere.

Unlike the post-1993 situation, securitization of U.S. immigration policy is occurring. This is unlikely to result in fundamental alteration of legal immigration policy. It will foster more credible enforcement of existing laws and better coordination of immigration, foreign and security policies. A principal casualty of securitization was the U.S.-Mexico migration initiative, but that foundered before September 11, 2001, perhaps for the better. The long history of temporary foreign worker policies suggests that they are not conducive to improved bilateral relations, but the contrary. Studies of past legalizations in the United States and elsewhere suggest that they do not alter underlying labor market dynamics fostering illegal migration. Indeed, such policies attract further illegal migration. Nevertheless, Democratic Congressman Richard Gephardt of Missouri would call for legalization at a 2002 meeting of Hispanics, suggesting that the U.S.-Mexico initiative could rise like the biblical Lazarus, back from the dead.

---

[22] Daniel Pipes and Khalid Durán, "Muslim Immigrants in the United States," Washington, DC: Center for Immigration Studies backgrounder series, August 2002.

[23] Michael S. Teitelbaum and Myron Weiner, eds., *Threatened Peoples, Threatened Borders*, (New York: W.W. Norton, 1995).

In: Mexico: Economic, Political and Social Issues
Editors: Maria L. Castro and Irene P. Navarro
ISBN: 978-1-60456-847-9

Chapter 5

FREE TRADE AND WOMEN IN BUSINESS: WOMEN'S ORGANIZATIONS *CAN* MAKE A DIFFERENCE

Elsie Echeverri-Carroll[1], Daniela Brandazza[2] and Cecilia Giusti[3]
[1] Bureau of Business Research, McCombs School of Business,
University of Texas at Austin
[2] Standard and Poor's, Mexico
[3] Center for Housing and Urban Development,
Texas AandM University

ABSTRACT

Our objective in this paper is to bring to the attention of businesswomen's organizations in Latin America the importance of collecting data on the increasing participation of women in the economy as entrepreneurs and managers. Why is collecting this data important? As we will discuss in this paper, there are two reasons why having this data matters. First, we anticipate that women's gains in education and the labor market should put them in a good position to benefit from business opportunities opened by free trade. However, free trade also brings challenges to women entrepreneurs. Having the data will allow us to measure the net effect of free trade on women entrepreneurs. And, because governments do not necessarily collect this data, it is important for women's organizations to do so. Second, women's organizations in Canada and the United States have already provided an example of why it is important for them to compile data that the government may not be collecting. These organizations have used data that demonstrate the impact of women in business on the economy to successfully lobby legislators to pass policies that benefit women in business. Women's organizations in Latin America can use data they collect in the same way.

INTRODUCTION

In the mid-1980s, the protectionist tendencies of countries in Latin America gave way to free trade fever. Simplification of import procedures, reduction or elimination of quotas, and the rationalization of tariff structures were the most common reforms (Rodrik 1992). With the opening of the economies came a renewed effort toward regional and subregional integration. These efforts differed from those initiated in the 1960s,[1] which paralleled protectionist policies implemented in the context of the import substitution model. As Dornbusch (1992) points out, what was new in the 1980s was the willingness to practice free trade as a two-way street. In other words, Latin American countries granted free access to their markets to companies from developed countries.

What are the benefits of free trade? *Traditional* trade theory tells us that free trade allows countries with *different* factor endowments to specialize according to their comparative advantages. The increasing specialization resulting from trade will bring about a more efficient use of resources, lower prices for the consumer, and access to a greater variety of goods. According to the traditional trade theory, one of the gains of free trade for Latin America is an increasing specialization in business activities requiring a relatively abundant resource in the region: unskilled labor. Thus, the region would tend to focus on maquiladoras or export assembly facilities that use mostly female, unskilled labor.

A clear example of the relationship between free trade and specialization in unskilled labor production is Mexico. Maquiladora output and employment growth began to accelerate markedly with the advent of NAFTA in 1994. Over the first six years after the implementation of NAFTA, maquiladora employment grew 110 percent, compared with 78 percent over the previous six years (Gruben 2001). Data published by the Mexican government indicate that the number of maquiladoras increased from 2,085 in 1994, the year NAFTA was signed, to 3,450 maquiladoras in 2001; while the number of people employed by these plants increased from 540,000 to 1.2 million during the same period (CIEMEX WEFA 2002). More importantly, women accounted for 63 percent of direct labor in Mexican maquiladoras in 2001.

If the trend toward "maquilinization" were to prevail, unskilled women would benefit from job opportunities made available by free trade fever in the Americas.[2] Starting in the 1990s, UNIFEM and other international financial institutions, perhaps anticipating this trend, adopted as an important theme the issue of how unskilled women in Latin America are affected by free trade. One important initiative of such organizations is increasing funding of women-owned micro-enterprises in Latin America.

Emerging in the 1970s, the *new* trade theory highlights other benefits of free trade usually accruing to countries with *similar* factor endowments, the so-called non-comparative advantages. Krugman (1993) identifies three types of noncomparative advantages. First, trade expands the market for firms so they can take advantage of economies of scale.[3] Second, trade creates efficiency gains because inefficient firms are forced out of the market due to

[1] Examples of these economic integration efforts include the Latin American Free Trade Area (1961), Central American Common Market (1960), Caribbean Free Trade Association (1965), and Andean Group (1969).

[2] For an extensive analysis of the effect of NAFTA on the maquiladora industry, see Echeverri-Carroll (1995).

[3] Economies of scale refers to the notion of increasing efficiencies of the production of goods as the number of goods being produced increases. Typically the average cost of producing a good will diminish as each additional good is produced, since the fixed costs are shared over an increasing number of goods.

increasing international competition. Third, trade promotes agglomeration economies[4] because firms do not need to maintain production facilities in each country to comply with government requirements to create jobs locally in order to access to the local market. In the context of free trade, firms can locate their production plants in only one partner country and export to the others. More recent empirical studies find a fourth advantage related to international trade: access to international knowledge and its positive effect on innovations (Keller 1999; Echeverri-Carroll and Somuano 2001).

The new trade theory anticipates that most benefits will accrue to certain kinds of businesses:

- Firms that can sell in a larger international market and therefore enjoy economies of scale
- Firms with the capacity to access international knowledge networks
- Firms that can locate in countries where there is already an agglomeration of similar firms so they enjoy agglomeration economies associated with access to "free" knowledge, specialized services, and specialized labor.

In this regard, it is important to examine the ways that a more open economy affects not only women-owned microenterprises but also women-owned small and medium-sized enterprises (SMEs). Why? Our assumption is that the accumulation of human capital is a necessary condition for the development of international alliances. In this regard, women owners of SMEs can more easily penetrate international markets and international knowledge networks than owners of micro-enterprises because the level of human capital (education and experience) is probably higher in the SME owners than in the micro-enterprise owners.

Some of the relevant questions in this line of analysis are: Have women-owned SMEs expanded their presence in international markets as a result of free trade? If so, have increasing contacts with international markets served as a source of knowledge about new technologies? Or have women-owned SMEs been more negatively affected by international competition than those owned by men? Have women-owned SMEs profited from alliances with foreign firms, which mushroomed after free trade agreements? Have women benefited from an increasing international pool of ideas on how to open or expand a successful small business? And finally, what are the conditions necessary to transform a woman-owned micro-enterprise to a woman-owned SME?

Free trade affects not only women who *own* businesses, but also those seeking career advancement in business. We hypothesize that increasing international competition as a result of free trade will increase the probability that firms will base promotions to management positions on employees' contribution to productivity, not on factors such as gender (or social status, cultural background, etc.). Thus, an important question is: Have women reached higher managerial positions within large private organizations as a result of more open economies? Also, has the liberalization of services, and with it the expansion of educational opportunities, provided women access to increasing specialization in fields such as technology and engineering that have traditionally been dominated by men?

---

[4] Agglomeration economies refer to the benefits that similar firms get when they locate close to each other. In particular, firms that agglomerate enjoy benefits associated with knowledge spillovers (free access to knowledge because of spatial proximity) and access to specialized services and labor.

Our objective in this paper is to bring to the attention of businesswomen's organizations in Latin America the importance of collecting data on the increasing participation of women in the economy as entrepreneurs and managers. Why is collecting this data important? As we will discuss in this paper, there are two reasons why having this data matters. First, we anticipate that women's gains in education and the labor market should put them in a good position to benefit from business opportunities opened by free trade. However, free trade also brings challenges to women entrepreneurs. Having the data will allow us to measure the net effect of free trade on women entrepreneurs. And, because governments do not necessarily collect this data, it is important for women's organizations to do so. Second, women's organizations in Canada and the United States have already provided an example of why it is important for them to compile data that the government may not be collecting. These organizations have used data that demonstrate the impact of women in business on the economy to successfully lobby legislators to pass policies that benefit women in business. Women's organizations in Latin America can use data they collect in the same way.

In her book, *Bold Women, Big Ideas*, Koplovitz (2002) describes the advances of women in business in the United States: In the early 1970s, women owned less than 5 percent of American businesses, generating less than 1 percent of total revenues. Yet, by 1998, they owned 9.1 million enterprises in the country, contributing $3.6 trillion to the GNP each year, and employing over 27.5 million people. Furthermore, she points out that along the way, women demonstrated not only that they are good at business, but also that they are better credit risks than their male counterparts. These are the kind of statistics that allowed women entrepreneurs in the United States to lobby successfully for government measures in their favor; we will expand on this topic later in the paper.

Contrary to the case of the United States and Canada, the contribution of women-owned businesses to Latin American economies is unknown. We argue here that the lack of data about the progress of women in business in Latin America and their contributions to the national economy puts them in a weak situation to negotiate with the national government. To illustrate our hypothesis, we focus on Chile and the largest countries within the NAFTA and MERCOSUR free trade areas: the United States, Canada, Mexico, Brazil, and Argentina.

In this analysis of women entrepreneurs, we exclude the microenterprise. Although there is no universal definition of microenterprises, there is some agreement as to their general characteristics in developing countries: very small scales of operation, low levels of technology, low access to credit, and a lack of managerial capacity (International Labor Organization 2001, p. 2). In this paper, however, we focus on women who have had the opportunity to invest in human capital—defined mainly by their educational level and their work experience. We do so because we think that education and professional experience are necessary prerequisites for women to play significant roles as "sustainable" managers of their own SMEs[5] or large organizations and because, as already hypothesized, we think that there is a positive correlation between human capital and taking advantage of the benefits of trade as suggested by the "new" trade theory.

[5] Loecher (2000) indicates that there are about 200 definitions for the term Small and Medium Size Enterprise (SME). The OECD (2000) defines SMEs as non-subsidiary, independent firms that employ fewer than a given number of employees; but it acknowledges that this number varies across countries.

BUSINESS WOMEN'S GAINS IN CHILE AND THE MERCOSUR AND NAFTA COUNTRIES

Women have made important advances in their participation in the labor markets in the countries in our study. The economically active population refers to the proportion of the population that is either employed or seeking employment.[6] In 2001, as shown in Table 1, women accounted for about 46 percent of the labor force (economically active population) in Canada and the United States, 35 percent in Brazil, about 34 percent in Argentina and Chile, and 33 percent in Mexico. As indicated by the absolute change in percentages between 1980 and 2001, women have been particularly active in entering the labor market in Chile and Brazil.

Table 1. Labor Force Structure, 1980-2001, Selected Countries

Country	Female percentage of economically active population		Absolute change, 1980-2001
	1980	2001	
Argentina	28	34	6
Brazil	28	35	7
Canada	40	46	6
Chile	26	34	8
Mexico	27	33	6
United States	41	46	5

Source: World Bank, *World Development Indicators* (Washington, DC: World Bank), 2003.

Table 2 shows that women achieved higher levels of education in the 1990s than they did in the 1980s. Indeed, women show high levels of participation in both undergraduate schools (International Standard Classification of Education or ISCED level 6), and in graduate schools (ISCED level 7) in all the countries in our study. They are also steadily entering traditionally male-dominated programs, such as engineering and computer sciences. In the case of Brazil, for instance, the Fundaçao Carlos Chagas[7] reports that the percentage of women engineers increased from 4.4 percent in 1980 to 6.6 percent in 1991 while the percentage of women in computer science increased from 15.6 to 25.3 percent during the same period.

One would expect that a more competitive economy associated with free trade and significant investments in human capital (i.e., higher levels of education and experience through an increasing participation in the labor market) in the female population would have opened new opportunities for women to reach the upper management levels within companies. Data for the United States show, for instance, that two-thirds of women managers have graduate degrees. Indeed, we found evidence that more women are reaching top

[6] Outside the labor market are homemakers, retirees, the chronically ill, and others who are not seeking employment.

[7] The Carlos Chagas Foundation is a nonprofit organization located in São Paulo dedicated to collecting data on women in Brazil.

management positions in all the countries in our study. Nevertheless, a large gap remains between industrialized and developing countries in terms of gains made by women.

Table 2. Percentage of Female Graduates in Each ISCED Level, 1980s and 1990s

Country	ISCED 6 (Undergraduate School)		ISCED 7 (Graduate School)	
	1980s	1990s	1980s	1990s
United States	50.7 (1985)	54.6 (1995)	45.3 (1985)	51.7 (1995)
Canada	52.9 (1984)	57.9 (1996)	40.6 (1984)	47.6 (1996)
Mexico	—	51.2 (1997)	—	40.3 (1997)
Chile	51.1 (1984)	52.7 (1997)	42.2 (1984)	39.4 (1997)
Brazil	60.2 (1984)	54.6* (1994)	43.6 (1984)	—
Argentina	—	—	—	—

Source: UNESCO, *Statistical Yearbook* (Paris: UNESCO), 1987 and 1999.
* Percentage of female students *enrolled* (not graduates).

Since 1995, the United Nations has been developing the Gender Empowerment Measure (GEM). This index gauges the progress of women in both politics and business. The GEM rankings presented in Table 3 show that Canada and the United States ranked 4th and 10th, respectively, in 2001; the other countries in our sample fared comparatively worse. Excluding Argentina, for which data are not available, Brazil, at number 70 in 1997, ranks the lowest among our selected countries. Moreover, it is the only country in our study that shows deterioration in the index, dropping from 68th to 70th between 1995 and 1997. Mexico showed no gain between 1995 and 2001, ranking 37th both years. Chile improved from 61st to 49th during that period.

As noted, the GEM is an indicator of women's advances in both business and politics. Another proxy to measure the advances of women in business is the percentage of female administrators, legislators, and managers, also published by the United Nations. As Table 3 illustrates, women in Canada and the United States represented more than 40 percent of administrators, legislators, and managers in 2001, while about 20 percent of these occupations were held by women the Latin American countries in our study (with the exception of Brazil, which showed a precipitous drop between 1995 and 1997).

Despite the favorable relative position that the United States shows in the UN's indices, women still have a long way to go in this country.[8] According to Catalyst,[9] women account for only 5 percent of the senior management positions in Fortune 500 companies. Moreover, only five women are CEOs of Fortune 500 companies: Carly Fiorina (Hewlett Packard), Andrea Jung (Avon Products), Anne Mulcahy (Xerox), Marion Sandler (Golden West Financial Corporation), and Cinda Hallman (Spherion Corporation). At the same time,

[8] For an interesting discussion of women in management around the world, see Nancy Adler (1994).
[9] Catalyst is a nonprofit research organization working to advance women in business.

although the Latin American countries in our study rank relatively low according to the UN indices, some women in those countries have attained important management positions in the private sector. For example, Maria Silvia Bastos Marques, who has a Ph.D. in economics, worked in several important positions in the Brazilian government, including director of the Banco Nacional de Desenvolvimento Econômico, before becoming the CEO of Companhia Siderúrgica Nacional in Rio de Janeiro, the largest integrated steel-making complex in Latin America. In Mexico, Yvonne Sánchez-Navarro is vice president and plant manager of SCI Systems, a multibillion dollar electronics manufacturing company located in Guadalajara.

Table 3. Gender Empowerment Measures (GEM[1/]), Selected Countries, 1995-2001

Country	GEM rank		Percentage of female managers legislators, senior officials[2]	
	1995	2001	1995	2001
Canada	7	4	42.2	42.2
United States	11	10	42.7	44.3
Chile	61	49	20.1	18.5
Mexico	37	37	19.8	19.8
Brazil	68	70[3]	17.3	7.3[3/]
Argentina	N/A	N/A	N/A	N/A

Source: United Nations, *Human Development Report* (New York: Oxford University Press), 1998, 1999, 2001.

[1] GEM measures the use of women's capabilities.

[2] Data refer to the latest year available during the period 1994-1999.

[3] Data for Brazil are for 1997.

N/A = not available.

The stories of successful businesswomen in Latin America have rarely been told, with the exception of books by Heller (1996) and Arango et al. (1995). We believe there are several reasons that some women in Latin America have been able to reach important management positions: a large pool of cheap labor, little geographic mobility, and strong family ties have allowed women in Latin America to balance work and family more easily than their counterparts in more industrialized countries.

Large investments in human capital through education and experience have also prepared women to become business owners. Data on female entrepreneurs are relatively abundant in Canada and the United States.[10] For instance, the Center for Women's Business Research reports that in the United States in 2003, there were 10.1 million privately-held, 50-percent-or-more women-owned businesses, employing 18.2 million people and generating nearly $2.3 trillion in sales.[11] The Center also reports that growth continues to be a major component of the picture of women-owned businesses. Between 1997 and 2002, the number of privately-held, 50-percent-or-more women-owned firms grew by 11 percent, more than 1.5 times the rate of all privately-held firms (6 percent) and employment increased by 18 percent, more than twice the average (8 percent). Why are women-owned businesses growing so fast in the

[10] For a discussion of barriers and opportunities for women entrepreneurs in the United States, see Moore (2000).

[11] Center for Women's Research. Research Summary: "Nearly Half of Privately Held U.S. Businesses are Women-Owned." Release date: May 6, 2003. http://www.nfwbo.org.

United States? Catalyst lists two main reasons for this development: first, women want to pursue an entrepreneurial idea, and second, frustration or dissatisfaction with previous work experience (e.g., the glass ceiling) propels women to start their own businesses.

We do not know how many small enterprises are owned by women in Latin America. The National Association of Women Business Owners has conducted studies for Mexico and Argentina that lend some insight into the characteristics of women-owned businesses in these countries. However, these studies do not present any evidence of the relative importance of these businesses to the national economy. In this regard, the Inter-American Development Bank or IADB (2001, p. 3) notes: "Although much has been written about women's economic activity and entrepreneurship in Latin America and the Caribbean, there are few statistics that quantify the economic contributions of women."

Women's Business Organizations Can Make a Difference

To measure the economic contribution of businesswomen, we need to know the answers to these questions: How many SMEs in Brazil, Argentina, Mexico, and Chile do women own? Women-owned SMEs account for what proportion of total employment in these countries? How many women are occupying senior management positions in these countries? What proportion of graduate and undergraduate degrees in engineering and computer science are earned by women? Unfortunately, it is not possible at the moment to find answers to these questions.

Who is responsible for collecting data that gauge the advances of women in entrepreneurial activity or in managerial positions? The logical answer would be the national government. However, even in a wealthy country such as the United States, many of the most current statistics about businesswomen are collected and disseminated by women's organizations, not the government. Catalyst is responsible for many studies about the progress of women to senior management positions and to boards of directors. The National Association of Women Business Owners (NAWBO) and its research branch, the National Foundation for Women Business Owners (NFWBO), are responsible for compiling data on women-owned firms. These data have been instrumental in fostering an appreciation for women business owners among U.S. policymakers. NAWBO's most impressive advocacy feat is the passage of HR 5050, *The Women's Business Ownership Act of 1988*. This legislation created the Office of Women's Business Ownership within the Small Business Administration and the National Women's Business Council.[12] NAWBO also advocated for President Clinton's Executive Order, signed in 2000, calling for federal agencies to meet a 5 percent goal for procurement of goods and services from women-owned businesses. More importantly, it has not only been successful in advocating for new policy measures in favor of women-owned businesses, but also in following the success of these policies. For instance, in 1998, it conducted a study and found that only 22 percent of women-owned firms had landed

[12] The National Women's Business Council, a bipartisan federal government advisory panel, was created to serve as an independent source of advice and counsel to the president, Congress, and the Interagency Committee on Women's Business Enterprise, its public sector counterpart on economic issues of importance to women business owners.

subcontracts from government agencies or large corporations, compared to 31 percent of firms owned by men.

During the 1990s, the federal governments in all the Latin American countries in our study created important organizations within the national government structure to focus on women's issues. Examples include the Servicio Nacional de la Mujer (SERNAM) in Chile, the Consejo Nacional de la Mujer in Argentina, the Coordinación General del Programa Nacional de la Mujer in Mexico, and the Conselho Nacional dos Direitos da Mulher in Brazil. However, these governmental institutions have not been involved in collecting statistics to produce data on the impact of women in business on the economy. Rather, most of the public policy initiatives of these institutions are directed toward unskilled women. For instance, some policies focus on helping these women open their own microenterprises. Moreover, although there are important programs dedicated to the promotion of small- and medium-sized enterprises in Latin America, there is little recognition that women-owned businesses confront different economic and social conditions within this sector.

We suggest that women's organizations in Latin America should follow the example of their counterparts in industrialized countries and gather data that is not being collected by the government. The do-it-yourself spirit that animates women entrepreneurs to start their own businesses can be put to use in this endeavor. Rather than waiting for the government to collect this kind of data, women's organizations can take on that responsibility because it is in their interest to do so. As discussed above, the case of the U.S. provides evidence of the benefits that can accrue to both women in business and to the national economy when women's organizations take on the task of collecting data, a task usually performed by the government.

Women's business organizations serve very different functions in Canada and the United States than in Argentina, Brazil, Chile, and Mexico. In particular, Canadian and U.S. women's business organizations emphasize both networking and policy advocacy, while businesswomen's organizations in the Latin American countries mainly stress networking. The IADB (2001, p. 46) highlights two women's business organizations in Latin America because they are international in their focus and because they are comprised of women in small, medium, and larger enterprises rather than microenterprises: Federación Interamericana Empresarial (FIE) and Mujeres, Oportunidades, y Negocios. These organizations excel in providing online information to women on how to start or expand a business. They do not, however, provide data on the number of women-owned SMEs or the number of women in senior management positions. Women's business organizations can advocate to international institutions and the national government to consider the needs of skilled businesswomen, along with the needs of unskilled women. But, to be successful in this task, they need data. We suggest that women's organizations, working jointly with private companies, should take the first step in collecting these statistics.

CONCLUSIONS

Throughout this paper, we have highlighted that women in the Americas have made significant investments in human capital through education (i.e., earning more university degrees) and experience (i.e., participating more in the labor market) in both developed and developing countries. Gains in human capital investments have prepared women to play an increasingly important role as senior managers and SME owners in all the countries in our study. These advances are supported with data in countries such as the United States and Canada. In Chile, Brazil, Argentina, and Mexico, however, our knowledge on the advances of businesswomen is limited to information about individual cases, while data on their contribution to the national economies are not yet available.

Although women's business organizations in Chile, Brazil, Argentina, and Mexico have been successful in transferring information on how to create and expand new businesses among their members (especially online), they have been slow in collecting data on women in business. Their lack of data to confirm the important contribution of businesswomen to the economy has limited their ability to advocate effectively for policy measures directed toward this group.

Studying the impact of women in business on the economy is important for policymaking, but studying the impact of economic changes—in particular, the impact of free trade on women in business—is also important for economic growth. We expect that economic integration (exemplified by regional trade agreements) is opening opportunities as well as challenges, not only for unskilled women but also for women with skills and professional work experience who own SMEs or are managers. As we indicate in the beginning of this article, international financial institutions and national organizations, many funded by those financial institutions, have been actively studying the consequences of free trade on unskilled women, but there is little effort to understand the consequences on educated women with professional experience. We claim in this paper that women-owned SMEs and managers are crucial for developing a country's competitive advantage. Indeed, IADB (2001) finds a positive and significant relationship between women's participation in business ownership and GDP growth. But until we can get more data, we will have more questions than answers.

Acknowledgments

This article presents preliminary findings from ongoing research supported by the Bureau of Business Research of the McCombs School of Business and the Hewlett Foundation through the LBJ Center for Inter-American Policy Studies, both at the University of Texas at Austin. We are grateful for this support. We would like to thank Andrea Macera, a graduate student at the Getúlio Vargas Foundation and the LBJ School, for outstanding research assistance, and our colleagues Julia Apodaca and Bruce Kellison for their helpful comments and suggestions.

References

Adler, N.J. and Izraeli, D.N. 1994. *Competitive Frontiers: Women Managers in a Global Economy*. Cambridge: Blackwell.

Arango, L.G., Viveros, M., and Bernal, R. 1995. *Mujeres Ejecutivas: Dilemas Comunes, Alternativas Individuales*. Bogotá: Ediciones Uniandes.

Dornbusch, R. 1992. "The Limit of Trade Policy Reforms in Developing Countries." *Journal of Economic Perspective* 6: 69-85.

Echeverri-Carroll, E.L. 1995. "Flexible Production and the North American Free Trade Agreement: The Impact on U.S. and Japanese Maquiladoras." In Echeverri-Carroll E.L. (Ed.), *NAFTA and Trade Liberalization in the Americas*. Austin, Texas: Bureau of Business Research and IC^2 Institute.

Echeverri-Carroll, E.L. and Somuano, A. 2001. "Do Innovations Lead to Exports? The Special Case of High-Technology Firms." *Southwestern Journal of Economics* 4: 192-216.

Furchtgott-Rott, D. and Stolba, C. 1999. *Women's Figures--An Illustrated Guide to Economic Progress of Women in America*. Washington, D.C.: AEI Press.

Heller, L. 1996. *Porque Llegan las que Llegan*. Buenos Aires: Feminaria Editora.

Inter-American Development Bank (IADB) and National Association of Women Business Owners (NAWBO). 2001. *Women's Entrepreneurship in Latin America: An Exploration of Current Knowledge*. Washington, D.C.: IADB and NAWBO.

International Labor Organization. 2001. *Gender Issues in Micro-Enterprise Development.* http:www.ilo.org/public/English/bureau/gender/business/ent/index.htm.

Keller, W. 1999. Trade and the Transmission of Technology. Austin: University of Texas at Austin and National Bureau of Economic Research.

Koplovitz, K. 2002. *Bold Women, Big Ideas—Learning to Play the High Risk Entrepreneurial Game*. New York: PublicAffairs.

Krugman, P.R. 1993. "The Narrow and Broad Arguments for Free Trade." *American Economic Review* 83: 367-371.

Loecher, U. 2000. "Small and Medium-Sized-Enterprises—Delimitation and the European Definition in the Area of Industrial Business." *European Business Review* 12, 5: 261-264.

Moore, D.P. 2000. *Career preneurs*. Palo Alto, California: Davies-Black Publisher.

Organization for Economic Cooperation and Development (OECD). 2000. *OECD Small and Medium Enterprise Outlook*. Paris : OECD.

Rodrik, D. 1992. "The Limit of Trade Policy Reforms in Developing Countries." *Journal of Economic Perspective* 6: 87-105.

In: Mexico: Economic, Political and Social Issues
Editors: Maria L. Castro and Irene P. Navarro
ISBN: 978-1-60456-847-9

Chapter 6

WOMEN ENTREPRENEURS IN THE AMERICAS

Elsie Echeverri- Carroll*
McCombs School of Business, University of Texas at Austin USA
Daniela Brandazza
Standards and Poor's, Mexico, City, Mexico

ABSTRACT

Defining "entrepreneurs" as workers who declare their professional status to be that of employers or own-account workers (self-employed without full-time, paid employees), the Organization for Economic Co-operation and Development (OECD, 2000) reports that the share of women entrepreneurs as a percentage of all entrepreneurs increased from 29.7 percent in 1980 to 35.2 percent in 1990 in the United States and from 30.8 percent to 37.1 percent in Canada during the same period. The U.S. Economic Census defines "women-owned businesses" as privately held firms in which women own 51 percent or more of the enterprise. According to the most recent economic census data (1997), the number of women-owned firms increased 16 percent from 1992 to 1997. This is almost triple the rate of growth (6 percent) for all U.S. firms during this period. Estimates from the Center for Women's Business Research (1997) show the increase in women-owned businesses holding at 14 percent between 1997 and 2002.

Furthermore, this growth is consistent across all ethnic groups in the United States. This trend, however, is not necessarily well noted. As Robles (2002) has pointed out, "we are bereft of comprehensive knowledge and information about the U.S. minority enterprise population."

These statistics indicate noteworthy increases in the numbers of U.S. and Canadian women entrepreneurs. What factors have contributed to this growth? And do these factors also translate into success for their colleagues in Latin America? How does the experience of women entrepreneurs in Latin America compare to that of their counterparts to the north? What are the relative advantages and disadvantages of entrepreneurship in the emerging economies of Latin America?

* Phone: (512) 475-7811; Email: e.carroll@mail.utexas.edu.

Women-owned Firms Compared to All U.S. Firms, 1992 and 1997

Source: 1997 Economic Census, U.S. Bureau of the Census

THE ELEMENTS OF ENTREPRENEURSHIP

As the OECD (2000, p.10) points out, "appropriate education and adult training (experience) are key to fostering widespread entrepreneurial spirit." The Center for Women's Business Research (1997) reported that approximately 75 percent of U.S. women entrepreneurs earned a college degree. And, using a representative sample from 10 industrialized countries (including the United States and Canada), Reynolds et al. (1999) found a positive correlation of 0.78 and 0.61 between college education and business star-ups in 1980 and 1995. While higher education certainly fosters entrepreneurial activity, college education in the hard sciences seems to be a prerequisite for developing high-tech firms, which rely on skilled, highly innovative labor. Hight-tech start-up statistics reveal the scarcity of women entrepreneurs in this area. The March 15, 2000, issue of *Internet World Magazine* (2000) notes that of the 129 new chief executive officers named to U.S. Internet companies in 2000, only eight were women, and of 49 new chief technology officer positions filled in that same year, none were women. Such dismal numbers have caused U.S. policymakers to cite as an urgent national priority the increase in numbers of female graduates in technical fields, such as engineering and computer science.

To improve their chances to succeed as entrepreneurs, women need not only the knowledge and skills acquired through a college degree, but also the experience gained in the labor market. Many self-employed women obtain this experience in corporations, where they learn the various skills necessary to run their own businesses effectively. In particular, they develop—usually over the course of a ten- to twelve-year corporate tenure—managerial, financial, marketing, technical, and planning skills before leaving to form their own companies (Cooper and Dunkelberg 1987; Moore 2000; Moore and Buttner 1997). At the same time, women often tend to be pushed into entrepreneurship by negative aspects of the corporate working environment, such as the limitations of the "glass ceiling," discrimination, and inflexible schedules (Catalyst 1998).

Estimated Number of Minority Women-Owned Businesses in the United States, 2002

Minority	Number of firms	Percentage increase, 1997-2002
Hispanic	470,344	39.3
African-American	365,110	16.7
Asian/Pacific Islander	358,503	44.6
Native American/ Alaska native	77,483	44.6

Source: Center for Women's Business Research (based on U.S. Bureau of Census data), http: //www.nfwbo.org

In addition to these gains in human capital investments (i.e., increasing levels of education and work experience), what other variables lead to increased participation by women in entrepreneurial activities? Research shows that in the United States greater relative earnings potential in self-employment and a greater demand for time flexibility prompt women to choose entrepreneurship (Lombard 2001). Self-determined work schedules allow for better balance between professional and family responsibilities. Stadies for the United States reveal that a self-employed woman is more likely to be married and that her spouse will also be self-employed and have health insurance that covers the family (Devine 1994; Georgellis and Howard 2000). Never-married women in the United States accounted for only 7.3 percent of all self-employed females through the 1975-1990 period; married women (with spouse present), 75 percent during the same period (Devine 1994).

Women Entrepreneurs in the Emerging Economies of Latin America

Statistics on female entrepreneurs in Latin American countries are scant. The most reliable information can be found in a series of surveys conducted by the U.S. National Association of Women Business Owners and IBM for Argentina and Mexico and by SEBRAE, a Brazilian organization dedicated to the promotion of entrepreneurship in Brazil, for Sao Paulo. Although these surveys represent the first attempt to describe the economic and demographic characteristics of women business owners in these countries, they are not a representative sample. As OECD (2000, p.3) points out, "women entrepreneurship suffers from a lack of statistical information and research, thus limiting analysis and leading to the use of a priori estimates and hypotheses."

The exception here is Mexico, one of the few Latin American countries supplying data on women-owned businesses. Data from the OECD (2000) reveal that women-owned enterprises accounted for 16 percent of all enterprises in Mexico in 1990. This is approximately half the percentages reported for the United States (36 percent) in 1996 and Canada (30 percent) in 1994.

The research that does exist indicates that women in Latin America lag behind their U.S. and Canadian counterparts in several areas. For example, the gap in the share of female college matriculations remains significant between the United States and Canada and the largest Latin American countries. Data from UNESCO (cited by Echeverri-Carroll et al 2001) show that, on average, half of all U.S. and Canadian college graduates in the 1990s were females, while Chile and Mexico listed an average of approximately 40 percent (data for Argentina and Brazil are not available). A similar gap appears in the numbers for women's participation in the labor market. The World Bank reports that in 1998, women accounted, on average, for 45 percent of the labor force (economic active population) in the United States and Canada, but for only 33 percent, on average, in Argentina, Brazil, Chile, and Mexico (cited in Echeverri-Carroll et al 2001).

Given the relatively low incorporation of human capital (in both education and labor force experience), one would expect to find a relatively smaller number of Latin American women in entrepreneurial activities. Do Latin American women in fact experience unique disadvantages that negatively affect the rate of entrepreneurship? We suggest that they experience both advantages and disadvantages in comparison to their counterparts in the United States and Canada.

Relative Advantages

Employing outside services for domestic help and childcare lists as the top strategy adopted by U.S. and Canadian professional women to balance career and home duties (Catalyst 1998). Indeed, approximately 85 percent of professional women in both countries reported employing outside services. Certainly the abundance of cheap labor in Latin America makes this a viable strategy for professional women in that region as well. In addition, the close ties among family members and the proximity of extended family ensure help, especially with childcare, for many Latin American women working outside the home. The very high urban concentration that characterizes Latin American countries can also prove an advantage for Latinas, who tend to have little geographical mobility in their job searches and therefore usually remain in the same area as their extended families. Henderson (2001), for instance, reports that among a group of 72 countries, Chile and Argentina were in the list of countries with *highly excessive* urban concentration in 1990.

Relative Disadvantages

As in most societies, Latin American sociopolitical structures are marked by the separation of male and female roles. The public sphere is considered the domain of men, while women manage the organization of the home and the care of children (Craske 1999). However, the volatility of the Latin American economies in the 1980s and 1990s may have shaken such fixed notions regarding “women’s work,” as more women have been pushed into the labor market to compensate for the loss of purchasing power within the household.

However, a larger number of women in the workforce has not translated into an increase in the numbers of women entrepreneurs in Latin America. Why? The main reason may be the low level of entrepreneurial activity in general in Latin American countries. In a recent survey, researchers at Babson College estimated the rate of new business creation in ten industrialized countries, using a representative sample of 1,000 adults (Reynolds et al 1999). The results suggested significant differences among countries in new firm start-ups. When disaggregated by gender, the data show relatively similar start-up participation rates for men and women in the United States and Canada, countries with high levels of entrepreneurial activity. On the other hand, the start-up participation rates for women and men are highly disparate in countries showing low levels of entrepreneurial activity.

Finally, as noted, the lack of statistical information and research about women entrepreneurs in Latin America hinders their effectiveness with policymakers in the implementation of government procurement laws or policies that promote women business owners.

CONCLUSIONS

Relatively speaking, Latin American women face more obstacles in the pursuit of entrepreneurship than do women in the United States and Canada, and they enjoy fewer advantages than their counterparts to the north. However, we know little about the importance for Latin America women of factors that have proven important to the success of women entrepreneurs in the United States. For instance, is it also the case that the husbands of Latin American entrepreneurs tend to be self-employed? Do their husbands play a significant role as mentors or as support in providing the health insurance that many female small business owners cannot afford? Is it the case that Latin American professional women can more easily balance the demands of home and workplace because of the large supply of cheap labor in that region? We propose here that identifying and measuring the relative importance of these factors is the first step to promoting women entrepreneurship in the region.

ACKNOWLEDGEMENTS

We appreciate the support of the Hewlett Foundation through the Center for Inter-American Policy Studies at the LBJ School of Public Affairs and the Bureau of Business Research, both at the University of Texas at Austin.

REFERENCES

Catalyst, Closing the Gap: Women's Advancement in Corporate and Professional Canada, New York, 1998.

Center for Women's Business Research, "Fact of the Week, June 16, 1997," and "Number of Minority Women-Owned Businesses Expected to Reach 1.2 Million in 2002," http://www.nfwbo.org, 1997 and 2001.

Echeverri-Carroll E.L., D. Brandazza, and C. Giusti, "El Libre Comercio y las Mujeres en las Esfereas de Negocios en America," *InfoPyme* 4:1-4, 2001.

Organization for Economic Co-operation and Development, *Women Entrepreneurs in SMEs: Realizing the Benefits of Globalization and the Knowledge-based Economy*, Paris, 2000.

Reynolds, P.D., M. Hay, M.S. Camp, *Global Entrepreneurship Monitor*---1999 Executive Report, Kauffman Center for Entrepreneurial Leadership, London Business School, 1999.

Robles, B., "Latina Entrepreneurial Activity in the 1990s: Lessons for the 21st Century," Reflexiones, 2002.

In: Mexico: Economic, Political and Social Issues
Editors: Maria L. Castro and Irene P. Navarro

ISBN: 978-1-60456-847-9

Chapter 7

MODELING ASYMMETRIC CONSUMER BEHAVIOR AND DEMAND EQUATIONS FOR BRIDGING GAPS IN RETAILING[†]

Rajagopal*

Department of Marketing, Business Division,
Monterrey Institute of Technology and Higher Education, ITESM
Mexico City Campus, Tlalpan, Mexico

INTRODUCTION

In growing competitive markets the large and reputed firms are developing strategies to move into the provision of innovative combinations of products and services as 'high-value integrated solutions' tailored to each customer's needs than simply 'moving downstream' into services. Such firms are developing innovative combinations of service capabilities such as operations, business consultancy and finance required to provide complete solutions to each customer's needs in order to augment the customer value towards the innovative or new products. It has been argued that provision of integrated solutions is attracting firms traditionally based in manufacturing and services to occupy a new base in the value stream centered on 'systems integration' using internal or external sources of product designing, supply and customer focused promotion (Davies,2004). Besides organizational perspectives of enhancing customer value, the functional variables like pricing play a significant role in developing the customer perceptions towards new products.

Consumers plan to spread consumption of their total resources evenly over the remainder of their life span at a given time. Such consumption smoothing occurs though current demand

[†] Author expresses his gratitude to the anonymous referees for their valuable suggestion to improve the paper. Author also acknowledges the support provided by Amritanshu Rajagopal, student of Industrial and Systems Engineering of ITESM, Mexico City Campus in data collection, translation of questionnaires in Spanish language, computing the data, developing Tables and figures in this study.

* PhD (India) FRSA (London), Professor, Department of Marketing, Business Division, Monterrey Institute of Technology and Higher Education, ITESM, Mexico City Campus, 222, Calle del Puente, Tlalpan, Mexico DF 14380. E-mail: *rajagopal@itesm.mx*. Home page: *http://www.geocities.com/prof_rajagopal/homepage.html*

for the products and services and buying power may fluctuate over time. Thus, borrowing allows consumers with lower initial assets but higher expected future income to make utility-maximizing consumption choices within the overall, lifetime budget constraint. On the contrary, consumers may not be very capable of taking lifetime budget constraints into account when making repeated consumption choices that are distributed over time and are influenced by the self reference criterion (see Herrnstein and Prelec, 1992). It has been observed in previous studies that value to expenditure ratios increase consumer sensitivity in volume of buying and driving repeat buying decisions for the regular and high-tech products (Carroll and Dunn 1997). Consumers often have enough insight towards limiting their choices by employing self-rationing strategies. Consumers may show suboptimal behavior while adapting to the self-rationing strategies to limit their choice which may induce asymmetric consumer behavior in the long run (Loewenstein, 1996).

This paper attempts to discuss the interdependence of variability in consumer behavior due to intrinsic and extrinsic retail environment which influence the process of determining the choices on products and services. It is argued in the paper that suboptimal choice of consumers affect the demand of the products and services in the long-run and the cause and effect has been explained through the single non-linear equations. A system of demand equations which explains the process of optimization of consumer choice and behavioral adjustment towards gaining a long-term association with the market has also been discussed in the paper.

Related Contributions

Customer Value and Choice Probabilities

The prospect theory developed by Tversky and Kahnman (1981) towards framing decisions and understanding the dynamics of choices of consumers reveals that the consumers exercise options in consuming products to optimize their satisfaction and ultimate value. Value measurements have been used as one of the principal tools to assess the trend of consumer behavior for non-conventional products. Value syndrome influences the individual and group decisions in retail and bulk deals, and conditionalizes the decision process of consumers. Conditional consumption behavior suggests that consumption depends heavily on the utility function and on the source of uncertainty (Carroll and Kimball, 1996 and Deaton 1992). Repeat buying behavior of customers is largely determined by the values acquired on the product. The attributes, awareness, trial, availability and repeat (AATAR) factors influence the customers towards making re-buying decisions in reference to the marketing strategies of the firm. Decision of customers on repeat buying is also affected by the level of satisfaction derived on the products and number of customers attracted towards buying the same product, as a behavioral determinant (Rajagopal, 2005). A study using market-level data for the yogurt category developed an econometric model derived from a game-theoretic perspective explicitly considers firms' use of product-line length as a competitive tool (Dragnska and Jain, 2005). On demand side, the study analytically establishes link between customer choice and the length of the product line and includes a measure of line length in the utility function to investigate customer preference for variety using a brand-level discrete-choice model. The study reveals that supply side is characterized by price and line length competition between oligopolistic firms.

Each successive purchase decision is relatively unimportant to an individual consumer, which may be derived from the economic and relational variables associated with the product or services. The formal model of price competition analyzed here is derived from that of Chintagunta and Rao (1996), who similarly consider a dynamic duopoly with adaptive consumers. Besides price, brand and quality are other variables which drive consumers' perceptions on choice mapping and repeat consumption. Bergemann and Välikmäki (1996) examine the effect of strategic pricing on the rate of information acquisition by a buyer which reveals that optimal learning allows consumers to analyze their choice pattern. Erev and Haruvy (2001) also consider the implications of adaptive learning by consumers but again firms have fixed pricing policies. Recent theoretical explanations for sustained dominance include network effects, increasing returns to scale and learning by doing. There is now considerable evidence to explain consumer choice behavior such as in retail buying the choices are determined by an exogenous random process (Erev and Roth, 1998; Camerer and Ho, 1999; Erev and Barron, 2001). Consumer as a decision maker is endowed with propensities and values for each choice that is made. There are some critical issues associated to the price sensitive consumer behavior, whether customers are equally price-sensitive while purchasing products for functional (e.g. purchasing frozen vegetables, toiletries or paper towels) versus hedonic (e.g. purchasing a high technology computer or a video camera) consumption situations and whether perceived value derived during consuming the product influences price sensitivity. It may also be stated that higher price volatility makes consumers more sensitive to gains and less sensitive to losses, while intense price promotion by competing brands makes consumers more sensitive to losses but does not influence consumers' sensitivity to gains (Han et.al, 2001).

Behavioral Asymmetry and Customer Choice

Value of a customer may be defined in reference to a firm as the expected performance measures are based on key assumptions concerning retention rate and profit margin and the customer value also tracks market value of these firms over time. Value of all customers is determined by the acquisition rate and cost of acquiring new customers (Guptaet al, 2003). A long standing approach to examining how consumers react to price and income changes estimates a set of demand equations for the main commodities and bases deductions on coefficient values. At its simplest, economic demand theory assumes that consumers choose to allocate their limited spending power to purchases of goods to maximize their own satisfaction. This assumption of rational economic behavior imposes substantial constraints (aggregation, homogeneity, symmetry and negativity) on the specification of a system of equations. Consumer behavior is largely driven by tangible and intangible factors which include product attributes, pricing, willingness to pay (disposable income), product attractiveness and related variables. Value and pricing models have been developed for many different products, services and assets. Some of them are extensions and refinements of conventional models on value driven pricing theories (Gamrowski & Rachev, 1999; Pedersen, 2000). There have been some other models developed and calibrated addressing specific issues such as model for household assets demand (Perraudin & Sorensen, 2000).

Key marketing variables such as price, brand name, and product attributes affect customers' judgment processes and derive inference on its quality dimensions leading to customer satisfaction. The experimental study conducted indicates that customers use price and brand name differently to judge the quality dimensions and measure the degree of satisfaction (Brucks et.al., 2000). Most importantly, these are expected to raise their spending and association with the products and services of the company with increasing levels of satisfactions that attribute, to values of customers (Reichheld and Sasser, 1990). However, it has been observed that low perceived use value; comparative advantages over physical attributes and economic gains of the product make significant impact on determining customer value for the relatively new products.

Motivational forces are commonly accepted to have a key influencing role in the explanation of shopping behavior. Personal shopping motives, values and perceived shopping alternatives are often considered independent inputs into a choice model, it is argued that shopping motives influence the perception of retail store attributes as well as the attitude towards retail stores (Morschett et.al, 2005). In retail self-service store where consumer exercises in-store brand options, both service and merchandise quality exert significant influence on store performance, measured by sales growth and customer growth, and their impact is mediated by customer satisfaction. Liberal environment of self-service stores for merchandise decisions, service quality and learning about competitive brands are the major attributes of retail self-service stores (Babakus et.al, 2004). Retail self-service stores offer an environment of three distinct dimensions of emotions e.g. pleasantness, arousal and dominance. Customer value gap may be defined as the negative driver, which lowers the returns on the aggregate customer value. This is an important variable, which needs to be carefully examined by a firm and measure its impact on the profitability of the firm in reference to spatial (coverage of the market) and temporal (over time) market dimension (Marjolein and Verspagen, 1999).

Organizational Influences on Customer Values

Another study explores qualitatively the understanding of the importance of intangibles as performance drivers in reference to Swedish organizations using a combination of evolutionary theory, knowledge-based theory and organizational learning. The study reveals that customer values are created towards new products through individual perceptions, and organizational and relational competence (Johanson et.al., 2001). The firms need to ascertain a continuous organizational learning process with respect to value creation chain and measure performance of the new products introduced in the market. In growing competitive markets the large and reputed firms are developing strategies to move into the provision of innovative combinations of products and services as 'high-value integrated solutions' tailored to each customer's needs than simply 'moving downstream' into services. Such firms are developing innovative combinations of service capabilities such as operations, business consultancy and finance required to provide complete solutions to each customer's needs in order to augment customer value towards the innovative or new products. It has been argued that provision of integrated solutions is attracting firms traditionally based in manufacturing and services to occupy a new base in the value stream cantered on 'systems integration' using internal or external sources of product designing, supply and customer focused promotion (Davies,2004). Besides organizational perspectives of enhancing the customer value, the functional variables like pricing play a significant role in developing customer perceptions towards the new products.

Analysis of the perceived values of customers towards new products is a complex issue. Despite considerable research in the field of measuring customer values in the recent past, it is still not clear how value interacts with marketing related constructs. However there exists the need for evolving a comprehensive application model determining the interrelationship between customer satisfaction and customer value, which may help in reducing the ambiguities surrounding both concepts. One of the studies in this regard discusses two alternative models yielding empirically tested results in a cross-sectional survey with purchasing managers in Germany. The first model suggests a direct impact of perceived value on the purchasing managers' intentions. In the second model, perceived value is mediated by satisfaction. This research suggests that value and satisfaction can be conceptualized and measured as two distinct, yet complementary constructs (Eggert and Ulaga, 2002).

Improving customer value through faster response times for new products is a significant way to gain competitive advantage. In the globalization process many approaches to new product development emerge, which exhibit an internal focus and view the new product development process as terminating with product launch. However, it is process output that really counts, such as customer availability. A study proposes that with shortening product life cycles it should pay to get the product into the market as quickly as possible, and indicates that these markets should be defined on an international basis. The results of the study reveals that greater new product commercial success is significantly associated with a more ambitious and speedier launch into overseas markets as the process of innovation is only complete when potential customers on a world scale are introduced effectively to the new product (Oakley, 1996).

Retail sales performance and customer value approach are conceptually and methodically analogous. Both concepts calculate the value of a particular decision unit by analytical attributes forecast and the risk-adjusted value parameters. However, virtually no scholarly attention has been devoted to the question if any of these components of the shareholder value could be determined in a more market oriented way using individual customer lifetime values (Rajagopal, 2005). Value of a customer may be defined in reference to a firm as the expected performance measures are based on key assumptions concerning retention rate and profit margin and the customer value also tracks market value of these firms over time. Value of all customers is determined by the acquisition rate and cost of acquiring new customers (Gupta, Lehmann and Stuart, 2003).

Objectives and Design of Model

This paper emerges from a new indirect utility function and derives the corresponding system of equations, relating commodity demands to prices, income and customer values that satisfy the customer behavior by utility maximization (aggregation, homogeneity, symmetry and negativity). One of the assumptions made in developing the asymmetric model for measuring the consumer behavior and derived values is that consumers are determined by the sub-sets of tangible and intangible variables which include product attributes, awareness, product attractiveness, price, disposable income and competitive advantage. The analytical construct in this paper has been derived using the Linear Expenditure System (LES) and Linear Equations in Demand Estimation (LEDE) to measure the variability in consumer behavior.

This paper analyzes the belief-based or reinforcement learning attributes in forming typical consumer behavior through inter-personal communication, point of purchase information, advertisement or corporate image may have a significant impact on market organization. The model of dynamic oligopoly, where consumers learn about the relative perceived values of the different brands has also been discussed in the paper. The basic premise of the model is towards reinforcement type behavioral model, where more familiar products have a greater probability of being selected. Consequently, consumers can get locked into inferior choices without considering the novelty factor in reference to product attributes or brand. Such lock-in behavior may be cyclical and asymmetric in context to personality traits and demand for the product. Such situation may become significant when firms influence consumer opinion in the short run as consumers' initial estimate of a firm's quality is high (or low), it has an incentive to charge above (or below) the myopic price in order to slow (or speed up) learning and behavioral adaptation of consumer towards the competing products.

Construct of Model

Choice Variability and demand equation

Ofek Elie (2002) discussed that the values of product and service are not always the same and are subject to value life cycle that governs customer preferences in the long-run. If customers prefer the product and service for N periods with Q as value perceived by the customer, the value may be determined as Q>N, where Q and N both are exogenous variables. If every customer receives higher perceived values for each of his buying, the value added product $q \geq Q$, where 'q' refers to the change in the quality brought by innovation or up-graded technology. Customer may refrain from buying the products if $q \leq Q$, that does not influence his buying decisions. However, a strong referral 'R' may lead to influence the customer values, with an advantage factor β that may be explained by price or quality factor. In view of the above discussion it may be assumed that customer preferences have high variability that grows the behavioral factors in retail buyers' decisions (Rajagopal, 2006[a]):

$$D_{bn} = \sum_{t=1}^{N} \beta^t \mu\left(C_t, \hat{Z}\right) + \beta^{N+1} Q_t \tag{1}$$

Where, D_{bn} is expressed as initial buying decision of the customers, C_t represents consumption, $\hat{Z}$ is a vector of customer attributes (*viz.* preferential variables) and Q_t is the value perceived by the customer.

Customer behavior is largely derived from the customer value and it has a dynamic attribute that plays a key role in buying and is an intangible factor to be considered in all marketing and selling functions. The value equation for customer satisfaction may be expressed as a function of all value drivers wherein each driver contains the parameters that directly or indirectly offer competitive advantages to the customers and enhance the customer value.

$$V' = K_s, K_m, K_d, K_c\left[\prod \{V(x, t, q, p)\}\right] \tag{2}$$

In the above equation V' is a specific customer value driver, K are constants for supplies(K_s), margins (K_m), distribution (K_d), and cost to customers (K_c); x is volume, t is time, q is quality and p denotes price. Perceived customer value (V) is a function of price (p) and non-price factors including quality (q) and volume (x) in a given time t. Hence Π has been used as a multiplication operator in the above equation. Quality of the product and volume are closely associated with the customer values. Total utility for the conventional products goes up due to economy of scale as the quality is also increased simultaneously ($\partial_v/\partial_x>0$). The ∂_v customer value is enhanced by offering larger volume of product at a competitive price in a given time ($\partial_v/\partial_p>0$) and ($\partial_v/\partial_t>0$). Conventional products create lower values to the customers ($\partial_v/\partial_x<0$) while innovative products irrespective of price advantages, enhance the customer value ($\partial_v/\partial_x>0$). Value addition in the conventional products provides lesser enhancement in customer satisfaction as compared to the innovative products. Such transition in the customer value, due to shift in technology may be expressed as:

$$V'_{hj} = a\left[\sum \frac{T_p}{\left(1+V_p\right)^{(1+j'+i)}}\right] + b\left(X_j\right) \tag{3}$$

In this equation V'_{hj} represents enhancements in customer value over the transition from conventional to innovative products, a and b are constants, T_p denotes high-tech and high-value products, V_p represents value of product performance that leads to enhance the customer value, volume is denoted by X and (j') is the period during which customer value is measured (Rajagopal, 2006[b]).

In reference to optimization theory it may be stated that maximizing a valid or direct utility function subject to a budget constraint or alternatively, appealing to duality theory and commencing from a cost or indirect utility function, influences on consumer behavior (Shida, 2001). In the latter case, let U (p, y) be the indirect utility function, where p is a vector of prices and y is income. For validity, U (p, y) should be homogeneous of degree zero in income and prices (p), non-decreasing in y, non-increasing in p, and convex or quasi-convex in p. The demand equations can be obtained through:

$$q_i = \frac{\partial U}{\partial p} / \frac{\partial U}{\partial y} \tag{4}$$

In the above equation (q_i) is denoted as demand for the product. Simple utility function derived by generic consumer behavior may be understood as $\left[U = \frac{y}{P}\right]$ wherein P may be expressed as geometric mean of prices which derives dynamic consumer behavior with the variability factor of competitive advantage (α_j) over the products in a given retail environment and j is the vector adding to unity over n commodities. Such condition of consumer behavior may be explained as:

$$\log P = \sum \left(\alpha_j \log p_j\right) \tag{5}$$

The above equation helps in deriving the demand equation as below:

$$w_i = \left(\frac{p_i q_i}{y}\right) = \alpha_j \tag{6}$$

wherein, (w_i) represents the individual expenditure limits or disposable income for buying the products. However, these equations limit consumer responses to changes in prices, competitive advantages or disposable income to maintaining consistency in buying behavior due to change in the elasticity of aforesaid variables. While such a consumption pattern might sometimes be plausible, it adds to the asymmetric behavior of consumers in retail buying.

Propensity of consumption during leisure season may be largely determined as a driver of retail attractions in terms of appealing sales promotions and availability of innovative products. Choice of consumers is thus established by the propensity of consumption in the array of innovative products in the retail stores. The propensity of consumption of buyers may be denoted by $\theta = \left[\theta_{jt...n}^{\lim 0-\infty}\right]$, which is measured in reference to frequency of buying $\left(\theta^{\lim 0-\infty}\right)$ from a jth store in a given time *t*. The choice pattern of buyers in shopping during holiday season may be derived as:

$$x_i(t) = \frac{\exp\{\beta\theta_i(t)\}}{\sum_{j=1}^{n}\exp\{\beta\theta_j(t)\}} \tag{7}$$

In the above equation $\{x_i(t)\}$ is the probability of buying strategy *i* at time *t*. In the exponential expression β represents the degree of value optimization on buying. At higher levels of β, consumer will have higher probabilities of buying with increased propensity.

Consumer Choice for New Products

According to the customer choice model of Giannakas and Fulton (2002), individuals are assumed to consume optimum one unit of product of their interest within a given time. The construct of the model of customer behavior, assumes that prior to choice of new product, customer *i* derives perceived use value, for *t* conventional or new products having U_{vi} willingness to pay for the conventional product on the perceived used value of customer *i* at price *p*. In order to explain the customer preference to the product and estimating the brand value in reference to this study it may be derived that customer obtains the perceived use value $\left(U_{vi} - p^t\right)$ from consuming conventional product. The customer also exercises his option of buying a high value substitute (new products) at an alternate price p^a where $\left(p^a \geq p^t\right)$. Hence without availability of new products, the customer value Cs may be derived as:

$$Cs_i^t =_{\lim 0-\infty} \left[\left(U_{vi} - p^t\right), \left(U_{vi} - p^a\right)\right] = \left(U_{vi} - p^t\right) \tag{8}$$

Following the scenario when customers get access to new products in the market, customers enhance the perceived use value of the new product by factor E_{vi}. This parameter is subjective to the customer decision in view of their preferences towards consuming organic products. However, due to lack of awareness, advertising and sales promotions, many customers may not be able to establish their preferences explicitly towards synthetic and conventional products. If α represents the market segment for new products, the customers would access the products and perceive its value by $\left(\alpha E_{vi}\right)$. Accordingly, the customer value after the new products are made available in the market segment may be described as:

$$Cs_i^{AP} =_{\lim 0-\infty} \left[\left(U_{vi} - p^t\right) - \alpha E_{vi}, \left(U_{vi} - p^a\right), B_i^{vg}\right] \tag{9}$$

Wherein, the expression Cs_i^{AP} denotes the enhancement of customer value for new products in reference to the advertising and promotion strategies of the firms and B_i^{vg} represents the brand value of new products perceived by the customers. Further, Cs_i^{AP} may be understood as a function of interpersonal communication $\left(Cs_i^{IP}\right)$ comprising word of mouth and referrals, commercials $\left(Cs_i^{ma}\right)$ and point of sales promotions $\left(Cs_i^{ps}\right)$. Hence, the factors influencing the enhancement of customer value may be expressed as:

$$Cs_i^{AP} = f\left(Cs_i^{IP}, Cs_i^{ma}, Cs_i^{ps}\right)^{\lim_{0-\infty}} \tag{10}$$

Motivational forces are commonly accepted to have a key influencing role in the explanation of shopping behavior. Personal shopping motives, values and perceived shopping alternatives are often considered independent inputs into a choice model. It is argued that shopping motives influence the perception of retail store attributes as well as the attitude towards retail stores (Morschett et.al, 2005). Lliberal environment of the self-service stores for merchandise decisions, service quality and learning about competitive brands are the major attributes of retail self-service stores (Babakus et.al, 2004). Retail self-service stores offer an environment of three distinct dimensions of emotions e.g. pleasantness, arousal and dominance. The change in the customer value observed among the synthetic and new products in reference to advertising and promotional strategies used by the firms, may be described as:

$$Cs_i^{AP-t} = Cs_t^{AP} - Cs_i^t \tag{11}$$

The model assumes that if N_{rs} number of customers in a given retail store has preferred to use new products; the change in the customer value may be derived as:

$$\Delta Cs_i^{AP-t} = \sum_{i=1}^{Nrs_1 \ldots Nrs_n} \Delta Cs_i^{AP-t} \tag{12}$$

Customers choose the product which offers maximum utility in reference to the price, awareness and promotional advantage over other conventional products. Hence, the customer value for new products may be expressed as:

$$\Delta C_{Nrs=1}^{E_{vi}-t} = \alpha\left(C_i^{E_{vi}} - Cs_i^t\right) \tag{13}$$

Where, $C^{E_{vi}}$ represents the customer value in total derived by all factors. Value and pricing models have been developed for many different products, services and assets. Some of them are extensions and refinements of convention models on value driven pricing theories (Gamrowski and Rachev, 1999; Pedersen, 2000). There have also been some models that are developed and calibrated addressing specific issues such as model for household assets demand (Perraudin and Sorensen, 2000). Key marketing variables such as price, brand name, and product attributes affect customers' judgment processes and derive inference on its quality dimensions leading to customer satisfaction. The experimental study conducted indicates that customers use price and brand name differently to judge the quality dimensions and measure the degree of satisfaction (Brucks et.al. 2000). Value of corporate brand endorsement across different products and product lines, and at lower levels of the brand hierarchy also needs to be assessed as a customer value driver. Use of corporate brand endorsement either as a name identifier or logo identifies the product with the company, and provides reassurance for the customer (Rajagopal and Sanchez, 2004).

Cost of acquiring new products would be the difference in traditional good price, variation in the perceived use value and search cost as indicated by $\left(C_i^{sc}\right)$ for each customer. Hence, appreciation of customer value to obtain new products may be expressed as:

$$\Delta C_i^{Krs-t} = \alpha\left[\left(E_{vi} + p^a + C_i^{sc}\right) - Cs_i^t\right] \tag{14}$$

Where, C_i^{Krs} represents the cost of acquiring the new products from a given retail store. Competitive advantage of a firm is also measurable from the perspective of product attractiveness to generate new customers. Given the scope of retail networks, a feasible value structure for customers may be reflected in repeat buying behavior ($\hat{R}$) that explains the relationship of the customer value with the product and associated marketing strategies. The impact of such customer value attributes in a given situation may be described as:

$$\sum_{Nsr=1}^{n} Cs_i^{AP} = \hat{R} = C^{E_{vi}} \tag{15}$$

Repeat buying behavior of customers is largely determined by the values acquired on the product. Decision of customers on repeat buying is also affected by the level of satisfaction derived on the products and number of customers attracted towards buying the same product, as a behavioral determinant (Rajagopal, 2005).

New product attractiveness may comprise the product features including improved attributes, use of advance technology, innovativeness, extended product applications, brand augmentation, perceived use value, competitive advantages, corporate image, product advertisements, sales and services policies associated therewith, which contribute in building sustainable customer values towards making buying decisions on the new products (Rajagopal, 2006[a]). Attributes of the new products lead to satisfaction to the customers and is reflected through the product attractiveness (F_x). It has been observed that the new products have been considered as new and experimental products in Mexico by a significant number of consumers. Hence product attractiveness (F_x) may be explained along the associated variables in the following equation as:

$$F_x = \prod \left[\alpha E_{vi} \left(Cs_t^{AP}, q, Z_{xi}, p^a \right) \right]^t \tag{16}$$

Wherein, q denotes quality of the product and Z_{xi} represents services offered by the retailers towards prospecting and retaining customers who intend to buy the new products. Customer value may also be negative or low if attributes are not built into the new product to maximize the customer value as per the estimation of the firm. Perceived use value of customers by market segments αE_{vi} is a function of advertising and promotion Cs_i^{AP}, price appreciation p^a and retailer services Z_{xi} in a given time t and $\prod$ has been used as a multiplication operator in the above equation. The quality of the product and volume are closely associated with the customer values.

Introduction of new technological products makes it important for marketers to understand how innovators or first adopters respond to persuasion cues. It has been observed in a study that innovativeness and perceived product newness which are the major constituents of new product attractiveness were independent constructs that had independent effects on customer's attitude toward the brand and purchase intent for the new product (Lafferty and Goldsmith, 2004).

Customer Value Enhancement

A firm may introduce new product with high investment $M_t^{(i_1+i_2+i_3+\ldots i_n)j}$ in terms of product attributes (i_1), distribution (i_2), promotion (i_3) and other related factors ($\ldots i_n$) related with gaining competitive advantage in a given time (t) in the jth market. Let us assume that s

is the estimated market coverage for the new product, the customer value (V_{np}) may be initially positive and high, resulting into deeper market penetration (with s increasing). This may be described as:

$$M_t^{(i_1+i_2+i_3+...)j} = \frac{\partial s}{\partial t} = k \tag{17}$$

However, $V_{np} \leq \frac{\partial v}{\partial t}$ may become negative following product competition within the product line due to the product overlap strategy of the firm. In the above equation, volume of buying is represented by ∂v in a given time t. To augment the customer value and enhance market coverage for the new products in potential markets the firm may optimize the product line $[s]_{pt}^{j,h}$ by pruning the slow moving products in the jth chain in h market in order to reposition them in new market. The opportunity cost in moving the slow performance products may be derived by inputting the values of V′ from equation (ii) as:

$$[s]_{Pt}^{j,h} = \left[\frac{\partial v}{\partial t}\right]^{j,h} + \prod\{V(x,t,q,p)\} \tag{18}$$

Hence to enhance market coverage for the new product with enhancing customer value for the new product of the firm, the strategy may be described as:

$$s = \int \left[k + \{s\}_{Pt}^{j,h}\right] \partial t + \beta^t R \tag{19}$$

Where in s is market coverage of the new product, k is investment on market functions derived in a given time [equation (vi)] and R is the referral factor influencing the customer values with an advantage factor coefficient β in time t. The products constituting the optimal product line of the firm in a given time are represented by P_t in the above equation. The firm may measure the customer value shocks accordingly and shield the uncertainties occurring to the estimated market coverage due to declining customer values for the new products. As is common the new products are susceptible to such value shocks in view of the companies' own product line strategy.

Let us assume that new product attractiveness is F_x and initial product market investment is $M_t^{(i_1+i_2+i_3+...i_n)j}$, perceived customer value of the new product is V_{np} and competitive advantage driver for the customer is C_{at} at a given time, we get the following equation.

$$F_x = \sum_t^{jh} \left[M_t^{(i_1+i_2+\ldots i_n)j} \right] \left(V_{np} \right) \left(C_{at} \right) \tag{20}$$

Hence, the above equation may be further simplified as,

$$F_x = M_t^{i_n, j} \frac{\partial v'}{\partial t} = M_t^{in, j} \frac{\partial b'}{\partial s} \frac{\partial s}{\partial t} = M_t^{in, j} \frac{\partial v}{\partial s} \left(V_{np} \right) \left(C_{at} \right) \tag{21}$$

Where in $M_t^{i_n, j}$ denotes the initial investment made by the firm for introducing new products, V' represents the volume of penetration of new product in a given market in time *t* with estimated market coverage *s* and b' expresses the volume of repeat buying during the period the new product was penetrated in the market by the firm. The total quality for new products goes up due to economy of scale as the quality is also increased simultaneously $(\partial_v / \partial_s > 0)$ and $(\partial_{b'} / \partial_s > 0)$. In reference to the new products *x*, competitive products create lower values to the customers $(\partial_v / \partial_x < 0)$ while innovative products irrespective of price advantages, enhance the customer value $(\partial_v / \partial_x > 0)$. Value addition in the competitive products provides lesser enhancement in customer satisfaction as compared to the innovative products if the new products have faster penetration, re-buying attributes and market coverage.

$$\text{Therefore } \int s \partial s = \int V_{np} + C_{at} \tag{22}$$

In the above equation V_{np} denotes customer value for the new product and C_{at} represents the competitive advantage at a given time.

The prospect theory laid by Tversky and Khanman (1981) proposes that the intensity of gains plays strategic role in value enhancement as $G_{xt} = g_{pt} \left(\partial_x / \partial_p \right)$. In this situation *t* represents the period wherein promotional strategies were implemented to enhance customer values in reference to product specific gains (g_{pt}). However, in order to measure relationship/variability between repeat buying behavior and customer value, it would be appropriate to determine the cumulative decision weights (w) and substitute it in the equation (1) to get the following equation:

$$G_{xt} = w \sum_{k=1}^{jh} \left[g_{pt} \left(r_j m_j \right) + \beta^{n+1} Q_t \right] \tag{23}$$

The customer value however may be the driver function of gains on buying decision on new products and the influencing variables such as perceived use value and referrals.

Conclusion and Managerial Implications

Existing theoretical and methodological issues are reviewed in this study and a new framework has been proposed for future research in measuring customer value in specific reference to the new products as launching innovative and high technology products is a continuous process for the firms in the present competitive markets. The assumptions and methodology employed in this paper are quite different from those of conventional behavioral models. It would be interesting to analyze the robustness of convergence of the model in reference to asymmetric behavioral patterns of consumer and demand orientation. Some of the existing empirical evidences, both from laboratory and field consumer data, seem to give enhanced scope for analyzing the asymmetric behavior model discussed in the paper that predicts suboptimal consumer behavior even in the long run in view of shifts in retailing strategies. The framework for measuring customer values discussed in this paper provides analytical dimensions for establishing the long run customer relationship by the firm and to optimize its profit levels. To test some hypotheses concerning homogeneity in consumer behavior and its impact on derived demand for the product or services may be required to be taken-up with additional parameters to estimate model. While following the LES data to estimate demand functions, the results may not aggregate over consumers' asymmetric behavior, particularly in reference to expenditures. Hence, individual expenditures on goods over a group of consumers of varying incomes produce different equations with income when replaced by utility based qualitative parameters. However, it is believed that utility maximization, and the consequent constraints on demand equations, pertain strictly to individuals and consequently consider their application at aggregate level provided the demand equations aggregate over consumers qualitative parameters. It is necessary to standardize the qualitative parameters before applying in this model.

One of the challenges for a firm is to incorporate and validate the preferences of customers into the design of new products and services in order to maximize customer value. An augmented and sustainable customer value builds loyalty towards the product and brand and helps to stabilize customer behavior. Systematically explored concepts in the field of customer value and market driven approach towards new products would be beneficial for a company to derive long term profit optimization strategy over the period. Hence, a comprehensive framework for estimating both the value of a customer and profit optimization need to be developed. On a tactical level, managers need to consider as what is the optimum spread of customers on a matrix of product attractiveness and market coverage. The model discussed in this paper provides a holistic view of the customer behavior driven by the value matrices associated with product attractiveness, market coverage, brand and point-of-purchase services offered to the customers. Analysis of these variables would help strategists/managers to develop appropriate strategies to enhance customer value for the new products and optimize profit of the firm.

REFERENCES

Babakus E, Bienstock C C and Van Scotter J R (2004), Linking perceived quality and customer satisfaction to store traffic and revenue growth, *Decision Sciences*, 35 (4), 713-737

Bergemann D, Välimäki J (1996) Learning and strategic pricing, *Econometrica*, 64, 1125-1149

Brucks M, Zeithaml V A and Naylor G (2000), Price and brand name as indicators of quality dimensions of customer durables, *Journal of Academy of Marketing Science*, 28 (3), 359-374

Carroll D and Dunn W E (1997), *Unemployment expectations*, NBER, Working Paper # 6081

Carroll C D and Kimball M S (1996), On the concavity of the consumption function, *Econometrics*, 64(4), 981-992

Chintagunta, P.K., Rao, P.V. (1996), Pricing strategies in a dynamic duopoly: a differential game model, *Management Science*, 42, 1501-14

Davies A (2004), Moving base into high-value integrated solutions: A value stream approach, *Industrial and Corporate Change*, 13 (5), October, 727-756

Deaton A (1992), *Understanding competition*, Oxford University Press, Oxford

Erev I and Barron G (2001), *On adaptation, maximization and reinforcement learning among cognitive strategies*, Working Paper, Columbia University

Erev I and Roth A E(1998), Predicting how people play games: reinforcement learning in experimental games with unique, mixed strategy equilibria, *American Economic Review*, 88, 848-881

Gramrowski B and Rachev S (1999), A testable version of the pareto-stable CAPM, *Mathematical and Computer Modeling*, Vol. 29, 61-81.

Herrnstein, R and Dražen P (1992), "Melioration," in George L and Jon E (Eds), *Choice over time*, New York: Russell Sage, 235-263.

Loewenstein, G (1996), Out of control: Visceral influences on behavior, *Organizational behavior and Human Decision Processes*, 65 (March), 272-292.

Marjolein C and Verspagen B (1999), *Spatial distance in a technology gap model*, Maastricht Economic Research Institute on Innovation and Technology (MERIT), Working Paper No. 021

Morschett, D; Swoboda, B and Foscht, T (2005), Perception of store attributes and overall attitude towards grocery retailers: The role of shopping motives, *The International Review of Retail, Distribution and Consumer Research*, 15 (4), 423-447

Ofek E (2002), *Customer profitability and lifetime value*, Harvard Business School, Note, August, 1-9 (Publication reference 9-503-019)

Pederson C S(2000), Sparsing risk and return in CAPM: A general utility based model, *European Journal of Operational Research*, Vol. 123 (3), 628-639.

Perraudin W R M and Sorensen B E (2000), The demand of risky assets: Sample selection and household portfolios, *Journal of Econometrics*, Vol. 97, 117-144

Rajagopal (2006[a]), Measuring customer value gaps: An empirical study in mexican retail markets, *Economic Issues*, 11(1), March, 19-40

Rajagopal (2006[b]), Measuring customer value and market dynamics for newproducts of a firm: An analytical construct for gaining competitive advantage, *Global Business and Economics Review*, 8 (3-4), 187-205

Reichheld F F and Sasser W E (1990), Zero defections: Quality comes to services, *Harvard Business Review*, Sep-Oct, pp 105-111

Shida M (2000), Fundamental theorems of morse theory for optimization on manifolds with corners, *Journal of Optimization Theory and Applications*, 106 (3), September, 683-688

Tversky A and Kahnman D (1981), The framing decisions and psychology of hoice, *Science*, No.211, 453-458

In: Mexico: Economic, Political and Social Issues ISBN: 978-1-60456-847-9
Editors: Maria L. Castro and Irene P. Navarro

Chapter 8

COMING TO TERMS WITH ABORTION IN MEXICO

*Andrzej Kulczycki**
University of Alabama at Birmingham, Department of Maternal and Child Health, Birmingham, AL

ABSTRACT

Over half a million clandestine abortions are believed to occur annually in Mexico, many under unfavorable health conditions that lead to the death of several hundred women. Since it first came under scrutiny in the early 1970s, this situation has proved politically sensitive and difficult for both society and state. An uneasy truce has masked over the subject, broken by periodic controversy. The abortion debate became nationwide following several contrasting legal initiatives and high-profile adolescent rape cases as the country entered systemic change in 2000. This paper assesses accessibility to abortion services, the medical demography of abortion, recent attempts to make abortion safer and rarer, the evolution and social construction of the abortion debate, and the strategies and relative influences of the key actors involved. It further examines the international dimensions to this controversy and the barriers to bringing policy more into line with actual abortion practice. Despite increasing political pluralism, societal and elite awareness of existing problems, for now the issue is not judged sufficiently pressing to merit major action due to a host of reasons discussed. On the other hand, incremental changes in post-abortion care have occurred and the question of abortion can no longer be ignored.

INTRODUCTION

In Mexico as throughout Latin America, abortion frequently occurs under unfavorable health conditions and in a context that defines it as sinful and illegal.[1] Although its incidence

* Address for correspondence: Andrzej Kulczycki, PhD, University of Alabama at Birmingham, Department of Maternal and Child Health, 320 Ryals Public Health Building, 1665 University Boulevard, Birmingham, AL 35294-0022. E-mail: andrzej@uab.edu; Tel.: (205) 934-9875; Fax: (205) 934-8248

[1] Only Cuba, Barbados and Puerto Rico in the Caribbean, and Belize in Central America, permit abortion on broad social grounds (David and Pick de Weiss, 1992). All other Latin American countries list punishments for

is unknown, abortion is a politically sensitive and difficult issue for both society and state. Since the early 1970s, the intermittent appearance of abortion in public discourse has allowed for the gradual demystification of a once taboo subject. It is not yet possible to articulate all aspects of the issue, however. As a result, the question of what to do about abortion is mired in a state of negotiated reality, with the attendant problems only tacitly recognized and partially addressed.

Over the last three decades, considerable energies have been periodically expended on changing laws and policies relating to abortion. Yet it is unclear if there is a gradual tendency towards decriminalization, as certain trends suggest, or whether further change in that direction remains unlikely because groups hostile to the provision of abortion services have actively mobilized about the issue. The most important of these actors is the Catholic Church. With the second largest Catholic population in the world, Mexico remains crucial to the development of Catholicism. Even if far fewer Mexicans practice their faith than are baptized, the Church's influence permeates social values and may have increased in the public arena following the relaxation of anti-clerical laws in 1992. Under John Paul II, who visited Mexico five times during his papacy, the Church hierarchy and Church-backed groups became more assertive in rallying against abortion, which they equate with the destruction of family values and structures.

Mexico's population has grown from under 15 million in 1921 to about 105 million in 2004. In spite of a rapid fertility decline from 6.7 children per woman in 1970 to 2.5 in 2000-05, the population's annual increment is 1.4 million and its median age is only 25 years (UN, 2005). The youthful age structure indicates the need to extend contraceptive protection and accurate information so as to reduce the likelihood of unwanted pregnancy. Given these needs, the country's size and proximity to its rich northern neighbor, and its influence in Central America and other parts of Latin America, Mexico has developed into a major regional node in the worldwide operations of a number of family planning agencies. It hosted the 1984 World Population Conference at which the USA announced its controversial "Mexico City policy" that lasted until 1992 and was then reinstated in 2001.[2] This precluded foreign aid funds for any family planning agency that so much as mentioned abortion. Although no such agency engaged in abortion-related activities, the policy affected more sensitive components of family planning programs in Mexico, such as contraceptive provision to youth, indirectly contributing to more unwanted pregnancies. In 1994, Mexico endorsed the reproductive rights agenda proclaimed at the International Conference on Population and Development (ICPD, held in Cairo), facilitating the extension of post-abortion care though not the promotion of other abortion services. Such influences show that struggles over

abortions performed for non-therapeutic reasons. Nonetheless, across Latin America, it has long been noted that "the harshness of the written statutes is alleviated...by their virtual nonenforcement" in practice (Isaacs and Sanhueza, 1975: 39).

[2] President George W. Bush reinstituted the policy in early 2001, shortly after he assumed power. Also known as the 'Global Gag Rule,' the policy bars U.S. assistance for family planning from being provided to foreign nongovernmental organizations (NGOs) that use funding from any other source to perform abortion in cases other than a threat to the life of the woman, rape, or incest; to provide counseling and referral for abortion; or to lobby to make abortion legal or more available in their own country. Assistance is defined to include not just funds but the provision of technical assistance, customized training, and commodities, including contraceptive supplies. Governments receiving U.S. family planning assistance are not formally bound by the Global Gag Rule. See USAID, Contract Information Bulletin, "Restoration of the Mexico City Policy: White House Memorandum for the Acting Administrator of the U.S. Agency for International Development (Revised)," [CIB 01-08 (R), 29 March 2001], for the full text of the Mexico City Policy.

abortion in Mexico are affected by external developments that, in turn, are mediated by domestic actors.

Since the mid-1970s, successive Mexican governments have considered the question of abortion. Discourse on the subject was initially tightly controlled, but as political pluralism has slowly increased, so has the ability of different groups to express themselves and influence the course of debate. In 2000 the National Action Party (PAN) wrested control of the presidency through the ballot box after seven decades of rule by the Institutional Revolutionary Party (PRI). Well before Mexico had entered a more democratic era, however, civil society had developed to the point where it should be considered alongside traditional political structures when analyzing struggles taking place within the society and polity (Camp, 2002; Preston and Dillon, 2004). The new social agents included feminist and anti-abortion groups. Until recently however, their avenues for expression were restricted within a highly centralized policymaking system that has always functioned beyond purview, as if behind a mask.

This article assesses the existing abortion situation in Mexico and the surrounding policy context. It is based on multiple sources of evidence including 60 elite interviews conducted over the last decade with high-level policymakers, religious leaders, health care personnel, activists, researchers, lawyers, and other key informants, as well as extensive analysis of documents and data, newspaper articles, and interest group material. The article first assesses how access to abortion services varies and what is the demographic and health context of abortion. These empirical realities describe the situation in which abortion occurs, are variously perceived by different groups in society, and provide arguments to justify policies. We then review the course and social construction of the abortion debate and assess the roles played by different social agents who have attempted to determine its nature and outcome. The article examines both domestic and international influences on abortion policy, and analyses why there has been little substantive policy change on a subject long identified as a serious health and social problem inadequately resolved by existing policy measures. On the other hand, several steps have been taken recently to extend access to emergency contraception, improve post-abortion care and revise the legal context of abortion. The article also reflects on the prospects for further changes in how abortion is considered in the future.

Access to Abortion Services

The Mexican legal system classifies abortion as a crime in most cases. Although there is no federal regulation, most states follow the example of the Federal District's (i.e. Mexico City's) 1931 Penal Code (articles 329-324, prior to their amendment in 2000), so that their criminal codes differ little from each other (De la Barreda Solórzano, 1991). Abortion requires the approval of two physicians and is allowed only in the event of rape, incest, endangerment of the woman's life or imprudence (a term neither explained nor understood by the legal or medical profession, and which has no effect on access). However, legal and institutional mechanisms for women to benefit from these exceptions are lacking, while cumbersome and bureaucratic practices, social and cultural barriers restrict access further. Some rape victims do not know that they can legally seek an abortion, let alone the procedure for obtaining one (Ehrenfeld, 1999).

In 2000, the Federal District extended the grounds for a legal abortion to situations where a woman's health is in danger, where fetal defects exist, or when non-consensual artificial insemination occurred, and clarified the procedure for rape victims to obtain an abortion. It stipulated a maximum waiting period of 24 hours for a legal abortion where pregnancy is the result of rape, so as to ensure that health service providers cannot delay access to the procedure. The Supreme Court subsequently upheld these amendments, the so-called 'Robles laws' (or '*leyes robles,*' named after the incumbent city mayor who pushed the measure). It also reduced from 5 to 3 years the maximum prison sentence for women who obtained an abortion for other reasons. Penalties for performing or procuring an illegal abortion have been rarely enforced (González, 1992), but the wording of the extenuating circumstances of liability (which reduces imprisonment if the woman is not of "bad repute," manages to hide her pregnancy, and if it was the result of an illegitimate union) is common to most Latin American laws; the honor protected is essentially that of the husband the woman is considered to belong to. It would seem that the law preserves the mystification of motherhood and the myth of fidelity within marriage, while sanctions are not intended to be enforced if the abortion act is sufficiently masked.

The existing situation causes serious problems of social justice and public health. Women have needed to obtain court orders to have legally permissible abortions that physicians sometimes refuse to perform. The legal restrictions serve no useful purpose in reducing the incidence of abortion and contribute to many unsafe procedures. The black market increases the economic and psychosocial costs of abortion for women. Current laws remain exploitative and discriminate against poor women who cannot secure safe services that are available to the socio-economically advantaged. The government has still not enforced laws guaranteeing the right to abortion for rape victims.

Abortion is easier to obtain in a large city where there are more physicians and women have a greater chance of securing anonymity. The most widely used method is dilatation and curettage (with general anesthesia); more dangerous methods include the "sonda" (a rubber tube inserted into the uterus) and abortifacient herbs, particularly in rural areas. The "cihuapatli" (or "xoapactle") is one indigenous plant that is usually effective in strong doses and is widely known and used (Pérez-Palacios and Garza-Flores, 1994; Pick et al., 2003). Also, injections of menstrual regulators such as Metrigen, quinine tablets (a medication for malaria) and misoprostol (an anti-ulcer drug) are used to provoke abortions that are often ended in hospitals under emergency care, increasingly with manual vacuum aspiration (MVA).[3] MVA is a safe, low-cost and highly effective method of uterine evacuation that can be used by health professionals at rural and primary-level facilities that do not have operating theatres, general anesthesia or electricity. It therefore also makes it easier for providers to offer other reproductive health services, such as post-abortion family planning, at the treatment visit.

[3] Misoprostol, a medicine for treating gastric ulcers and also known by its commercial name of Cytotec, is a potent and effective drug when used as an abortifacient, and at later gestation ages, for inducing labor (Goldberg et al., 2001). First widely adopted to provoke first-trimester abortions in Brazil, in Mexico misoprostol has since the late 1990s become increasingly available on the black market and (unofficially) administered by gynecologists. MVA, which uses a handheld syringe to produce a vacuum to dislodge the contents of conception, requires only local anesthesia, a shorter patient stay and fewer hospital resources than does dilatation and curettage, the traditional method for treating incomplete abortion (Johnson et al., 1993).

THE MEDICAL DEMOGRAPHY OF ABORTION

In Latin America, initial research interest in abortion waned once it was pointed out in the late 1960s and early 1970s that abortion was common and could be reduced through contraception (e.g. Gaslonde, 1976; Viel, 1988). It resurfaced in the early 1990s, but the pool of knowledge on abortion in Mexico, as for Latin America, remains small and sketchy. Abortion is greatly underreported owing to the illegality of the procedure, its social stigma, and the failure to distinguish between spontaneous and induced abortions.[4]

In the late 1960s studies conducted on women covered by the health services of the Mexican Social Security Institute (IMSS) highlighted the growing number and costs of abortion complications in public sector hospitals, and revealed that most women having abortions were multiparous housewives who had an insufficient income or had already too many children in the family. In 1971 an estimated 700,000 abortions occurred nationally (Ordóñez, 1975). This figure, while not rigorously computed, reflected informed opinion at a time when contraceptive use was still low. Typically, abortion rates are highest when societies are approaching the middle stages of fertility transition, that is, when reproductive preferences are falling but family planning services are not yet widely adopted due to limited availability or awareness (Kulczycki et al., 1996). By the 1970s and 1980s, induced abortion may have accounted for as much as one-quarter of deliberate fertility control (Frejka and Atkin, 1996).

Estimates of the annual number of induced abortions performed in the early 1990s range from as low as 110,000 (CONAPO, 1996) to as high as 850,000 (López García, 1994). Mendoza (1991) estimated that about 256,000 abortions were performed in Mexico during 1986 (little more than twice the reported number of hospitalizations for abortion) and that abortion rates peaked sometime earlier. However, the calculation estimated abortion only as a residual of other fertility determinants.[5] A higher incidence most likely prevailed because contraceptive use and efficacy were then still relatively low, while birth rates were declining steadily. These difficulties notwithstanding, every existing assessment of abortion incidence in Mexico has serious limitations due to the paucity of available data on the topic. Table 1 lists estimates of the annual incidence of induced abortion since the mid-1980s. Governmental sources typically yield lower estimates, both because they tend to be based only on hospital reports of abortion-related complications and because they may reflect a preference to downplay the issue so as not to politicize it further. Estimates produced by other researchers concur that at least 500,000 abortions occur annually.

---

[4] For example, the 1987 National Fertility and Health Survey indicated that only 14% of women of childbearing age had at least one abortion at some time, and of these women only 13% admitted to an induced abortion (Núñez, 2001). This is significantly less than can be inferred from international studies and considerably understates the problem.

[5] The calculation used Bongaarts's model of the proximate determinants of fertility. This framework is typically applied to analyze fertility patterns but also offers an indirect method for estimating abortion levels in situations where measures are available for the other major determinants of fertility (contraception, marriage, and postpartum infecundability) and are lacking only for abortion. However, the abortion rate is estimated by inference and the utility of this approach is heavily qualified. Small measurement errors in the three other proximate determinants and interactions between the determinants can have large effects on the estimated abortion index. In addition, without further modification, the Bongaarts' model excludes consideration of abortion, sexual activity and pregnancy among the unmarried, so that model estimates reflect the situation among married women only.

Table 1. Recent estimates of the total number of induced abortions performed annually in Mexico, various years

Reference Date	Number of abortions	Source
1986	256,000	Mendoza (1991)
1990	533,100	Singh and Wulf (1994)
c. 1990	850,000	López Garcia (1994)
1990-92	220,000	CONAPO (1995)
1995	110,000	CONAPO (1996)
1998	145,436	INEGI (2000)

Note: Full references are given at the end of the article.

Another study suggested that 533,100 abortions occurred in Mexico in 1990 (Singh and Wulf, 1994), equivalent to an abortion rate of 23 per 1,000 women aged 15-49 (slightly lower than that in the USA at the time). The calculation rests on the opinions of health workers and researchers from Mexico City and surrounding rural areas, as well as on a somewhat arbitrary (but plausible) inflation factor of five abortions for every one treated in public hospitals. Physicians interviewed by the present author at several hospital sites in different Mexican cities, along with other informed observers, believe that the incidence of abortion has probably not risen since due to increases in contraceptive use and efficacy, as well as the relatively high cost of a safe abortion. Among currently married women aged 15-49, contraceptive prevalence increased from 30% in 1976 to 67% in 1995 (CONAPO, 1997), and is now believed to be approximately 70%.

Most likely, there is substantial recourse to abortion in Mexico -- over half a million abortions performed per year -- but abortion rates are somewhat lower than in much of Latin America. The decision to continue with an unwanted pregnancy may be easier in Mexico, where children are important to a woman's perception of integrity in a relationship. Nonetheless, about 40% of pregnancies in Mexico were thought to be unwanted (Singh and Wulf, 1994). There has always been much cross-border traffic by women seeking abortions, which has been very poorly documented. Mexican clinicians ran thriving abortion practices that served many American women before the US Supreme Court legalized abortion (Weddington, 1992), after which thousands of Mexican women began traveling north for abortions. Researchers, family planning and other health-care providers in Ciudad Juárez confirmed to the author that the single young women who mostly work in the *maquiladoras* (northern border assembly plants) frequently resort to abortion to keep their jobs.

Research conducted in Mexico City, Acapulco, and Oaxaca among women who had undergone induced abortions found they had typically done so because of economic constraints and conflicts with their partners that might impede a child's upbringing. Some women also said they became pregnant at a young age whereas others indicated they had no wish to have another child (Pick de Weiss and David, 1990; Elu, 1999). Poor women and those with low levels of education typically sought induced abortions from untrained providers. They were more likely to suffer complications than were wealthier, better educated and older women who were more likely to afford decent care. Other research indicates a lower incidence of abortion among rural residents (Núñez, 2001).

Making Abortions Safer and Rarer

Abortion-related deaths are often hidden as deaths from hemorrhage, infection, anemia, renal failure, or other causes. Patients with minor complications frequently do not request hospital treatment and most private hospitals do not record incomplete abortions. Even official statistics indicate, however, that abortion-related complications are the fourth leading cause of maternal mortality, accounting for 7% of all such registered deaths (Aguirre, 1997; Núñez, 2001). In addition, abortions (both spontaneous and induced) are the third most common reason for hospitalization among childbearing age women; approximately 120,000 women receive abortion-related care each year in public sector facilities (INEGI, 2001).

In the early 1990s, IMSS, the Secretariat of Health (SSA), and the IMSS Solidarity Program (IMSS-Sol) extended use of MVA for emergency treatment of abortion complications and the provision of post-abortion contraceptive counseling and services. By 2001, over 25,000 health care providers had been trained to offer post-abortion care services at nearly 60% of all public hospitals nationally. This development has undoubtedly improved maternal health, reduced treatment costs and the likelihood of repeat abortions, although firm data are lacking (Chambers et al., 2001; Langer et al., 2002; Billings et al., 2003).

In the late 1990s, the government allowed several non-governmental organizations (NGOs) to disseminate information about emergency contraception to reduce the incidence of unintended pregnancy and the consequent need for abortion.[6] Awareness among family planning providers and clients increased in Mexico City (Ellertson, 2002). However, emergency contraception remained largely inaccessible and little understood. In January 2004, the government approved the use of emergency contraceptive pills, but to date, access to such pills and knowledge of their potential benefits remains poor.

The Course of the Abortion Debate

Debate on abortion can be traced to the 1920s (Ortiz-Ortega, 2001), but did not begin in earnest until five decades later. We can distinguish six phases in the course of the abortion debate since the mid-1970s. Abortion first moved onto the agenda through the efforts of the emerging feminist movement and as a result of the discussion surrounding the state's introduction of a new population policy. The government justified its new family planning program in part through the need to reduce the high number of abortions. A government-commissioned study favored legalizing abortion (CONAPO, 1976), but submitted its testimony just before a presidential succession when little was likely to be accomplished. The suggestions were not followed and the "expert dialogue" soon ended (Tarrés, 1993).

A second phase began after left-wing parties were legalized at the end of the decade. An uneasy alliance between feminists and communists proposed a measure on "voluntary motherhood" (*maternidad voluntaria*), but differences soon deepened among its sponsors. As before, the proposed legal changes were never publicly discussed by government circles

[6] Emergency contraception, sometimes referred to as the 'morning-after pill,' essentially consists of a higher dose of regular hormonal contraception. If taken within 72 hours of unprotected sexual intercourse, emergency contraceptive pills may prevent pregnancy by delaying or inhibiting ovulation, inhibiting fertilization, or inhibiting implantation of a fertilized egg (Trussell, 2004).

(Leal, 1980). The Church, buoyed by Pope John Paul II's first visit to Mexico in 1979, voiced its objections more publicly than when the state instituted a national family planning program. A church-linked organization, Pro-Vida, was formed to forestall legalization of abortion and set out to assume a role as a guardian of the nation's moral conscience.

The third conjuncture (a "dialogue of the deaf") occurred when the incoming president proposed to decriminalize abortion (De la Madrid, 1982). The initiative was closed off once its detractors rallied more strongly than did its supporters. The deep economic crisis dominated the political scene and created political opportunities best exploited by conservative groups. A fourth and very different debate took place after police raided an abortion clinic in Mexico City over Holy Week 1989. Several of the arrested women publicly denounced the police action and expressed their support for legalized abortion services; so did over 700 elite women who signed a widely publicized declaration which showed that feminists and non-feminists could cross ideological, party and class lines over this issue.[7] This triggered another debate on abortion and legal inequities. Unlike before, this took place in the public sphere and was not consciously manufactured by the government. Also, those opposed to such a policy shift were divided. Some PAN deputies abstained out of principle, being against the arbitrary use of force, whereas the bishops and Pro-Vida were now cast in a radical light for having supported the raids.

A fifth period concerns the huge controversy that flared up when it was announced in December 1990 that the Chiapas state legislature had revised its abortion law two months earlier to permit first trimester abortion on broad grounds. Legislators said they acted on behalf of thousands of women who suffer injury, infertility or death from clandestine unhealthy abortions. The state attorney repeated to the author that 200,000 abortions occurred each year in Chiapas,[8] an implausibly high number first publicized by the state governor. The incident re-galvanized feminist voices in support of abortion rights, but the Catholic Church and Church-linked organizations reacted sharply and the central government did not want to risk new obstacles in the way of mending church-state relations. Within two weeks, the Chiapas state legislature had suspended the process. For the first time public discussion of abortion was not confined to specific groups or forums. The extensive media comment included television discussion involving prominent figures holding diverse views about abortion, a subject still taboo until then (Monsivaís, 1991). The federal government defused the issue by shifting it to the National Human Rights Commission which avoided ruling on whether the revision violated human rights.

In 1993 abortion was again discussed in political circles as the focus of special sessions of the Chamber of Deputies' Health Commission, but all the major presidential candidates in the 1994 election avoided the issue. The government adopted a low-key stance at the 1994 ICPD, when Church officials pressed it to forcefully oppose the liberal consideration of abortion policy proposed in the preparatory conference document (Vera, 1994). After winning several state elections, PAN-controlled congresses attempted to declare the right to life from

[7] This declaration, published as a full-page advertisement in major national newspapers on 5 April 1989, began with the words "ninguna mujer aborta por gusto" ('no woman has an abortion for the heck of it'). Those signing it included well-known politicians from the ruling party, the government, opposition figures, feminists, artists and professionals.

[8] Interview, Chiapas State Attorney, Tuxtla Gutiérrez, August, 1992. Although the figure cited is improbably high and reliable data are unavailable, abortion-related morbidity and mortality are higher in Chiapas than in most other states (Aguirre, 1997) and may be disproportionately undercounted, as suggested to the author in interviews with senior health and family planning personnel.

the moment of conception in Chihuahua (1994), Baja California (1998), and Nuevo León (1999).[9] These proposals were defeated. In 1998, the Minister of Health sparked controversy when he suggested that all views on abortion should be heard and considered by legislators, who should be able to interpret what society wants (GIRE, 2001). The issue then resurfaced dramatically on the national stage in the run-up to the landmark 2000 presidential election won by PAN, raising expectations that conservative social causes would be championed by the new government.

This sixth phase in the abortion debate, by far the longest, began with the revelation that a 13 year-old rape victim in Baja California would give birth after being pressured by hospital physicians, state officials, anti-abortion activists, and Catholic clergy to drop her request for a legal abortion. The case of "Paulina" provoked a furor among feminist and human rights advocates, became something of a *cause célèbre* among many intellectuals and well-known writers, and gained international attention (GIRE, 2000; Poniatowska, 2000). Controversy continued when in Sinoloa a 12 year-old girl ('Lucila') impregnated by her father was initially denied a legal abortion that state authorities later permitted so as to reduce media attention. Shortly after the national election, PAN legislators from the new president's home state of Guanajuato approved without prior public debate a ban on abortion in rape cases. This stirred national outrage and protests by many civic groups, forcing the governor to veto the measure and the president-elect to distance himself from it. Then the Morelos state legislature decriminalized abortion in cases of rape, fetal anomalies, or when the mother's life is in danger, and reformed the state penal code to further permit abortion if a woman had an accident or received unauthorized artificial insemination. Also, Mexico City's mayor warned of a growing religious intolerance and of a backlash against recent advances for women, and proposed changes to the Federal District's law. These were promptly enacted, allowing abortion when pregnancy threatens the health of a woman, results from rape or unauthorized artificial insemination, or when the fetus has serious malformations. In 2002, following a legal challenge, the Supreme Court narrowly ratified the Federal District's initiative (the 'Robles laws') permitting women to obtain abortions in such difficult circumstances. The ruling raised expectations that other Mexican states might follow suit, but none had done so as of this writing three years later.

Most recently, the government amended federal family planning guidelines to allow use of emergency contraceptive pills. It justified its move with health department statistics showing that around 40% of Mexico's 2.1 million annual pregnancies were unplanned. Church leaders criticized the decision, as did more outspoken conservative politicians. However, emergency contraception has no effect if a woman is already pregnant and so is less controversial than mifepristone (also known as the 'abortion pill' RU-486 and by its U.S. commercial brand name, mifeprex). The government stood by its decision, but so far has done little to promote this therapy.

[9] This demand reflected similar guarantees instituted as constitutional amendments in the neighboring Central American states of Guatemala and Honduras, as well as in Ecuador.

The Social Construction of Abortion

A consistent feature of the abortion debate in Mexico is that it is poorly informed by basic facts. An analysis of newspaper coverage during 1974-1982 revealed major inconsistencies in abortion numbers, rates, and cause-related mortality (Infante Castañeda and Cobos-Pons, 1989). Estimates of the incidence of abortion ranged from 50,000 to 6 million, those of maternal deaths varied from 5,000 to 400,000, and 39% of the figures cited did not mention their sources. Newspapers continue to cite widely ranging statistics, underscoring the failure of the health and research communities to address these matters further. Indeed, public health concerns are not accorded high priority and tend to enter political discourse only rhetorically. As the case of AIDS illustrates, strong latent prejudices about behavioral practices have often reduced public health campaigns to generalities, platitudes or fear tactics, particularly where issues touch on the sexual sphere.

Opinion polls indicate no consensus on abortion exists. Whereas adults aged 21-35 and residents of Mexico City hold the most liberal attitudes, fewer than half those polled in major urban areas agree that the decision to have an abortion belongs to the woman alone, or that women need not take stock of the Church's opinion when deciding about abortion (Lamas, 1992). Beyond Mexico City and outside of intellectual circles, few think of abortion as an aspect of freedom and rights. Knowledge of current abortion laws remains low; a poll conducted in Mexico City and six other geographic regions in 2000 indicated that 54% of men and women aged 15-24 did not know the legal status of abortion in their state, and of these respondents, most thought that abortion was unconditionally illegal (Becker et al., 2002). Surveys have exposed various social and cultural myths about abortion, but these are proving very hard to dispel, like other mores about appropriate and standard sexual behavior. Research findings may help move the issue of abortion on to the public platform, but they have not swayed public opinion, which to date has exerted little direct influence on Mexican policymakers.

Public debate on abortion has tended to be episodic and marked by many polemical arguments, underscoring a profound "clash" of views. There is no clear framework for thinking about abortion, reflecting the lack of societal consensus and the multiplicity of views and opinions that have been exchanged. Some public officials think of abortion as a public health problem or relate it to the issue of population growth, but there is considerable resistance — from feminists and the Church alike — to defining abortion as a demographic issue. Groups seeking to remove restrictions on abortion services have based their arguments on public health and social justice considerations, as well as a woman's right to control her own body. The Catholic Church, which has acted as an umbrella for conservative opposition to abortion, has attempted to keep debate focused instead on the ontological status of the fetus and insists that abortion is a moral rather than a socio-political question. It argues that life begins at the moment of conception and that abortion kills an innocent person. Its teaching presupposes that a woman's love and life are self-sacrificial before the fetus. To this, the Church adds that abortion should not be legalized because nearly all Mexicans are (baptized) Catholic and, perforce, follow and agree with this teaching.

Even though the issue has been politicized to some extent, more often, interest in abortion is not shown directly. This stems from past restrictions imposed on civil society; the primordial association of abortion with blood and "the feminine," and its inelegance for a heavily male-dominated culture; the divisive and difficult nature of the issue; and the preference of many Mexicans for more indirect ways of expression and negotiation rather than open conflict. That the subjective is a key element in Mexican political praxis helps explain why the question of abortion has been raised only obliquely by several political administrations. It is also why many reform advocates — such as the reproductive rights group GIRE (*Grupo de Información en Reproducción Elegida*), founded in 1992 — now seek to negotiate the decriminalization of abortion, rather than outspokenly demand the liberalization of abortion *per se*. In the process, they are trying to make abortion the concern of society, not just of feminists, and to communicate an alternative position by stressing the language of choice and greater tolerance.[10]

The state has not formed its own discourse on abortion, in contrast to its concern about population growth and for family planning which, it asserts, reduces abortion. The state has mediated between the actors engaged in the dispute and set the parameters of the debate. However, its increasing inability to defuse promptly conflict over abortion shows its diminishing control over the course of the debate. Successive governments have tested the waters for reform and, on occasion, declared that abortion is a public health issue, only to then postpone possible action. In the 1990s, the state slowly extended post-abortion care services in public sector health-care facilities. President Vicente Fox, who ruled Mexico until his term ended in late 2006, voiced his personal opposition to abortion (as did his wife and adopted children), but like his predecessors, he refused to take sides publicly in the dispute.

Public ideas about gender roles, motherhood, and sexuality also underpin considerations of abortion. A strong undercurrent to this debate is the concern with women's roles and lives, as in most countries (Kulczycki, 1999). In particular, abortion contradicts the idealization of motherhood that lies at the core of women's identity. Despite expanded opportunities and goals, a woman's role is still popularly conceived as mother and homemaker, and double standards of sexual morality remain common. Consequently, many people find calls for abortion rights threatening to a social and cultural order that is symbolized by the evocative Catholic symbols of motherhood and suffering, particularly in Marian imagery and devotion. Moreover, the political culture continues to privilege the rights of the group over the individual, making it difficult to advance the limited autonomy and minority status of women.

The Role of Social Actors in the Abortion Debate

The Mexican Catholic Church

Before the Church regained full legal status and the state restored diplomatic relations with the Vatican in 1992, church-state relations were governed by a *modus vivendi* whereby the authoritarian state did not enforce anticlerical laws while the Church stayed clear of the political forum and was expected to help keep social order (Loaza-Lajous, 1990; Metz, 1992; Puente, 1992). At the same time the clergy maintained influence by developing a network of lay organizations, such as the National Parents' Union; by implicitly supporting PAN, the

[10] Marta Lamas, co-founder and director, GIRE, and editor of the journal *Debate Feminista*, points to the writings of the German social theorist and political philosopher, Jurgen Habermas, for inspiration on communicating such an alternative position (interview, M. Lamas, July 1992).

voice of national conservatism which has favored Church activism; and by educating Mexican elites through private church schools and colleges. Large lay movements account for much of the Church's vitality and include the Knights of Columbus (a Catholic men's fraternal service organization) as well as elitist and arch-conservative orders such as the Legionnaires of Christ and Opus Dei; these assist Pro-Vida, by far the most energetic of anti-abortion groups.[11] Consequently, the Church can still count on many devout followers, in spite of growing secularization and the spread of evangelical Protestantism.

Mexican bishops assumed a greater public role in the 1980s due to the political bankruptcy and economic mismanagement of PRI, as well as the electoral gains made by PAN. They were also emboldened by Pope John Paul II's strong advocacy of human rights. The relaxation of state-imposed restrictions on church activities enabled the hierarchy to speak out more on social issues and to mobilize considerable support at the local and national level when deemed important, as during the 'Chiapas' and 'Paulina' controversies over abortion. However, there are continued sensitivities surrounding church-state relations and clergy opinion over issues neither strictly moral nor religious.

The Episcopal Commission for the Family promotes Church teaching on the family. Its board includes representatives of various Catholic groups and religious orders who vigorously oppose abortion under any circumstances. The commission's President — since appointed as Archbishop of Mexico City, the largest diocese in the world, and the leader of the Catholic Church in Mexico — explained to the author that it seeks to stop publications and media messages "dealing with AIDS, sex education, non-natural methods of family planning, as promoted by NGOs and sometimes by the government, and which are part of the worldwide plan to undermine such [Catholic] values."[12] Through its pastoral letters, the Church has called for the protection of all human life and has rallied against abortion and "artificial contraception," contrasting "family planning" to "responsible parenthood."

It is by no means certain if Mexican Catholics are listening closely to these injunctions. Most Catholics neither attend church regularly nor practice their faith rigidly (Blancarte, 1991). Beyond the public level, the Church has become more tolerant of family planning activities and has muted its criticism of condom use as a HIV/AIDS preventive measure. Pro-Vida representatives admitted privately to the author that even some priests are unsure what Pro-Vida stands for. Since it was founded in 1978, when pro-life groups began to flourish in the USA, Pro-Vida has frequently assailed family planning programs and mobilized against initiatives deemed antithetical to "family values." By 1993, its formal structure extended to nearly all 31 states beyond the capital. Pro-Vida publicly exposes physicians and clinics said to be carrying out abortions. One former director of Mexico's largest family planning program described Pro-Vida to the author as "the civil armed force of the Catholic Church."[13]

In 2000, encouraged by the rise of the conservative PAN to the center of political life and by a president personally opposed to abortion, Pro-Vida invited U.S. anti-abortion protestors to Mexico. This led to giant pictures of aborted fetuses being held up in the capital's main square and outside alleged clandestine abortion clinics. The move won little support and evidently backfired. It was widely perceived as provocative and to constitute outside meddling in Mexican affairs and in what many Mexicans, especially women, consider to be a

---

[11] Interviews with Pro-Vida state representatives, July and August 1992, and October 2001. See also Loaeza-Lajous (1990) on Opus Dei's activities in Mexico.

[12] Interview with Bishop N. Rivera (President, Episcopal Commission for the Family), Tehuacán, July 1992.

[13] Interview with a former director of the IMSS family planning program, Mexico City, July 1992.

private matter. That same year Pro-Vida assumed a limited presence in discussion of the 'Paulina case.' This may be because many press articles reported that two of the group's members illegally entered the hospital where Paulina was admitted so as to show her a video similar to *The Silent Scream* in an attempt to persuade her not to have an abortion.

Dissenting Catholicism

Several Catholic groups have recently attempted to open up debate about their Church's teaching on women, sexuality, and reproductive health, including abortion. The most prominent, *Católicas por el Derecho a Decidir* (Catholics for a Free Choice), is a small but active group that publishes a quarterly opinion journal on these matters, along the lines of its U.S. parent organization. It soon earned the wrath of the institutional Church due to its calls for church reform and its work to win public support for widening the legal grounds for abortion, though the groups does not advocate to make the procedure available on demand. The alternative strand of Catholic thought it represents is not well known in Mexico, and it possesses few resources compared to the Church hierarchy.

Despite these limitations, the group has managed to garner considerable media attention and to highlight some inconsistencies in the Church's position on sexuality, birth control, and abortion. On World AIDS Day, 2001, the Church hierarchy even granted it permission to hold a religious celebration in Mexico City's cathedral as part of the group's campaign to promote condom use to prevent the spread of AIDS.[14] Other groups, calling for a greater dialogue within the Church, command less public presence and refrain from directly questioning official teaching on abortion. Their existence, however, shows that a plurality of opinions exists within the Church, despite initial appearances to the contrary.

The Feminist Push for Abortion Rights

Feminists have been by far the most vocal advocates of legalizing abortion. Feminist activism grew in the 1970s, aided by awareness of the success of the feminist movement in the USA and Western Europe, the government's new rhetorical commitment to gender equality that marked its reversal on population policy, and the staging of the 1975 UN conference on women in Mexico City. Demands for the legalization of abortion figured prominently in the formation of various action groups, notably the *Coalición de Mujeres Feministas*, and in the leading feminist journal, *Fem*. However, differences developed over whether to push for decriminalization alone or abortion on demand; what time limit to seek under which an abortion should be permitted without restriction; and how best to pursue such claims.

The loose-knit feminist coalition has been beset by deep, long-standing internal divisions, strategic errors, and organizational problems.[15] The purist convictions held by feminist leaders, and their understandable fears of being coopted and neutralized by the PRI, made it

[14] As reported in *La Jornada*, 2 December, 2001.

[15] The author's assessment is based primarily on discussions held with feminist activists and researchers, as well as other academics and well-informed observers. See also Tarrés (1993); and Lamas et al. (1995).

even more difficult to succeed in a de facto one-party system. The cooperation with the communist parliamentary fraction in 1979 heavily stigmatized feminists; the 1990 controversy over abortion in Chiapas showed they could not rely on the political left for support and that they have not managed to exploit their opportunities. A decade later, the case of 'Paulina' and the attempted ban on abortion for rape victims in Guanajuato stung women's groups into protest and facilitated passage of the 'Robles laws.' Since Mexico entered systemic change however, women's groups have become disillusioned by government cutbacks in women's programs and lack of progress on many issues. The feminist movement remains splintered and elitist in a class-ridden society,[16] failing to absorb young people and to speak meaningfully to the mass of women it claims to represent. Their concerns are more often rooted in basic economic needs and reflected in the demands of many other women's activists that, for the most part, are not integrated into an understanding of gender oppression.

In an attempt to be more effective and to avoid speaking as separate cliques talking among themselves, several women's rights activists formed the group GIRE about the same time that the state modified the legal status of religious institutions. GIRE seeks to advance a reproductive rights agenda that stresses the public health and social justice reasons for revising abortion policy.[17] It has jointly sponsored with Gallup, the US-based polling organization, several well-publicized surveys of attitudes on abortion in Mexico as part of its aims to promote action-oriented research and disseminate information. By 1996, four years after its foundation, GIRE employed 16 staff members, commanded good contacts with journalists who increasingly reported its opinions in juxtaposition to those of the Church, and had developed contacts with sympathetic lawyers. Five years later however, partial loss of donor support forced GIRE to scale back its activities, and it has struggled since to build on its initial successes.

Health Care Providers

Earlier research on abortion influenced public health and medical opinion in support of family planning across Latin America (Mundigo, 1996). Once family planning programs were established however, Mexican physicians stayed remarkably mute about abortion. Although they feel they can legitimately decide on matters of women's health and fertility, many male professionals in dominant positions do not ascribe high priority to abortion problems. Moreover, Mexican physicians are largely apolitical, neither working individually nor through their professional organizations to effect change. Some physicians maintain silence on abortion because they illegally profit from it, while others stay quiet for fear of being stigmatized with doing so, or because they would rather not confront medical and legal institutional norms. Interviews with some physicians also revealed a resistance on the part of health care providers to giving proper care. This may stem from personal convictions about appropriate reproductive conduct and is manifested in different ways; even the quality of hospital registration forms differs between those women admitted for an incomplete abortion

[16] Feminism has been mostly a force among urban middle-class women, as in many Latin American countries (Jaquette, 1994). The middle class, however, is a very diverse grouping that also contains many women opposed to feminism.

[17] As emphasized in interviews held with the group's founders and personnel, July 1992, March 1996, and October 2001; and as reflected in its promotional materials.

and those admitted for a caesarean section or a normal delivery, underlining that abortion patients are usually treated as second-class patients.

Recent health ministers have sought to strengthen efforts aimed at reducing maternal mortality and reinforcing post-abortion services throughout state health institutions. In 1998, the Minister of Health emphasized the need to discuss abortion as a public health problem, prompting Pro-Vida to organize a street protest outside his ministry (GIRE, 2001). The National Institute of Public Health convened in 2001 a conference on the health aspects of unwanted pregnancy and abortion in the region. The meeting was attended by health officials and nongovernmental abortion-rights advocates from 20 Latin American countries, and was also picketed by Pro-Vida protestors. Health officials, in addition to finding it easier to deal with less conflictual issues, must contend with many other pressing health problems, not least extending health coverage to at least half the population that is poor.

Family planning agencies have not played a more pro-active role in abortion care for various political and cultural reasons. Several family planning leaders expressed to the author a concern that their programs lack adequate political protection from attacks by powerful groups opposed to their activities. Also, despite having embraced the new reproductive health agenda, family planning agencies tend to exhibit a "cultural bias" against involvement in abortion-related work. Their focus is on the technical aspects of contraceptive service delivery, not on the termination of an existing pregnancy. All are worried about engaging in public debate about abortion.

International Influences on the Abortion Debate

Mexico has been affected by the growing international awareness that abortion is a major health problem for women. By the early 1990s this became evident in the activities of several small players in the abortion debate. IPAS, a U.S.-based NGO that works to improve abortion care in poorer countries, helped provide training in post-abortion care and in the use of MVA equipment in public-sector hospitals to assist those suffering complications from incomplete abortion (Billings et al., 2003). Both the New York-based Population Council and the Ford Foundation sponsored reproductive health programs that included research on abortion, and the MacArthur Foundation supported the lobbying efforts of several NGOs promoting reproductive rights. In its own small way, this activity seems to have refocused attention on the issue by bringing together individuals working in separate institutions and adding to the discussion of public health and women's choices. These developments notwithstanding, research findings have been poorly disseminated, institutional coordination between the various programs and groups has proved elusive, and the state has paid little attention to their concerns.

Feminists have still not developed significant transnational linkages that could pressure the government to reconsider the question of abortion. Before Mexico entered systemic change, any such alignments would have been watched carefully by governments wary of NGOs. The diffusion of discourse on reproductive rights has provided a new opportunistic focus for activists and like-minded researchers. GIRE has used this rubric to rearticulate and strengthen women's demands, viewing abortion rights as part of a broader reproductive health agenda. It has cooperated closely with the New York-based Center for Reproductive Law and

Policy to highlight the areas of reproductive rights within the emerging international framework of documents and treaties that cover such issues.

Mexico has revised its population policy in light of the reproductive health agenda of the ICPD. But the concept of reproductive health has not yet reached most of the population, nor is it familiar to all service providers, and its operationalization has been stymied by budgetary cuts (Palma and Palma, 2000). Mexican officials are keenly aware that U.S. presidents moved vigorously in the 1980s and again in 2001-02 to restrict access to abortion. This may account for some of their own reluctance to consider abortion-related problems and has impeded efforts to tailor contraceptive services to the needs of post-abortion patients.[18] It would be wrong to overstate these influences though, as research efforts to publicize emergency contraception and post-abortion care may have swayed the government to approve such services. Nevertheless, over the course of the last decade, researchers at several organizations have told the author that their managers had communicated a preference for them not to study abortion-related issues.[19]

The Vatican views Mexico as pivotal to the diffusion of orthodox belief in Latin America, as well as a bridge linking religious movements in the region with those in the USA. John Paul II consistently criticized the use of contraceptives and abortion, inspiring Mexico's hierarchy to do likewise. The Pope's remarks on birth control underscore the degree to which the Vatican, the Mexican hierarchy, and Pro-Vida consider Mexico to be a strategic point in the worldwide struggle over abortion. Prominent churchmen and anti-abortion activists insist the government is under strong international pressures to reduce demographic growth by all means, including abortion, and point out that Mexico is a regional node for family planning organizations working in Latin America. They repeatedly stated to the author that legalization of abortion would open the door to similar moves within the region.[20] Pope Benedict XVI, a close ally and successor to John Paul II, is known to hold similar views on abortion.

In the late 1980s Pro-Vida held its first national congresses, meetings of its youth wing, and two international conferences attended by leading figures from the Mexican church and the U.S. anti-abortion movement. It has since proved adept at initiating and developing strong contacts with senior Church members. At the Vatican's request, it organized the first Latin American regional pro-life conference in Monterrey, 1992, attended by representatives from 22 Latin American and Southern European countries, as well as by cardinals from Mexico, Latin America, and the Vatican. In 1996, the Pontifical Council for the Family convened in Mexico City a meeting attended by politicians, legislators and leaders of anti-abortion groups from every American country. Conference participants judged both meetings favorably for

[18] As corroborated in meetings with various family planning officials. Post-abortion contraceptive services have long been deficient and equated with IUD insertion or sterilization, but have recently been improved (Family Health International, 1997; Chambers et al., 2001; Langer et al., 2002).

[19] Such advice carries implications for funding and employment security, and is almost certainly communicated down to managers from a higher level. In 1992, the director of CONAPO unexpectedly called off scheduled interviews with the present author on three occasions, underscoring a deep political sensitivity to discussing abortion that has not been shared by his successors. In 2002-03 Mexican researchers mentioned to the author similar concerns about studying abortion, although international NGOs have pushed research aimed at reducing the public health consequences of unsafe abortion.

[20] As highlighted in the author's interviews with J. Serrano Limón (Director, Pro-Vida); Bishop N. Rivera (President, Episcopal Commission for the Family); and A. Elena Cantú (Pro-Vida state representative, Monterrey), July-August, 1992. See also the official account of the first Latin America regional pro-life conference (Pro-Vida, 1992).

their publicity, networking and exchange of information, and the prospect of increased co-operation between national churches and church-linked organizations. Pro-Vida personnel acknowledge the momentum they have derived from U.S. anti-abortion groups, the help given by some U.S. Catholics in setting up Pro-Vida's Women's Aid Centers, and the written and audio-visual materials sent by the U.S.-based Human Life International and others. They now envisage playing a similar supportive role in Central and Latin America.

Barriers to Reforming Abortion Policy

There are many reasons why abortion does not command higher agenda status and why major revisions in abortion policy are not being more seriously pursued at the national level. They include the strong opposition of church-based groups and conservative sectors, the failure of potential reformers to successfully press the issue, and the lack of a societal consensus over abortion. A full explanation for this state of affairs, however, must take into account other structural impediments to policy reform. This is illustrated by the failure of feminism to find a niche within Mexican political culture, which still lacks a tradition of issue mobilization and citizenry participation in debates, and remains heavily male-centered. The discussion below focuses on five sets of obstacles: women's marginalization; the low priority given to health matters, particularly to women's reproductive health; cultural rationalizations of the personal dilemmas posed by abortion; the limited amount and dissemination of research documentation; and a series of political obstacles. We also consider the significance of recent legal initiatives for the future evolution of abortion policy.

The ability of women to transform their realities is impeded by cultural attitudes on sexuality and on gender roles internalized by most men and women. This situation is compounded by the alienation of women's groups from the socio-political arena and inadequate societal and governmental attempts to improve their status. For example, the National Commission for Women has long been an office without a budget, clear functions or authority, so that it cannot develop public policies for women, let alone tackle sensitive issues such as abortion. The state has tended to pay lip-service to women's health problems, despite having instituted its family planning program under a rhetoric that stressed individual choice, equal rights, the promotion of health among women and children, and avoidance of unwanted pregnancies and illegal abortions. Family planning has been accepted by most people out of economic necessity rather than out of concern about women's health or their self-autonomy. This makes it difficult to accept abortion for public health reasons. Moreover, few people think of health issues as politically important and, besides, there are more significant health problems than abortion. Recent discourse on reproductive rights has added to discussion about abortion, but groups seeking to liberalize abortion services are finding it difficult to sustain debate and extend it to such issues as sexual health and education.

There are certain culturally accepted ways of resolving the contradictions posed by abortion which have reduced the visibility of the phenomenon. Anthropological data from several semi-rural and rural communities, as well as from pharmacies and markets in Mexico City, show that abortifacients have been redefined as medicines for keeping a woman's period regular (Shedlin and Hollerbach, 1978; Ingham, 1986; Pick et al., 2003). Past neglect of the topic by researchers has additionally contributed to its oversight. The illegal status of abortion, its controversial nature, and the poor quality of available data have led many researchers to pass over the subject. Many are also ambivalent about it. Researchers have, however, highlighted some of the costs of incomplete abortions and thereby exercised influence with policymakers and reform advocates. In particular, all three of Mexico's major public sector health institutions have recently extended use of MVA across their health-care systems after research confirmed the procedure could cut treatment costs and enhance health facilities' capacity. In addition, the distribution of emergency contraceptive pills will most likely slowly improve now that it has been approved.

A series of political obstacles blocks more serious consideration of abortion law reform. They include the lack of political incentive for policymakers to carry out reform; the fear of opposition to such a measure; an inherited political culture that has not fostered political participation; and the use of the issue for other ends. With elite and societal consensus on the subject lacking and no politically significant sector calling for the legalization of abortion, policymakers see no obvious political advantage to changing the status quo. The perceived threat of a reaction to any reform measure from conservative circles contributes further to government inaction. Groups seeking to liberalize abortion law are also impeded by the low levels of mobilization and political participation, and the skepticism and cynicism shown toward a political system which though no longer authoritarian, is still not as open as is claimed.[21]

The abortion issue has also been used as a political game for different ends by various political circles. For example, right-wing groups have used it to rally support from those concerned about 'family values,' to secure Church favor, and to exert political influence. Leftist deputies used the controversy over the move to legalize abortion in Chiapas as part of a tactical game to oust the authoritarian State Governor and treated abortion *per se* as a secondary issue. Not until 2000 did they become involved in the forefront of efforts to liberalize abortion laws, and only then in the capital city as a reaction to the attempted adoption of restrictive legislation in Guanajuato. Various groups and commentators have also linked conflict over abortion to more frequent morality battles between liberals and social conservatives that have included arguments over gay rights and increased sexual content on television. Such political games underscore the complexity of the policy-setting on abortion and make for a stew of apparent contradictions.

The move by the Guanajuato state legislature heightened fears about the social agenda of the incoming government, but these have not materialized. Likewise, no other state has followed the example of the more liberal 'Robles laws' in Mexico City. Nevertheless, the symbolic significance of the Supreme Court considering the issue of abortion for the first time warrants further comment. Abortion-rights advocates believed that the capital's legal initiative and its ratification by the country's highest judicial authority might set a precedent, enabling easier access to safe abortion without fear of retribution. However, the new law essentially re-confirmed what had already been permitted and added a few minor indications for abortion in difficult circumstances; it did not address the gap between other aspects of abortion law and practice. Even though sexual assault has been for decades a legal indication

[21] Many commentators from a range of perspectives have drawn attention to the civic distrust in Mexican political culture. See, for example, Octavio Paz's writings about 'mestizaje'(Paz, 1997); Camp (2002); and Preston and Dillon (2004).

for abortion, the sharp divisions apparent among the Supreme Court's members indicated the lack of consensus within the judiciary for extending further the grounds for abortion.

The Supreme Court's judgment served notice nationally that Mexico City's rules are constitutional and pushed health authorities to enable women to take advantage of them. The Federal District's health authorities promised to ensure abortion services under the law, but there are many barriers to its implementation. The new law gives the state prosecutor responsibility for authorizing abortions for rape victims, a time-consuming process, and despite establishing an institutional mechanism to enable such women to have an abortion, powerful social and religious norms militate against the expansion of sexual and reproductive rights. Like adolescents' access to sexual and reproductive health information and services, abortion lacks a consistent legal and policy framework that reflects a commitment to the exercise of women's reproductive rights.

Presently, Mexico is in the early stages of multiparty democracy. Leftist deputies have not pursued measures that would decriminalize abortion further, and it is unclear if they would were a more liberal party to gain power in 2006. Officials continue to turn a blind eye to clandestine abortion, whereby women with financial resources and connections may secure a safe abortion whereas the poor often have to risk their health by making do with sub-optimal procedures. Abortion remains a deeply contentious political issue and an unsettling question for most Mexicans. Without more fundamental social and political change, only minor efforts will be made to confront the reality that abortion is a greater problem than it need be.

CONCLUSION

Data on abortion in Mexico are extremely limited. Nevertheless, the broad outline of existing problems is reasonably clear. For women, abortion has long been a major cause of ill-health, including death that was hidden from public discourse. The pretense that it did not happen because it was outlawed perpetuated existing problems, although such a contradiction may not seem at all strange or troubling to much of society.[22] Most people appear to hold mixed and confused feelings about abortion, and their actions may often contradict their beliefs. Successive governments could have enforced changes in abortion policy on several occasions before Mexico entered systemic change, but appear to have found the issue too sensitive with no clear political gain. In contrast to their active leadership in providing family planning services, which has helped reduce abortion, ambivalent government elites have passed over the problems associated with restrictive abortion laws whose penalties are seldom enforced, but which keep the procedure expensive and clandestine, with adverse public health consequences.

Abortion has become more problematic in Mexico not only due to the clash between groups seeking to determine the course of related public policy. The problem has been accentuated by unmet family planning needs, the neglect of women's reproductive health, changes in women's status and behavior and, more slowly, in public attitudes toward women

[22] The theme that even mutually contradictory truths can be true, including those which are unknown and which otherwise belong to the imaginary realm, is not only pointed out by Mexican writers. It is also evident in the novels of Gabriel García Márquez, as well as other Latin American authors.

and sexuality, as well as growing awareness of the public health risks stemming from the restrictive laws. The exposure of various social myths surrounding abortion and sexuality, the growth in research interest and publicity, and external influences have contributed as well.

Abortion has been debated periodically over the last three decades. In between such points in time, the issue of abortion seems to have vanished underground rather like the practice itself, with policymakers seemingly aloof to the circumstances surrounding it. Until the controversy surrounding a regional initiative to reform abortion laws in late 1990 demystified the subject further, discussion of abortion was largely confined to elite and technocratic circles. Debate became truly national in 2000 following several controversial legal initiatives and the well-publicized cases of two adolescent rape victims unlawfully denied abortions. However, the question of abortion policy reform has been funneled away from agenda status by a "system of bias" that limits serious consideration of policy alternatives judged by the government to be at once too disruptive, controversial, and bearing insufficient political gain. This is not to say that such a policy shift will not occur one day. For example, new discourses, such as reproductive rights, may come to challenge this status quo and a more propitious moment for enacting change may emerge. Moreover, conflict over abortion is likely to be more difficult to contain as society becomes more open and women develop greater choices and secure more influence. The 'abortion pill' mifepristone is not currently approved for use in Mexico, but may yet become available unofficially through the porous border with the USA.

Presently, post-abortion care services are being steadily institutionalized in public-sector health facilities across the country. This incremental change represents an important public health advance. It is also relatively non-controversial and an ethical imperative. Debate about abortion is now more open, but broad access to the procedure is not up for discussion. The country's leaders are unlikely to consider more substantive policy changes in the near future for fear of provoking bitter conflict and because they have little compelling political reason to do so. This is why for the time being at least, new ways of coming to terms with abortion are unlikely to advance much further.

References

Aguirre, Alejandro (1997) "Mortalidad maternal en México: medición a partir de estadísticas vitals," *Estudios Demográficos y Urbanos*, 12(1-2): 69-99.

Becker, Davida, Sandra G. Garcia and Ulla Larsen (2002) "Knowledge and opinions about abortion law among Mexican youth," *International Family Planning Perspectives*, 28(4): 205-213.

Billings, Deborah L., Jamie F. Velásquez and Ricardo Pérez-Cuevas (2003) "Comparing the quality of three models of postabortion care in public hospitals in Mexico City," *International Family Planning Perspectives*, 29(3): 112-120.

Blancarte, Roberto (1991) *El poder salinismo e Iglesia Católica. ¿Una nueva convivencia?* (México City: Editorial Grijalbo).

Camp, Roderic A. (2002) *Politics in Mexico: The Democratic Transformation* (New York: Oxford University Press), 4th edition.

Chambers, Virginia M., Andrea S. Rivera, Jaime F. Velazquez, Eduardo P. Cruz and Ramiro M. Ponce (2001) "Expanding postabortion care in Mexico's public health institutions: lessons from a decade of experience", paper presented at the 129th annual meeting of the American Public Health Association, October, Atlanta.

CONAPO (Consejo Nacional de Población) (1976) *Grupo Interdisciplinario para el Estudio del Aborto en México. Informe final* (Mexico City: CONAPO).

CONAPO (1995) *Programa Nacional de Población 1995-2000* (Mexico City: CONAPO).

CONAPO (1996) *Indicadores básicos de salud reproductive y planificación familiar* (Mexico City: CONAPO).

CONAPO (1997) *Encuestra Nacional de Planificación Familiar* (Mexico City: CONAPO).

David, Henry P. y Susan Pick de Weiss (1992) "Abortion in the Americas," in Abdel R. Omran, Joao Unes, José A. Solis, and Guillermo Lopez (eds.) *Reproductive Health in the Americas* (Washington, D.C.: Pan American Health Organization), pp. 323-354.

De la Barreda Solórzano, Luis (1991) *El delito del Aborto: Una careta de buena conciencia* (Mexico City: Miguel Angel Porrúa).

De la Madrid, Miguel (1982) "Miguel de la Madrid on population policy in Mexico," *Population and Development Review*, 8(2): 435-438.

Ehrenfeld, Noemí (1999). "Female adolescents at the crossroads: Sexuality, contraception and abortion in Mexico," in Axel I. Mundigo and Cynthia Indriso (eds.), *Abortion in the Developing World* (London: Zed Books), pp. 368-386.

Ellertson, Charlotte, Angela Heimburger, Dolores Acevedo-Garcia, Raffaela Schiavon, Guillermina Mejia, Georgina Corona, Eduardo del Castillo, Ana Langer (2002) "Information campaign and advocacy efforts to promote access to emergency contraception in Mexico," *Contraception*, 66(5):331-7.

Elu, Maria del Carmen (1999) "Between political debate and women's suffering: Abortion in Mexico," in Axel I. Mundigo and Cynthia Indriso (eds.), *Abortion in the Developing World* (London: Zed Books), pp. 245-258.

Family Health International (1997) *Postpartum and Postabortion Family Planning in Latin America: Interviews with Health Providers, Policymakers and Women's Advocates in Ecuador, Honduras and México* (Research Triangle Park, NC: Family Health International and Pan American Health Organization).

Frejka, Tomás and Lucille C. Atkin (1996) "The role of induced abortion in the fertility transition of Latin America," in José M. Guzmán, Susheela Singh, Germán Rodruez and Edith A. Pantelides (eds.), *The Fertility Transition in Latin America* (Oxford: Clarendon Press), pp. 179-91.

Gaslonde, Santiago (1976) "Abortion research in Latin America," *Studies in Family Planning*, 7(8): 211-217.

GIRE (2000) *Paulina en el Nombre de la Ley* (Mexico City: Grupo de Información en Reproducción Elegida).

GIRE (2001) *Trazos de una polémica: El aborto en 1998*, Mexico City: Grupo de Información en Reproducción Elegida.

Goldberg, Alisa B., Mara B. Greenberg, and Philip D. Darney (2001) "Misoprostol and pregnancy," *The New England Journal of Medicine*, 344(1): 38-47.

González, Lucero M. (1992) "La penalización del aborto en México," *Mujeres y Política*, UAM Xochimilco, no. 1.

INEGI (Instituto Nacional de Estadística Geografía e Informática) (2000) *Estadísticas del Sector Salud y Seguridad Social* (Aguascalientes, Mexico: INEGI), no. 16, p. 133.

INEGI (2001) *Mujeres y Hombres en México* (Aguascalientes, Mexico: INEGI).

Infante Castañeda, Claudia and Yolanda Cobos-Pons (1989) "El aborto induicido en cifras: análisis de la difusión de las estadísticas en la prensa," *Salud Pública de México*, 31(3): 385-393.

Ingham, John M. (1986) *Mary, Michael and Lucifer: Folk Catholicism in Central Mexico* (Austin, TX: University of Texas).

Isaacs, Stephen L. and Hernán Sanhueza (1975) "Induced abortion in Latin America: the legal perspective," in PAHO, *Epidemiology of Abortion and Practices of Fertility Regulation in Latin America: Selected Reports* (Washington, D.C.: Pan American Health Organization), PAHO Scientific Publication no. 306, pp. 39-49.

Jaquette, Jane S. (ed.) (1994) *The Women's Movement in Latin America: Participation and the Transition to Democracy* (Boulder, CO: Westview Press), 2nd edition.

Johnson, Brooke R., Jane Benson, Janet Bradley, and Aurora Rábago Ordoñez (1993) "Costs and resource utilization for the treatment of incomplete abortion in Kenya and Mexico", *Social Science and Medicine*, 36(11): 1443-1453.

Kulczycki, Andrzej, Malcolm Potts, and Allan Rosenfield (1996) "Abortion and Fertility Regulation," *The Lancet*, 1996; 347: 1663-1668.

Kulczycki, Andrzej (1999) *The Abortion Debate in the World Arena* (New York: Routledge).

Lamas, Marta (1992) "El aborto en México," *Nexos*, 15(176): 51-59.

Lamas, Marta, Alicia Martínez, María L. Tarrés, and Esperanza Tuñon (1995) "Building bridges: the growth of popular feminism in Mexico," in Amrita Basu (ed.) *The Challenge of Local Feminisms: Women's Movements in Global Perspective* (Boulder, CO: Westview Press), pp. 324-347.

Langer, Ana, Angela Heimburger, Cecilia Garcia-Barrios, and Beverly Winikoff (2002) "Improving postabortion care in a public hospital in Mexico," in Nicole Haberland and Diana Measham (eds.). *Responding to Cairo: Case Studies of Changing Practice in Reproductive Health and Family Planning* (New York: Population Council), pp. 236-256.

Leal, Luisa M. (ed.) (1980) *El problema del aborto en México* (Mexico City: Editorial Porrúa).

Loaeza-Lajous, Soledad (1990) "Continuity and change in the Mexican Catholic church," in D. Keogh (ed.) *Church and Politics in Latin America* (New York: St. Martin's Press), pp. 272-298.

López García, Raúl (1994) "El aborto como problema de salud pública," in Elu, Ma. del Carmen and Ana Langer (eds.) *Maternidad sin riesgos en México* ('Maternity without Risk') (Mexico City: Instituto Mexicano de Estudios Sociales), pp. 85-90.

Mendoza, Doroteo (1991) *Impacto demografico del aborto induicido en Mexico*, Division of Reproductive and Maternal/Child Health, IMSS, Mexico City, unpublished paper.

Metz, Allan (1992) "Mexican church-state relations under President Carlos Salinas de Gortari," *Journal of Church and State*, 34(1): 111-130.

Monsivaís, Carlos (1991) "De cómo un día amaneció Pro-Vida con la novedad de vivir en una sociedad laica," *Debate Feminista*, 2(3): 82-88.

Mundigo, Axel (1996) "The Role of Family Planning Programmes in the Fertility Transition of Latin America," in José M. Guzmán, Susheela Singh, Germán Rodruez and Edith A.

Pantelides (eds.) *The Fertility Transition in Latin America*, Oxford: Clarendon Press, pp. 192-210.

Núñez Fernández, Leopoldo (2001) *Incidencia, diferenciales, y actitudes del aborto en México: metodologías alternativas*, Master's thesis (unpublished), Mexico City: El Colegio de México.

Ordóñez, Blanca R. (1975) "Induced abortion in Mexico City: Summary conclusions from two studies conducted by the Mexican Social Security Institute", in PAHO *Epidemiology of Abortion and Practices of Fertility Regulation in Latin America: Selected Reports*, PAHO Scientific Publication no. 306, Washington, D.C.: Pan American Health Organization, pp. 26-29.

Ortiz-Ortega, Adriana (2001) *Si los hombres se embarazaran, ¿el aborto sería legal ? Las feministas ante la relación Estado-Iglesia católica (1871-2000)* (Mexico City: Edamex/Population Council).

Palma Cabrera, Yolanda, Juan G. Figueroa Perea, Alejandro Cervantes Carson and Carlos Echarri Cánovas (1989) *México. Encuesta Nacional sobre Fecundidad y Salud* (Mexico City: Ministry of Health, Division of Family Planning; and Columbia, MD: Institute for Resource Development/Macro Systems).

Palma, Yolanda and José Luis Palma (2000) "Mexico," in Shephard Forman and Romita Ghosh (eds.) *Promoting Reproductive Health: Investing in Health for Development* (Boulder, CO: Lynne Rienner), pp. 111-145.

Paz, Octavio (1997) *The Labyrinth of Solitude: Life and Thought in Mexico* (New York: Grove Press).

Pérez-Palacios, G. and J. Garza-Flores (1994) "The contributions of Mexican scientists to contraceptive research and development," in P.F.A. Van Look and G. Pérez-Palacios (eds.), *Contraceptive Research and Development 1984 to 1994: The Road from Mexico City to Cairo and Beyond* (Delhi: Oxford University Press), pp. 233-246.

Pick, Susan, Martha Givaudan, Marsela Alvarez Izazaga, and María Elena Collado (2003) "The role of pharmacists and market herb vendors as abortifacient providers in Mexico City," in Alaka M. Basu (ed.). *The Sociocultural and Political Aspects of Abortion: Global Perspectives* (Westport, CT: Praeger).

Pick de Weiss, Susan and Henry David (1990) "Illegal abortion in Mexico: Client perspections," *American Journal of Public Health*, 80(6): 715-716.

Poniatowska, Elena (2000) *Las mil y una... (la herida de Paulina)* (Barcelona: Plaza & Janés Editores).

Preston, Julia and Samuel Dillon (2004) *Opening Mexico: The Making of a Democracy* (New York: Farrar, Straus and Giroux).

Pro-Vida (1992) *1 Encuentro Latinoamericano Pro-Vida, Monterrey, México, 22-24 April,* 1992 (Mexico City: Comité Nacional Pro-Vida/Pontifical Council for the Family).

Puente, María A. (1992) "The Church in Mexico", in Enrique Dussel (ed.) *The Church in Latin America: 1492-1992* (Maryknoll, NY: Orbis Books), pp. 217-229.

Shedlin, Michele G. and Paula E. Hollerbach (1978) "Modern and traditional fertility regulation in a Mexican community: the process of decision making," *Studies in Family Planning*, 12(6/7): 278-296.

Singh, Susheela and Deirdre Wulf (1994) "Estimated levels of induced abortion in six Latin American countries," *International Family Planning Perspectives*, 20(1): 4-13.

Tarrés, María L. (1993) "El movimiento de mujeres y el sistema político mexicano: análisis de la lucha por la liberalización del aborto, 1976-1990," *Estudios Sociológicos*, 11(32): 365-397.

Trussell, James, Charlotte Ellertson, Felicia Stewart, Elizabeth Raymond, and Tara Shochet (2004) "The role of emergency contraception," *American Journal of Obstetrics and Gynecology*, 190, S30-S38.

UN (2005) *World Population Prospects: The 2004 Revision*. New York: United Nations.

Vera, Rodrigo (1994) "El gobierno Mexicano, indeciso sobre el aborto, ante la Conferencia Internacional de El Cairo," *Proceso*, no. 925, 25 July, pp. 52-55.

Viel, Benjamin V. (1988) "Latin America," in Paul Sachdev (ed.) *International Handbook on Abortion*. New York: Greenwood Press, pp. 317-332.

Weddington, Sarah R. (1992). *A Question of Choice*. New York: Putnam.

In: Mexico: Economic, Political and Social Issues
Editors: Maria L. Castro and Irene P. Navarro

ISBN: 978-1-60456-847-9

Chapter 9

An Interaction Model of HIV/AIDS Prevention Based in Hispanic Parent-Adolescent Communication about Sex

Raquel Benavides-Torres[1,2], Claude Bonazzo[1], Edith Cruz-Quevedo[2]
[1]University of Texas at Austin, USA
[2]Universidad Autónoma de Nuevo León, Monterrey, México

Abstract

Acquired Immunodeficiency Syndrome is a global epidemic. Seventy six percent of the total cases are in the age range of 18-35, which provide suspicions that most of the infections occur during adolescence. Adolescents often engage in sexual risk behaviors because they do not have enough information to make the best decisions concerning their sexual behavior. The adolescents' parents play a very important role in the sexual development and promotion of HIV/AIDS prevention. Parent-adolescent communication about sex is an important medium for adolescents because it provides them with a source of information and values that allow them to make safer sex decisions. Due to the fact that communication is a bi-directional process, it is important to take into account the parent-adolescent interaction. Therefore, the purpose of this paper is to explain an interaction model for HIV/AIDS prevention based in parent-adolescent communication about sex with the Hispanic population using the Self-Efficacy Theory. The model conceives the parent-adolescent dyad for HIV/AIDS prevention. There are two central elements that support this model. The first is the interaction of parent and adolescent to achieve the same goal, which is HIV/AIDS prevention. The second is focused on the general cultural characteristics of Hispanic families, such as: allocentrism, time orientation, gender roles, and fatalism. The principle concepts in this model are parent-adolescent interactions, preventive behaviors, and HIV/AIDS prevention as an outcome. The parent-adolescent interactions include: cultural characteristics, attitudes, beliefs, and knowledge. Together parent's and adolescent's efficacy expectations may result in the activation of preventive behaviors. The preventive behaviors for adolescents are abstinence, condom use, and partner discussion. The preventive behaviors for parents are quality and quantity of communication about sex. The maintenance and perseverance of parent-adolescent behaviors are regulated by outcome expectations such as, prevention of diseases, perceived benefits, partner protection for the adolescent, closeness and sexual risk reduction for parents. Thus, the adolescent's and parent's belief about the positive results of their behavior should result in the repetition of the preventive behavior. This repetition will increase the probability of preventing HIV/AIDS in Hispanic adolescents. This model illustrates the importance of working with efficacy and outcome expectations to improve the parent-adolescent behaviors for HIV/AIDS prevention. Health care providers may use this model to develop effective prevention programs in the community, guide the development of parent and adolescent skills in an educational context, and modify it to fit other STD's.

Keywords: HIV/AIDS prevention; communication about sex; self-efficacy; adolescents; parents.

Introduction

Acquired Immunodeficiency Syndrome (AIDS) is a global epidemic. Around the world, more than 27 million people have died, and 16 thousand people become infected every day (Joint United Nations Program on HIV/AIDS [UNAIDS], 2006a). In 2005, more than 39 million of people become infected by Human Immunodeficiency Virus (HIV), as a result AIDS has become a public health emergency (UNAIDS, 2006b). In the Latin American and Caribbean countries, the cases of HIV reported in 2005 totaled more than 1,308,000 and more than 90,000 deaths (UANAIDS, 2006c; UNAIDS, 2006d). The Hispanic population in the United Sates has grown rapidly and this has increased the probability of contracting the HIV virus. In 1993, HIV/AIDS cases among Hispanics totaled 18% and six years later they increased to 20% (Center for Diseases Control and Prevention [CDC], 2006). The fact that AIDS in the 18-35 age group are 72% of the total cases provide suspicions that most of the infections occurred during adolescence because of the long HIV incubation period (CDC, 2005; Pilcher et al., 2001; UNAIDS & World Health Organization [WHO], 2001).

The HIV infections among Hispanic adolescents are influenced by different factors. For example, like all adolescents, Hispanic adolescents go through developmental stages that are characterized by taking risks that allow them to define and discover their identity. In addition, many adolescents do not think about the possibility of getting pregnant or contracting HIV/AIDS (Guttmacher et al., 1997). A behavioral risk for HIV typically taken by Hispanic adolescents is the practice of unprotected sex with multiple partners (Villaseñor-Sierra, Caballero-Hoyos, Hidalgo-San Martín, & Santos-Preciado, 2003). One explanation given for this type of risk behavior is that Hispanic adolescents do not have enough information to make the best decisions concerning their sexual behavior (Romo, Lefkowitz, Sigman, & Au, 2001). One of the most important sources of information for adolescents are their parents. When using a parent-adolescent communication model about sex, parents may clarify adolescents doubts and may encourage them to make safer sex decisions. DiClemente, Wingood, Crosby, Cobb, Harrington, and Davies (2001) reported that adolescents whose parents talk with them about sexual matters and provide sexual education, or contraceptive information at home are more likely than others to postpone sexual activity. In addition, when these adolescents become sexually active they have fewer sexual partners and are more likely to use contraceptives, condoms, and other protective methods (DiClemente et al., 2001).

However, most Hispanic families do not discuss sexual issues as openly as European American families (Romo et al., 2001).

Bandura (1986) affirmed that people's beliefs about the outcome of a specific behavior may affect their execution. Moreover, the belief related to the confidence of doing a certain action is what he called self-efficacy. Similarly, Weeks (1998) in his metanalysis, concluded that the belief about positive parent-adolescent communication (e.g., decrease of sexual risk behaviors for HIV/AIDS) may predict the parental communication with the adolescent. In addition, adolescents believe the most convenient source of information on sexual topics are parents (Bhattachaya, Cleland, & Holland, 2000; Durán, García, Ramírez, & Sifuentes, 2000; Palacios, 2001). Thus, parents and adolescents efficacy expectations and benefits about the advantage of parent-adolescent communication about sex and sexual health behaviors may have an important impact for HIV/AIDS prevention.

In the last 25 years, theorists have worked hard to develop the evidence base practice. Some of these efforts have been delineating the role health care professionals have in the prevention of various diseases such as HIV/AIDS. Social theories can be used to help understand the phenomenon of HIV/AIDS prevention in adolescents, but it is central to legitimate the use of these theories in our population of interest (Villarruel, Bishop, Simpson, Jemmont, & Fawcett, 2001). In the case of HIV/AIDS prevention, the use of different models changes in diverse populations. A cursory review of literature revels that studies have used models that have not been adapted for Hispanics. It is crucial to understand that this population has some specific characteristics that must be addressed appropriately (Marin, 1991). An HIV/AIDS prevention model that is based on sexual communication needs to include Hispanic cultural values that may affect the process and outcomes of an intervention (Benavides, Bonazzo, & Torres, 2006). Unless the impact of these components is addressed, it will be difficult to have effective HIV/AIDS prevention strategies for Hispanic adolescents. Therefore, the purpose of this paper is to explain an interaction model for HIV/AIDS prevention based in parent-adolescent communication about sex with the Hispanic population using the Self-Efficacy Theory.

Self-Efficacy

The first person to introduce the self-efficacy construct was Albert Bandura, who used a Social Cognitive Theory as a basis for his analysis. In this theory, the behavior, characteristics, and environment of a person are represented as constantly interacting (Bandura, 1986, 1997). Cognitive, social, and behavioral skills must be organized for action to take place and control is used in the events that may occur in people's lives. The belief of personal efficacy using these skills is strongly related to their execution. Perceived self-efficacy is defined as "people's judgments of their capabilities to organize and execute courses of action required to attain designated types of performances. It is concerned, not with the skills one has but, with judgments of what one can do with whatever skills one possesses" (Bandura, 1986, p.391). In this theory the behavior is acquired and regulated by cognitive processes.

The basic premise in the Self-Efficacy Theory, according to Bandura (1977, 1986), is that the expectation of personal mastery or, in other words, the efficacy expectations, and the outcome expectations determine whether an individual will engage in a particular behavior. The principle concepts in Bandura's model are characteristics of a person, the behavior of the person, and the outcome of the behavior. These combined concepts involve two kinds of expectations that are efficacy expectations and outcome expectations. An efficacy expectation focuses on one's capability to produce the behavior. An outcome expectation is a person's belief about the outcomes that result from a given behavior. People are motivated to perform behaviors that they believe will produce desired outcomes (Bandura, 1977).

The Self-Efficacy Theory mainly focuses on the behavior of an individual. However, taking into consideration the usefulness of this model for HIV/AIDS prevention this theory is applicable as a dyad model for parents and adolescents in the Hispanic population. The HIV/AIDS prevention model based in parent-adolescent communication about sex in Hispanics (Figure 1) illustrates their interactions in the model. The emphasis of creating an interactive model is due to the fact that communication is used for the transmission of information from one source to another (King 1981). Therefore, communication about sex is a dyadic process between parents and adolescents as this model explains.

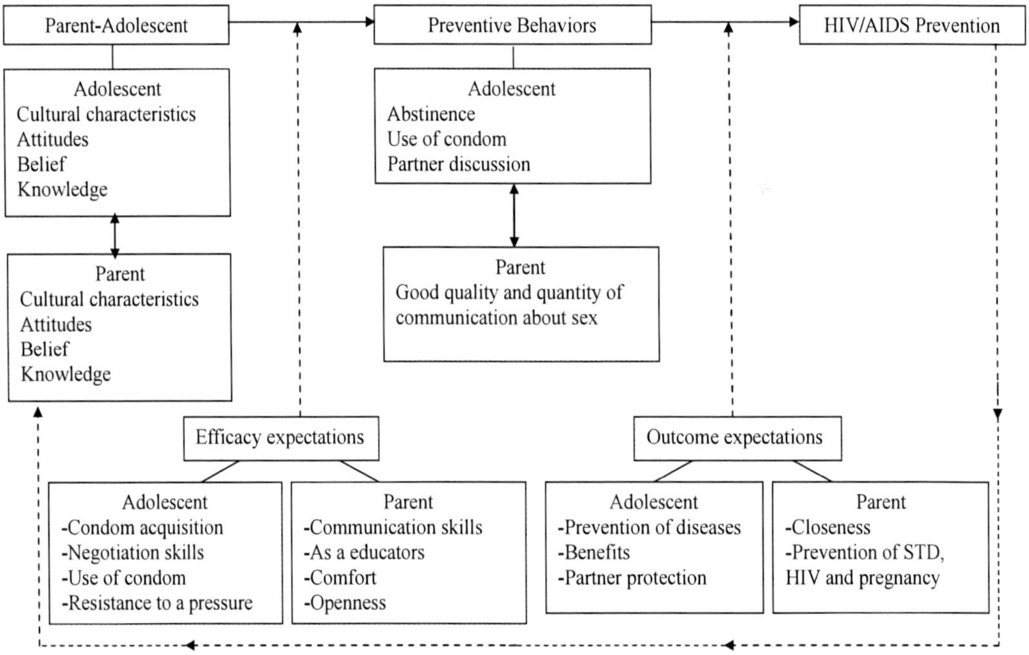

Figure 1. An interaction model of HIV/AIDS prevention based in parent-adolescent communication about sex in Hispanics.*

* The principle concepts in the model are parent-adolescent interactions, preventive behaviors, and HIV/AIDS prevention. As mentioned above the model describes cultural characteristics, attitudes, beliefs, and knowledge for adolescents and parents. Together with parent's and adolescent's efficacy and outcome expectations may result in the initiation of HIV prevention.

Model of HIV/AIDS Prevention Based in Parent-Adolescent Communication about Sex

Two principle characteristics support the parent-adolescent communication model for Hispanics. The first characteristic is the interaction of parent and adolescent to achieve the same goal, which is HIV/AIDS prevention. However, while the primary goal in this model is HIV/AIDS prevention, this model may be are useful for pregnancy and STD prevention in adolescents as well. The other characteristic that distinguishes the model is its focus on Hispanic families. The model was elaborated with the review of literature focusing only on Hispanic and Latino populations, with emphasis on the cultural characteristics of Hispanics and their importance. The primary concepts in the model are parent-adolescent interactions, preventive behaviors, and HIV/AIDS prevention as an outcome.

The parent-adolescents interactions include: cultural characteristics, attitudes, beliefs, and knowledge for adolescents and parents. Together parent's and adolescent's efficacy expectations may result in the activation of preventive behaviors. The preventive behaviors for adolescents include abstinence, use of condom, and partner discussion. The preventive behaviors for parents are quality and quantity of communication about safe sex behaviors. The maintenance of parent-adolescent behaviors is regulated by outcome expectations, such as prevention of diseases, perceived benefits, partner protection for the adolescent, closeness and sexual risk reduction for the parents. An outcome expectation is the capacity to characterize the future consequences of an action (Bandura, 1977; 1986). In other words the adolescent's and parent's belief about positive outcomes because of their behaviors should result in the recurrence of the preventive behavior. This repetition will increase the probability of preventing HIV/AIDS in the Hispanic adolescent

Parent-Adolescent Interactions

Cultural Characteristics

The concept of cultural characteristics of Hispanics is an important feature to consider when working with the Hispanic population. One of the cultural characteristics common in Hispanic communities is the identification of the individual as member of the community. Even when Hispanics come from Mexico, Cuba, Puerto Rico, or other countries of Latin America, and have different traditions, religions and demography; many share cultural characteristics that make them members of a particular group (Pajewski & Enriquez, 1996; Rizo et al., 2004). Therefore, this paper explains the importance of considering Hispanics' cultural characteristics. The most common cultural characteristics that may influence the execution of a prevention model when working with Hispanics are allocéntrism, time orientation, gender roles, and fatalism.

Allocéntrism

According to Marín and VanOss (1991), *allocéntrism* is a characteristic referring to the feeling of being part of a group. Accordingly, with this cultural characteristic, adolescents and parents may think similarly to a group of friends in their community and that community may influence their behavior when it comes to safe sex behaviors. Allocéntrism involves feelings of unity, reciprocity, and trust. "La familia" (family), is a close group unit and the primary component of Hispanic society. In most Hispanic families, the authority figure and provider is the father, while the mother is responsible for the home (Hispanic Ministry in the Southeast, 2003). This concept of allocentrism illustrates that the adolescent may make some decisions according to family values and perspectives of the larger community. Due to the value placed on the family, adolescents will be more likely to consider parental opinions or suggestions and attempt to meet their expectations.

Time Orientation

Another cultural characteristic of Hispanics is *time orientation*. Hispanic society is characterized by its orientation to the present and generally prefer not to plan for the future (Marin & VanOss, 1991). Because the present is viewed more valuable than the future, adolescents and parents engage in prevention behaviors after the fact. For example, an adolescent will go to see the doctor after having sex with somebody suspected of having an STD (McQuinston & Flaskerud, 2000; Pajowsky & Enrriquez, 1996) instead of planning ahead to prevent the infection of STD's. Adolescents may not be concerned about a possible risk but they could be interested in the issues about having sex such as experiencing pleasure, enjoying the moment, and attempting to represent themselves as a typical man or woman. In this model, parents must believe that 'right now' is the best time for starting a discussion with their adolescent about sex. Parents should realize that talking to their son or daughter in the present about future behaviors may prevent adolescents to be at risk of contracting HIV or AIDS (Jemmott, Jemmott, & McCaffree, 1999).

Gender Roles

Gender roles are another important cultural characteristic that needs to be taken into consideration when working with Hispanics. Machismo (chauvinism) is a male characteristic, meaning to be strong, in control, and the provider for the family. This machismo affects both men and women, because these attitudes promote the seeking of multiple sexual partners and rare usage of condoms placing them at risk for STD's including HIV/AIDS (VanOss, 2003; Marin & VanOss, 1991). Women are described as submissive and possess less social power than men. Women generally do not talk about their feelings related to sex, as a result, negotiating sexual safety in a relationship is difficult and can encourage sexual abuse (VanOss, 2003; Werner-Wilson & Jay, 1998). Thus, parent–adolescent communication could be influenced by this cultural characteristic; communication issues such as understanding, confidence and even language can be different depending on adolescent's gender as well as the parent's gender.

Fatalism

Fatalism is a cultural belief that emphasizes the inability of an individual to alter fate. In other words, it is the belief that one cannot control the current circumstances in order to change the future (Hondagneu-Sotelo, 1993). An example of fatalism in adolescents is "I am young and gay, so AIDS is going to get me eventually. I might as well enjoy myself while I am here." Parents should recognize their adolescent's sexual self-concept and attempt to transmit a contrary meaning to a fatalistic attitude. For instance a parent could respond to their son or daughter with, "If you practice safe sex like using condoms or abstinence, you can enjoy life for a longer time". Here the parent actively helps the adolescent redefine their situation and demonstrates how the adolescent can take control of the situation with a better outcome.

Attitudes

Attitude is the value given toward a specific behavior and is essential for increasing the probability of performance of that behavior. Evidence supports the notion that increased communication may have a positive impact if parents' attitudes about sexual intercourse are more liberal and accepting of their adolescent's sexual activity (Kirby, 1998). Positive attitudes toward pre-marital sex have become more permissive between Hispanics with a higher level of acculturation to American norms (Meir, 2002). As shown above, parents' and adolescents' attitudes about sex have important implications for the realization of an action. Attitudes reflect expectations (anticipatory effects) and expectancies (values of the expectations) in a given situation. According to Bandura (1977, 1986), expectations are learned from previous experience, from observing others' experience in a similar situation, from social persuasion and from emotional responses. Expectations are the beliefs a person has on a given behavior; value is then placed on the expectation with incentives (expectancies) that help understand what results can be expected with the given behavior (Bandura, 1986). For example, if educators help the parents relay the beliefs to the adolescent that instilling healthy sexual behaviors will prolong their lives and prevent unwanted grief, than the adolescent can begin to formulate the expectancies of how important safe sex is in their quality of life and the life of their partner. Therefore, in a parent-adolescent communication model, sources of learning expectations must be considered; health educators should use and teach parents by involving them in the following types of interaction: role playing, examples, exploration of contextual influences and emotional responses.

Beliefs

Beliefs, as it relates to parent-adolescent communication, are convictions about parent's and adolescent's capacity to execute an action. Social Cognitive Theory, as applied to condom use in Hispanic adolescents, posits that if a parent approves the behavior (i.e.using condoms) then it is more likely that the adolescent will believe it is appropriate to use condoms in a sexual encounter (Villarruel, Gallegos, Loveland & Duran, 2003). Behavioral beliefs in adolescents regarding condom use are: protection from HIV and STD's, pregnancy, concerns about partner and peer reaction, and not having any feeling when using a condom. Beliefs about abstinence in adolescents include: favorable parental reaction, maintaining one's self-esteem, and concerns about pleasure in the future (Villarruel, 1998). In the parents' case, there are different beliefs related to the right amount and time for having discussions about sex with their adolescent. Parents' beliefs as sex educators have been associated with greater quantity and quality of communication about sex (Rosental & Feldman, 2000). In the case of adolescents, beliefs are influenced by people that the adolescent interacts with on a daily basis such as, a partner, parents or peers. If they disapprove of condom use, an adolescent may be less likely to use condoms than if their partner or peers approve of the use. Among Hispanics, the influence of parents, siblings, and extended family members are thought to be particularly strong. The parent's opinion about sexual behavior and condom use is rated more highly than the opinion of peers (Jemmott, Jemmott, & Villarruel, 2000).

Knowledge

The knowledge component is an important factor in the performance of an action. Many of the sexual risk behaviors that adolescents carry out are for the reason that many do not have enough information to make good decisions about sexual interactions. In the parents' case, they may not talk with their adolescent because they assume that they do not know enough about how to relay that information to their son or daughter (Benavides, 2002). The perceptions of the amount of information that parents share with adolescents about sexuality relates to adolescent sexual behaviors. Hispanic adolescents who receive more information from their parents about sexuality are less likely to become pregnant (Baumeister, Flores, & Marin, 1995). Different studies have shown that most adolescents think that they must receive information about sex from their parents, while parents think that talking about sex will encourage adolescents to have sex (Palacios, 2001). Therefore, if parents have accurate knowledge about HIV prevention and HIV transmission and learn that providing adolescents accurate information does not increase or encourage their sexual behaviors, adolescents may potentially acquire more information and increase their knowledge about prevention.

Preventive Behaviors

Adolescent Behaviors

There are three behaviors that this model demonstrates as important factors in HIV prevention. The first is abstinence, which is the only 100% secure method for HIV prevention. The second is condom use, which includes not only using it but also the correct and consistent use of it. In addition to abstinence and use of condoms, talking with their partners is another protective factor in HIV prevention. When adolescents have good communication with their partner they are able to negotiate about abstinence and/or condom use and learn about each other's past sexual experience (i.e., past partners and sexual practices). Communication about sex between parents and adolescents is one of the central points in HIV/AIDS prevention. Adolescents who have open communication with their parents are more likely to negotiate with their partner and are more likely to use a condom (DiClemente et al., 2001).

Parent Behavior

Parent-child communication about sex is the desired behavior proposed in this model for parents. It is important to understand that communication involves not only discussion about physical development but also emotional. Communication about sex in this model has two components. The first component is quantity. This is the act of providing information that the adolescent needs on safe sex and the amount of conversations that clarifies doubts. The quantity of information is a concern between parents. This model posits that nobody is a better source of information than the parents and parents will know the right amount of information to give their adolescent. Quality is another crucial component of parent-child communication because it not only involves talking about sexual physical changes but it also involves learning the emotional aspect sexual intercourse. Talking with a high degree of quality includes using specific examples and depth of information (dates, first intercourse, peer pressure, etc.) in an understandable way for the adolescent and allowing for the adolescent to elaborate on that information. As mentioned above, communication has several benefits if it is a consistent behavior parents use with their adolescent.

HIV/AIDS Prevention

Prevention of HIV and AIDS is the outcome or goal of this model. Cognitive processes control and regulate behaviors in adolescents and parents. As Bandura (1977) mentioned, motivation is related to behavior persistence, which is strongly related to cognitive processes in an individual. In this part of the model the outcome expectations are very important for the attainment of safe behaviors in adolescents. Outcome expectations in adolescents include positive future outcomes such as, prevention of HIV, STD, and pregnancy; benefits of abstinence; use of condoms; negotiation with the partner; and the expectation of maintaining safe relationship with a partner. The capacity to demonstrate positive outcomes may produce the tendency to repeat a specific behavior that results in HIV prevention. In the parent's case, communication about sex is the behavior that the model proposes to maintain. There are different outcome expectations that affect the repetition of parents' actions. Parents who perceive that the communication has positive outcomes will talk with their child more often (Dilorio, Dudley, Leer & Soet, 2000). Parents who perceive that the communication will prevent HIV, STD and pregnancy are more likely to talk with their adolescent about sex. In addition, most parents who believe that communication may increase closeness between them and their son or daughter are more likely to communicate about sex (Hutchinson & Conney, 1998). In summary, the final outcome, HIV prevention, will take place if personal factors, self-efficacy expectations, behaviors, and outcome expectations address the need to achieve HIV prevention.

Things to be Aware of when Working with the Hispanic Population

Although the Hispanic population as a panethnic category do share common beliefs, attitudes, and behaviors, it is important to acknowledge that differences do exist between the Hispanic subgroups. In a study that sampled Mexicans, Puerto Rican, Cubans, and Dominicans and data collected over the span of 5 years showed that ethnic variations did exist between subgroups with respect to overall health outcomes (Zsembik & Fennell, 2005). The majority of the differences were attributed to differences in socioeconomic status, cultural heritage, interaction styles, and lifestyles characteristics. This is especially important when it is likely that a health provider or educator will interact with members of the family on a regular basis to establish the model in the context of the parent-child communication. Some of the differences between the subgroups relevant to the proposed model can be found in language, legal status, parenting styles, and health patterns.

Language is one of the essential components to carrying out a prevention model. It is through language that we convey facts and practices that will help prevent HIV infection and will allow health care educators to communicate with parents and adolescents. But for some Hispanics meanings of concepts or ideas vary depending on the cultural heritage. An educator must take this into account because of the possibility for miscommunication or unintended offensiveness. For example, the word "bicho" has varying meanings throughout Latin

American countries and the Caribbean. For Mexicans the word bicho is referred to as an insect. In Puerto Rico the word is considered a vulgar reference to a male penis. In El Salvador it is commonly used as slang for "kids." In Nicaragua and parts of Costa Rica the word bicho is used to refer to a female vagina. If educators are going to be talking about sensitive issues it is important to be familiar with what country the family is from.

Another important difference that can impact the interaction between the educator and family is legal status. It has been shown in the literature that some Hispanics fear participating in prevention programs and government sponsored research because of the belief that they may be sent back to their home country (Brooks, Newman, Duan, & Ortiz, 2007; Zuniga, 2004). This is largely a product of living in the US illegally. But there are some Hispanics/Latinos who are here legally because of political policies of asylum or their home country is a US colony or territory. For instance, Puerto Ricans are considered US citizens and Cubans can obtain political asylum and have many of the same rights as any American.

There are research that has shown that Hispanics differ in parenting styles (De Von Figueroa-Moseley, Ramey, Keltner, & Lanzi, 2006) and health patterns (Zsembik & Fennell, 2005). Puerto Rican parents have been found to have more nurturant behaviors and overall consistency than Mexican Americans and El Salvadorians. With respect to health patterns, it was found that differences exist between Mexicans, Puerto Ricans, Cubans, and Dominicans. Mexicans with higher levels of socioeconomic status and acculturation had worse health than any other group. In contrast, Puerto Ricans with lower levels of socioeconomic status and acculturation tended to have the worse health. Cubans and Dominicans were mixed in their health because of the variation of health disparities and advantages. It is important to take into account these differences because it will provide the tools for a more effective prevention model and ultimately diminish the possibilities of not having a clear understanding of the people you serve.

Implications for Future Research and Practice

It is necessary to work with parents and adolescent at the same time when establishing an HIV/AIDS prevention program. This model can be used to create programs that empower parents and adolescents. This interactive model for HIV/AIDS prevention based in parent-adolescent communication about sex in Hispanics can be used as a reference to create HIV/AIDS prevention programs. When health professionals and parents feel that sexual issues have power over adolescents and are challenged to explain how to address the cultural characteristics expressed above, they can translate effectively the Hispanic's values into a model that focus on a partnership. Using this model in a partnership process emphasizes the working relationship between parents and health professionals to promote safe sex among adolescents. A partnership will allow Hispanic parents to improve their capacity and empower themselves. As a result, the parents are able to act more effectively when communicating with their adolescents about sex. Furthermore, helath care providers and educators need to encourage parents to communicate more effectively about sexual issues to prevent or to reduce HIV/AIDS problems and to promote healthy sexual behaviors (Benavides, Bonazzo, & Torres, 2006).

To understand the context in which the parent and adolescent are involved it is crucial to have effective interventions. Additionally, health care providers are responsible to clarify and empower parents to feel confident to talk with their adolescents about sexual issues. Parents have the need to know if they are communicating the information to their adolescent in a correct and suitable manner, so educators must transmit a felling of mastery. When using this model, health care providers may play the role of facilitators in order to encourage parents and adolescents to communicate about prevention so that the adolescent begins to practice better sexual health behaviors. Adolescents and parents may feel that they do not have the capacity to perform a specific action and the health care provider can facilitate that action to ensure quality of communication and self-efficacy. It is imperative to understand that adolescents spend more time with parents than anyone else, so health care providers need to empower parents to communicate about sex (Nelson et al., 2000). Working with parents in the community implies the commitment to be an authentic partner, which will require them to become parent enablers (Courtney, 1996). Moreover, parents need to know their role and responsibility for HIV prevention and understand that the facilitators will act as a guide when they take action. Facilitators must provide parents and adolescents the necessary information and help them both to develop new communication skills and knowledge about HIV prevention using their cultural characteristics to their own benefit.

Conclusion

It is important that health care providers legitimize models from other disciplines in order to understand the HIV/AIDS prevention phenomenon in adolescents. It is recommended that self-efficacy theory be used in HIV/AIDS prevention based on parent-adolescent communication about sex in Hispanics. This model, designed for individual use, has been adapted for the parent-adolescent dyad. Health care providers may use this model in order to create new programs with the parent as a central participant on HIV prevention. This model may be modified to fit other types of STD preventions and takes into account the importance of incorporating the understanding of cultural characteristics. Without a clear understanding of the population of interest health care providers run the risk of an ineffective prevention program. Taking into account the nuances and particular characteristics found within a population affords the possibility of success and healthier adolescent sexual behaviors.

References

Benavides, R. A. (2003). *Comunicación y creencias sexuales de padres de adolescentes*. Unpublished master's thesis, Universidad Autónoma de Nuevo León, Monterrey, México.

Benavides, R., Bonazzo, C., & Torres, R. (2006). Parent-Child Communication: A Model for Hispanics on HIV Prevention. *Journal of Community Health in Nursing,* 23, 81-94.

Bandura, A. (1977). Self-efficacy: Toward a unifying theory of behavioral change. *Psychological Review*, 84, 191-215.

Bandura, A. (1986). *Social foundations of thought and action: a social cognitive theory.* Englewoods Cliffs, NJ: Pretince Hall.

Bandura, A. (1997). *Self-efficacy: the exercise of control.* New York: Freeman.

Bhattacharya, G., Cleland, C., & Holland, S. (2000). Knowledge about HIV/AIDS, the perceived risks of infections, and sources of information by Asian-Indian adolescents born in the USA, *AIDS Care,* 12 (2), 203-209.

Brooks, R.A., Newman, P.A., Duan, N. & Ortiz, D.J. (2007). HIV vaccine trial preparedness among Spanish-speaking Latinos in the US. *AIDS Care, 19*, 52-58.

Courtney, R., Ballard, E., Fauver, S., Gariota, M., & Holland, L. (1996). The partnership model: working with individuals, families and communities toward a new vision of health. *Public Health Nursing,* 13, 177-186.

Department of Human Health and Human Services & Center for Diseases Control and Prevention (CDC). (2002, May 11). HIV/ AIDS among Hispanics in the United States. Retrieved on March 2004 from *http://www.cdc.gov/hiv/pubs/facts/hispanic.htm*

De Von Figueroa-Moseley, C., Ramey, C.T., Keltner, B., & Lanzi, R.G. (2006). Variations in Latino parenting practices and their effects on child cognitive developmental outcomes. *Hispanic Journal of Behavioral Sciences,* 28, 102-114.

DiClemente, R., Wingood, G., Crosby, R., Cobb, B., Harrington, K. & Davies, S. (2001). Parent-adolescent communication and sexual risk behaviors among African American adolescent females. *Journal of Pediatrics,* 139, 407-412.

Dilorio C., Dudley, W., Leer C., & Soez, J. (2000). Correlates on safer sex communication among collage students. *Journal of Advanced Nursing,* 32, 658-665.

Durán, M., García, M., Ramírez, J. & Sifuentes, D. (2000). Conocimiento, actitudes y necesidades de apoyo en adolescentes para prevención del VIH/SIDA. *Revista de Desarrollo Científico de Enfermería,* 8(10), 291-294.

Guttmacher, S., Lieberman, L., Ward, D., Freudenberg, N., Radosh, A. & Des Jarlais, D. (1997). Condom availability in New York City public high schools: Relationships to condom use and sexual behavior. *American Journal of Public Health,* 87, 1427-1433.

Hispanic Ministry in the Southeast (2003). Family. Retrieved from http://www.hispanic-ministry.org/hispanic_culture/hispanic_culture01.html.

Hondagneu-Sotelo, P. (1993). New perspectives on Latina women. *Feminist Studies, 19*(1), 193-106.

Hutchinson, M. K. & Conney, T. M. (1998). Patterns of parental-teen sexual risk communication: implications for intervention. *Family relations, 47*, 185-194.

Jemmott, J. B., Jemmott, L. S., & McCaffree, K. (1999) An Abstinence-Based Approach to HIV / STDs and Teen Pregnancy Prevention. Retrieved on February 2004 from *http://www.selectmedia.org/curriculum.asp?curid=1*

Jemmott, J. B., Jemmott, L. S., & Villarruel A. M. (2000). Latino colleges students and condom use: a test of theory planed behavior. (manuscript submitted for publication).

Joint United Nations Programme on HIV/AIDS (2006). A Global view of HIV infections. Retrieved on March 2007 from *http://data.unaids.org/pub/GlobalReport/2006/2006GR-PrevalenceMap_en.pdf*

Joint United Nations Programme on HIV/AIDS (UNAIDS) & World Health Organization (WHO). (2001). El VIH y el SIDA en las Américas: una epidemia con muchas caras. *Pan-American Journal of Public Health,* 8, 422-430.

King, I. (1981). *Enfermería como profesión: filosofía, principios y objetivos* (Imogene King, Trads.). México, D.F., México.: Limusa.

Kirby, D. (1999). Sexuality and sex education at home and school. *Journal of Adolescence,* 32, 153-159.

Marin, G., & VanOss, B. (1991). *Research with Hispanic populations*. Newbury Park, CA: Sage publications.

Marin, B. (2003). HIV prevention in the Hispanic community: sex, culture, and empowerment. *Journal of Transcultural Nursing,* 14, 186-192.

McQuiston C., & Flaskerud, J.H. (2000) Sexual prevention of HIV: A model for Latinos. *Journal of the Association of Nurses in AIDS Care*, 11, 70-79.

Meir, A. (2002). Adolescents' transition to first intercourse, religiosity and attitudes about sex. *Social Forces,* 81, 1031-1052.

Nelson, G., Amio, J., Prilleltensky, I., & Nickels, P. (2000). Partnerships for Implementing School and Community Prevention Programs. *Journal of Educational & Psychological Consultation*, 11, 121-125.

Palacios, Y. (2001). *Fuentes de información y conducta sexual de los adolescentes*. Tesis de licenciatura no publicada, Universidad Autónoma de Nuevo León, Monterrey, México.

Pilcher, C. D., Eron, J. J., Vemazza, P. L., Battegay, M., Yerly, S., Vom, S. et al. (2001). Sexual transmission during the incubation period of primary HIV Infection. *Journal of the American Medical Asociation,* 286, 1713-1714.

Pajowsky, A., & Enrriquez, L. (1996). *Teaching from a Hispanic perspective: A handbook for a non Hispanics educators*. Phoenix, AZ: The Arizona adult literacy and technology resource center, Inc.

Rizzo, N., Ciardelli V., Colleoni, G., Bonavita, B., Parisio, C., Farina, A., & Bovicelli, L. (2004). Delivery and Immigration: The Experience of an Italian Hospital. *European Journal of Obstetrics & Gynecology and Reproductive Biology,* 116,170-172.

Romo, L. F., Lefkowitz, E. S., Sigman, M. & Au, T. K. (2001). Determinants of mother-adolescent communication about sex in Latino families. *Adolescent & Family Health,* 2, 72-82.

Villarruel, A. (1998). Cultural influences on the sexual attitudes, beliefs and norms of young Latina adolescents. *Journal of Social Public Nursing,* 3(2), 69-79.

Villarruel, A. M., Bishop, T. L., Simpson, E., Jemmott, L. S., & Fawcett, J. (2001). Borrowed theories, shared theories, and the development of nursing knowledge. *Nursing Science Quarterly,* 14, 158-163.

Villarruel, A., Gallegos, E., Loveland, C., & Duran, M. (2003). La uniendo fronteras: Collaboration to develop HIV prevention strategies for Mexican and Latino youth. *Journal of Transcultural Nursing,* 14, 193-206.

Villaseñor-Sierra, A., Caballero-Hoyos, R., Hidalgo-San Martín, A, & Santos-Preciado, J. (2003). Conocimiento objetivo y subjetivo sobre el VIH/SIDA como predictor del uso de condón en adolescentes. Salud Publica de Mexico, 45(s1), s73-s80.

Weeks, J. (1998). The sexual citizen, *Theory, Culture & Society*, *15*(3), 35 – 52.

Zsembik, B.A. & Fennell, D. (2005). Ethnic variation in health and the determinants of health among Latinos. *Social Science and Medicine,* 61, 53-63.

Zuniga, M. (2004). *Culturally competent practice with immigrant and refugee children and families*. New York, NY: Guildford Press.

INDEX

#

A

B

C

D

E

F

G

H

I

J

N

O

P

Q

R

S

U

V

W

Y